Lecture Notes in Computer Science

Lecture Notes in Computer Science

Edited by G. Goos and J. Hartmanis

439

P. Gorny M.J. Tauber (Eds.)

Visualization in Human-Computer Interaction

7th Interdisciplinary Workshop on
Informatics and Psychology
Schärding, Austria, May 24–27, 1988
Selected Contributions

Springer-Verlag

Berlin Heidelberg New York London
Paris Tokyo Hong Kong Barcelona

Editors

Peter Gorny
Universität Oldenburg, FB 10
Postfach 2503, D-2900 Oldenburg, FRG

Michael J. Tauber
Fachbereich Mathematik-Informatik, Universität Paderborn
Warburgerstr. 100, D-4790 Paderborn, FRG

CR Subject Classification (1987): B.4.2, H.1.2, D.2.2, J.4

ISBN 3-540-52698-6 Springer-Verlag Berlin Heidelberg New York
ISBN 0-387-52698-6 Springer-Verlag New York Berlin Heidelberg

Printing and binding: Druckhaus Beltz, Hemsbach/Bergstr.
2145/3140-543210 – Printed on acid-free paper

Preface

This volume presents a selection of the contributions to the Seventh Workshop on Informatics and Psychology at Schärding, Austria, May 1988. The theme of the workshop was Visualization in Human-Computer Interaction. The workshop was organized by the Austrian Computer Society (OCG) in cooperation with the German Chapter of the ACM.

Visualization is nowaday recognized as an important aspect of user-oriented human-computer interfaces. Both informatics and psychology are concerned with this topic. Informatics on one side is working on the technology which makes visualization and interaction based on visual concepts feasible. However, there is another important trend in informatics: the development of prototypical solutions. Visual programming, visual languages, graphical interfaces, visual representations and many other key-words characterize the current efforts in this field. Psychology on the other side is working on the question of how people represent knowledge visually and how they can take advantage of visual representations when solving tasks.

The contributions to the book address the problem of visualization from different point of views. Brandenburg discusses the computational problem of constructing nice graphs from a theoretical viewpoint. The paper of Mahling et al. demonstrates the value of visualization for expressing semantics of the problem domain in a powerful way. Fehrle et al. show how visual representations of knowledge can be generated in the context of an advice-giving system. The following papers (Riekert, Möbus/Schröder, Polak/Guest, Schneider-Hufschmidt) give examples of how visualization supports a better understanding of complex structures and processes. The example systems visualize the complex structure of an object-oriented representation of knowledge (Riekert), a functional language (Möbus/Schröder), how PROLOG works (Polak/Guest), and processes like tracing and stepping in an object-oriented programming environment (Schneider-Hufschmidt). The next two papers present application systems which are centered around a visual representation of the application domain (Anghern et al., Pejtersen/Goodstein). Psychological aspects are discussed by Kunkel/Strothotte, van der Veer/Wijk, and Preece. Gimnich presents a data model for a direct manipulation interface to databases. Harrison/Dix discuss a formal model that expresses the relation between conceptual states and display states and allows the definition of concepts like visibility, observability, and direct manipulation in a strong way. Viereck's paper is concerned with a software engineering approach to the development of human-computer interfaces.

The workshop was the tenth in the series of workshops on informatics and psychology. In the course of a celebration of this event, Milos Lansky, who was one of the initiators of these workshops, was invited to give a talk on his current work on doing intrinsic geometry with a turtle graphic language like LOGO. His paper is the last in this volume.

The editors have refrained from giving a survey of a very important part of the Schärding workshop: the discussions which traditionally occupy about half of the program. We would like to thank all participants who have contributed to these discussions with their ideas and experiences.

Finally, we express our gratitude to two institutions on either side of the Austrian/German border: to the University of Passau for the support of the workshop and to the town of Schärding for being an excellent host for the conference.

Oldenburg and Paderborn

Peter Gorny
Michael J. Tauber

Program Committee:

Franz J. Brandenburg, University of Passau
Shi-Kuo Chang, University of Pittsburgh
Peter Gorny, University of Oldenburg
Steve P. Guest, University of Technology Loughborough
Gabriele Rohr, IBM Science Center Heidelberg
Mathias Schneider-Hufschmidt, Siemens München
Michael J. Tauber, University of Paderborn
Gerrit C. van der Veer, Free University Amsterdam
Roland Wagner, University of Linz

Contents

Nice Drawings of Graphs are Computationally Hard

Franz J. Brandenburg

Lehrstuhl für Informatik, Universität Passau
Innstr. 33, D 8390 Passau, F. R. Germany
e-mail: brandenb@unido.unipas.uucp

Abstract

How to draw a graph? And more importantly, how to draw it nicely? As a formal approach to this problem we propose graph embeddings. A graph embedding is a mapping from a guest graph into a host graph. Graph embeddings are very rich in their descriptive capabilities. These should suffice to capture all instances from real applications in an appropriate way. Graph embeddings offer various parameters for optimizations, which are used to describe aestetics in a formal and uniform way. Thus, we measure the niceness of a drawing by the values of its aestetic parameters, such as area, width, expansion, maximal and total edge length, or non-planarity. However, in this general framework and from an algorithmic point of view optimal embeddings or equivalently nice drawings of graphs are intractable. In general, they are NP-complete, which means that one must pay for nice drawings with a high computational effort. This fact holds even for trees. To the contrary, there are drawings of trees which satisfy the upper and lower bounds up to some constant factor and are computable in polynomial time.

1. Introduction

Abstraction is an important human capability, and by the process of abstraction one can model complex real world situations and get a simplified view. There are many levels of abstraction depending on the complexity of the real world situations, on the intellectual capabilities of the individual observer and on his tools for an abstract description. Let us restrict our view to situations in computer science and engineering and to a very high level of abstraction, where we model a piece of reality by diagrammatic representations consisting only of points and curves. All other features are ignored or, if necessary, they can be added to our model in terms of labels attached to the points and the curves. For example, on a plan showing existing and non-existing flight connections, cities become points which are pairwise connected by straight lines iff there is a direct connection between the related cities. In a similar way we draw switching diagrams or VLSI circuits. Most frequently, such simple diagrams of points and curves are used as a designer's first draft of the system he is going to build. He expresses the more static objects of his system by points and indicates dependencies and interactions between the objects by curves or lines. Typical examples of such designs are entity relationship diagrams used in database design or modules and their interrelations in system design. We use this technique every day to teach our students complex phenomena and so apply and verify the ancient Chinese proverb "a picture is worth a thousand words".

We see graphs as a pure mathematical objects. They are used to model real world situations and are the result of an abstraction. As such, graphs are at the same abstract level as mathematical functions, numbers, or algorithms. For manipulations and storage, both in the brain and by a computer, these objects need a formal representation. Adequate representations for graphs are e.g. a drawing or a formal description by a list of the vertices and adjacency lists for the edges. Clearly, we prefer diagrammatic representations because of human perception and pattern recognition capabilities, whereas adjacency lists can easily be stored and manipulated by computer programs. Speaking in mathematical terms a translation from a diagrammatic representation of a graph into an adjacency list representation simply means forgetting the coordinates of the points and curves, and vice versa a drawing is obtained from the list representation by attaching coordinates to the vertices and routing the edges, and then using a graphics system to plot and visualize the object.

However, there is another serious problem. In general, a formal translation between two different types of representations of the same object is semantic preserving. As a common example consider the translation of programs by a compiler from high level to low level languages. As we see the situation for layouts, a translation from an adjacency list representation to a diagram adds information and in the opposite direction one looses information. Drawing a graph adds information because it introduces an additional partial order on the vertices. This is the natural partial order in two-dimensional space and stems on the relation "to the right and below". Hence, the translations between drawn graphs and their adjacency list representation may change the interpretation and meaning of the underlying object.

The main quality desired for diagrammatic representations is readability. We say that a diagram is readable, if its meaning is easily captured by the way it is drawn. The pictorial representation shall focus our view to the more important parts of the drawn object and shall illustrate its global structure. This, however, is vage and depends on various features including the intended meaning of the diagram and on the interpretation given by the individual observer. Moreover, there are innumerably many different ways of how to draw a graph. Some of them are readable and match the observer's intention, while others look chaotic and confuse or mislead or fool him. So it is not at all clear that the visual representation of a graph by a diagram is always superior to a formal adjacency list. Our goal are automatic tools for readable diagrams, i.e. algorithms which translate the internal adjacency list representation of a graph into a nice drawing. How can this be achieved? What are the criteria to distinguish a good drawing from a bad one? How can we measure the quality of a drawing of a graph? Clearly, these criteria or measures must be formalizable and checkable by an algorithm? They must be general enough to capture a wide range of applications. Conversely, they should fit to each specific problem. They should be agreed upon by many observers and independent of momentary impressions of an individual observer. However, each observer has an individual interpretation of a drawn picture and sees his global structure. Hence, our properties contradict each other. And, last but not least, we are left with incomplete information. Graphs are seen as abstractions of real world situations. They reflect only a simplified view. Often the simplification is obtained by ignoring certain characteristics which are irrelevant for the particular view. Thus we loose semantic information. However, by a visual representation, the drawn object is enriched by layout information. This is due to the fact that the pictorial representation activates human pattern recognition capabilities. These enable the observer to see general structures and to add global structural information to the observed object. For example, a node placed in the center of a picture seems more important than the nodes at the boundary. Conversely, nodes at the boundary may be seen as communication ports to the outside world. Hence, nodes placed in the intermediate region catch least attention and seem of least importance. Or, drawing a graph from top to bottom so that is looks like a tree with some back edges gives the immediate impression of a hierarchy, but this may be false. And, drawing a graph with all vertices on a circle and neighbors connected by an edge makes the Hamiltonian cycle visible. Given such a representation, the NP-complete Hamiltonian cycle problem is easy.

Hence, the global structure of a drawn graph superposed by an observer is subject to the individual and thus beyond the scope of formal theories. It cannot be captured in formal terms. Thus we are left with the problem of approximating an unknown goal, namely, how to draw a graph and drawing it nicely? How can we formalize and measure niceness? Are there general criteria for a good visualisation? What are formal parameters that enforce the readability of diagrams and that can be optimized for best possible layouts? How difficult is the optimization? For an automatic and universal graph drawing system we need satisfactory answers on these questions. Without we cannot build the necessary tools. However, we believe that such a system must be an open system and allow the individual user to add parameters, restrictions and tools according to his personal needs. This is because of the incomplete information and the individual global structure observed from a drawn graph. A general layout system with pre-determined aestetics and layout parameters can only supply basic layout strategies. In particular, it cannot capture demands arising from incomplete information.

In a formal way we approach the problem of nice drawings of graphs by graph embeddings. An embedding maps the vertices of the guest graph one-to-one into the vertices of the host graph and the edges of the guest graph are mapped to paths of the host graph. For a given class of guest graphs this gives flexibility at three levels. Firstly, we can choose the class of host graphs H. This choice determines the overall structure of the layout. Examples for H are the class of all graphs, which means no restriction and is useless in general, or the graphs with bounded degree to model a bounded number of local communication paths, or the planar graphs to force planarity, or the grids to model the discrete plane, or the trees to model hierarchies or the chains or cycles to force total resp. cyclic order. Clearly, planarity is the classical area for layouts of graphs, while grid embeddings capture the grid model in VLSI theory. Furthermore, certain vertices of the guest and host graphs can be distinguished and mapped into each other. For example, vertices may be distinguished as I/O ports and placed at the boundary of the diagram. This gives flexibility in the design phase but imposes further constraints on the embeddings. Secondly, we fix the type of the embeddings and consider e.g., directed embeddings, edge disjoint embeddings and vertex disjoint embeddings. Finally, and most importantly, we investigate the embedded guest graph, study its properties and compare certain parameters of the guest and the host graphs. The goal is choosing an embedding that optimizes the parameters under consideration. Such parameters are e.g., expansion, i.e. the size of the embedded guest graph, area, which is the size of the smallest enclosing rectangle on the grid, or the width in one dimension. Or, the maximal and the total or average edge lengths, the crossing number for non-planarity, or the number of bends for non-straightness.

There is a straightforward connection between the embedding problem and the problem of drawing graphs nicely: We suppose a "natural" layout of the host graphs! Then the embedding determines the layout. But what are natural layouts of the host graphs? This is up for discussion and has been approached in various contexts. See, e.g. [7] for a recent bibliography. Clearly, we know how to draw the grids and similarly, there are unique layouts for other regular networks, such as triangular or hexagonal tessalations or other regular structures. See Figure 1 or [1]. However, this is no longer true for graphs as simple as binary trees. For trees there are at least two distinct drawing strategies, namely the classical level by level layout with the root on top and the leaves at the lowest level and the H-tree layout introduced in VLSI theory. See Figure 2 and Figure 3. In either case an arbitrary binary tree can be drawn as a subtree of a complete binary tree, i.e. by the natural embedding of binary trees into complete binary trees. Is that pleasing? Is this a way to draw trees nicely? Our answer is no! And an immediate explanation is given by considering chains as degenerated complete trees, and drawing them as subtrees of complete trees.

Several proposals have been made of how to draw trees nicely. See, e.g., [8, 11, 20, 25, 30-33]. These approaches are either satisfied with layouts that are optimal up to some constant factor or introduce heuristic algorithms or consider restricted classes such as complete trees. In our formal approach we shall see that the problem of drawing trees nicely is an intractable problem, if we insist on sharp and optimal bounds. In formal terms, intractability means NP-completeness, see [12]. That is, the problem is computationally hard and at our current knowledge it cannot be solved with less then an exponential amount of time. From the pure theoretical point of view these are bad news, but in the concrete the situation is less serious, because of the following reasons. Firstly, the size of a screen is limited and so the trees or graphs exposed on a terminal are bounded in size. We suppose that this bound is comparatively small to allow computations that are even exponential in the bound. Secondly, we believe that there are - yet unknown and problem specific - strategies to structure a given large graph and subdivide it into smaller pieces. This may go even recursively, which introduces graph grammars as a systematic tool. Then smaller pieces can be handled according to the "divide and conquer" paradigm, which yields a hierarchical strategy for the solution of our problems. And finally, there exist good layouts for graphs and in particular for trees which meet the lower and upper bounds up to some constant factor. For example, by the separator technique, each tree can be drawn on area $O(n)$, where n is the size of the tree, and this is optimal up to some constant factor.

Clearly, planarity is the classical area for graphical representations of graphs. By definition, planarity guarantees the existence of a layout in the plane, which is nice in the sense that it avoids crossings of the edges. Intuitively, planarity embodies clearness and illustrates no collisions and no overlap. There are several and distinct characterizations of planar graphs, see e.g. [9]. The most illustrative one is based on the avoidance of the Kuratowski graphs $K_{3,3}$ and K_5, which are drawn differently in Figures 4 and 5. For the decision of planarity there are several fast $O(n)$ algorithms, see [9], which, however, do not directly produce nice planar layouts. On the other hand, if a graph is non-planar, it is an intractable problem to compute its maximal planar subgraph [12, GT27] or its crossing number [13].These are penalties for the violation of planarity, and parameters for the badness of a drawing, and are hard to compute. For nice drawings of planar graphs, Fary [10] proved that every planar graph has a straight-line layout in the Euclidean plane, and recently de Fraysseix et al. [6] developed an $O(n \log n)$ algorithm for straight-line embeddings of planar graphs with vertices on grid points and occupying $O(n^2)$ space. Grid embeddings of planar graphs with vertices on grid points and edges running along grid edges, were established e.g. in [24, 31]. These need $O(n^2)$ area, which is best possible. For further references see [7, 8, 30].

Another aestetic for planar graphs is convexity, which means, that the overall appearance and all inner faces are drawn as convex polygons. By Steinitz´ Theorem, see [14], every 3-connected planar graph has a convex drawing. Tutte [29] gave a fast method for producing a convex drawing, Thomassen [28] established necessary and sufficient criteria for a convex representation of 2-connected planar graphs and Chiba et al. [5] developed fast $O(n)$ algorithms, which draw planar graphs as convex as possible. However, Chiba´s algorithms do not always give pleasing pictures; they may bunch subgraphs and do not balance e.g. the size of faces.

Our approach to a formalization of nice drawings of graphs is strongly influenced by VLSI theory, and we refer to [30] for foundations. Algorithmic problems in VLSI theory are often formulated as graph problems or graph layout problems. Technology imposes certain constraints, which induces the grids as host graphs for layouts. Cost for production and performance of the chips determine certain parameters for optimizations, which stem from embeddings into grids. The problem size of several thousand objects evokes a need for good algorithms. Hence, VLSI layout problems can be seen as problems of drawing graphs nicely, and vice versa. Also, VLSI theory has introduced new techniques for condensed layouts, such as separators, and has shown certain trade-offs for the layouts parameters under optimization.

2. Graph Embeddings

In this section we introduce the basic terminology and establish NP-completeness results for general embeddings. For basic concepts from graph theory see [9]. For complexity and NP-completeness see [12]. General VLSI layout algorithms are in [18] and [30], .and [18] discusses some layout problems.For further details see the references in [7, 15, 16, 19, 30].

Definition:

A *graph* $G = (V, E)$ consists of finite sets of vertices V and edges E. Edges $e = (u, v)$ may be directed from vertex u to vertex v or undirected between u and v.

The *size* of a graph G, $|G|$, is defined by the number of its vertices.

For convenience we suppose that graphs are simple, i.e. there is at most one edge between any two vertices and there are no self-loops $e = (u, u)$.

Usually, using graphs to model real world situations and also for their visual representation according to some graphics standard, the vertices and the edges of graphs are labelled by symbols, numbers, or strings. These labels may indicate features such as size, shape, style or length of the vertices and the edges, or have some other problem dependent meaning. Forthcoming we consider only unlabelled graphs and for the moment we shall ignore such parameters. They make our problems even harder, e.g. vertices of a certain size may be seen as obstacles for routing the edges.

Definition:

The *degree* of a vertex is the number of its incident edges. It is the number of its direct neighbors.

A *path* p in a graph G is completely specified by a sequence of vertices and edges traversed by the path. Formally, $p = (v_0, e_1, v_1, e_2,..., e_k, v_k)$, $k \geq 1$ and for $1 \leq i \leq k$, e_i is an edge between v_{i-1} and v_i. p is called a path from v_0 to v_k and is of length k. It is *directed*, if each e_i is a directed edge from v_{i-1} to v_i.

A graph is *connected*, if there is a path between any pair of distinct vertices.

For the layout problem we are particularly interested in special classes of graphs such as trees, grids and planar graphs. A *tree* is a connected graph with $|G|-1$ edges. By distinguishing a particular vertex as the root we obtain a *rooted tree*. The root imposes a direction on the edges and induces a partial order on the vertices. A rooted tree represents a hierarchy.

A *chain* is a graph consisting of a single simple path p, i.e. $v_i \neq v_j$ for $i \neq j$ and p as above.

A *grid* is a finite connected region from the discrete plane with vertices (x, y) and edges of unit length between immediate neighbors (x, y) and $(x+1, y)$ or (x, y) and $(x, y+1)$.

Planar graphs are the classical field of graph layouts. A graph is planar, if it has a representation in the plane without crossovers of the edges.

Definition:

For graphs G and G', an *embedding* of G into G' is a mapping f : G —> G', which maps the vertices of G one-to-one into the vertices of G' and maps the edges from E incidence preserving into the paths of G'.

The embedding is *directed*, if G and G' are directed graphs and each edge of G is mapped into a directed path of G'. The embedding is *edge-disjoint*, if the paths of distinct edges do not have an edge in common, and is *vertex disjoint*, if the paths of distinct edges do not have a common vertex except possibly at the ends.

Note that arbitrary embeddings map G into a larger graph G'. Embeddings respect the possibility of communication, which is local by edges in G and is global by paths in G'. For directed graphs and directed embeddings, communication is over one-way channels. Edge disjoint embeddings model channels of width one. However, they permit crossovers of embedded edges at intermediate vertices. Vertex disjoint embeddings are the most restrictive. If f is vertex disjoint and G is planar, then so is f(G), and if G is a tree, then so is its embedding f(G).

Various classes of host graphs and special embeddings can be used to express certain aestetics for drawings of graphs. For a concrete drawing we assume a standard drawing for the host graphs. The drawing of the guest graphs is then obtained automatically by the embedding.

Example:

The following are the most interesting and the most important classes as host graphs *G'* :

(1) The complete graphs.

   These are used e.g. for the straight line standard or when edges are drawn as arbitrary curves, and no further restrictions are imposed, such as edge length, crossing number, etc.

(2) The planar graphs.

   They are used to illustrate that arrangements are clear and without collisions.

(3) The grids graphs.

   These represent the discrete plane. Grids are the fundamental host family in VLSI theory.

(4) The trees and in particular the binary trees.

   In a natural way trees model hierarchy and express partial order.

(5) The chains and the cycles.

   An embedding into a chain forces a linear order, and a cycle implies cyclic order and gives the appearance of a regular n-gon.

(6) Graphs with bounded tree width.

   Informally a graph G has tree width $\leq k$, if its vertices can be divided into subsets of size $\leq k$ which cover each edge of G and are ordered as a tree. For a formal definition see [21].

   Among others, graphs with bounded tree width have the exiting property of polynomial algorithms for some NP-complete problems.

There are many ways to define the cost of an embedding. Therefore we measure certain parameters of the guest graph under the embedding. These parameters are related to time and space and to structural properties. The size of these parameters defines the embedding complexity of the guest graph, and is usually expressed as a function depending on the size of the guest graph. Then we look at the best possible embeddings and try to compute the optimal one. For a class of guest graphs G and a class of host graphs G' the *embedding problem* can now be stated as follows: for each graph G in G find an appropriate host graph G' in G' and an embedding f such that f : G —> G' and f optimized the parameters under consideration. For a visualization we take these parameters as formal values for the aestetics of the drawings. So we can measure the aestetic quality of a drawing and evaluate its niceness. Our goal is the computation of nicest drawings.

Definition:

Let $G = (V, E)$ and $G' = (V', E')$ be graphs and $f : G \longrightarrow G'$ an embedding.

The *expansion* of G under f is the size of the $|f(G)|$. Note, that $|G| \le |f(G)|$, since f is one-to-one.

If G' is a grid, then the *area* of G under f is the size of the smallest rectangle containing $f(G)$; the *width* is the maximal extension of $f(G)$ in X-dimension.

The *maximal edge length* or dilation is max$\{ |f(e)| \mid e \in E \}$, where $|f(e)|$ denotes the length of the path f(e). The *total edge length* is the $\Sigma_{e \in E} |f(e)|$, so that $\Sigma_{e \in E} |f(e)| / \#E$ is the average dilation.

If the host graph G' is a chain, then the dilation is called bandwidth of G, and if G' is a cycle, it is the cyclic bandwidth, see e.g. [19] for a discussion. Dilation can be used synonymously with time or stretching of the edges.

An embedding f has *crossing number* k, if there are at most k pairs of distinct edges (e, e'), whose paths f(e) and f(e') intersect at a vertex other than the endpoints. Intuitively, this means that planarity is violated k times.

For the grids as host graphs, further cost measures can be defined both under worst case or average case assumptions which are the maximum number or the sum, respectively.

The *bends* of the paths f(e) count the changes from x to y directions, and conversely. They are penalties for light communication. See [12, ND47] and [24, 26].

The *divergence* of an embedding is defined by max$\{ \|x_i - y_j\| \mid x_i$ is a vertex of f(e); y_j is vertex of f(e') and e and e' are distinct edges$\}$, where $\| \ \|$ is any grid distance.

Finally, the *density* is the ratio $d(f(e), f(e')) / d(e, e)$, where e and e' are non-incident edges and for paths p and p', d(p, p') is the length of the shortest path between any pair of vertices (v, v') lying on the paths p and p', respectively.

Many of these aestetic parameters for embeddings have been investigated in the recent literature. They can be used to define a variety of classical problems in a uniform way, including Hamiltonian path, bandwidth, clique, etc.

From the algorithmic point of view is seems that parameterized graph embeddings are very powerful and flexible and are uniform in the sense that their complexity is NP-complete when formulated as a decision problem. Hence, the computation of an optimal embedding is intractable. This has been proved in the concrete for various instances with later refinements and improvements. See [12, 15, 16, 19]. We shall add some refinements for trees in the next section.

It is a simple observation, that if the host graph G' is connected, then a graph G can be embedded into G' if and only if it fits in size, i.e. there exists an embedding $f : G \longrightarrow G'$ iff $|G| \leq |G'|$. However, in all other cases the existence of an embedding is hard to decide and intractable to compute.

Theorem 1

The following embedding problems $f : G \longrightarrow G'$ are NP complete:

  a) Given graphs G and G', which are disconnected sets of chains. Is there an embedding ?
  b) Given directed, connected graphs G and G'. Is there a directed embedding ?
  c) Given a chain G and a connected graph G'. Is there an edge disjoint embedding ?
  d) Given a chain G and a connected graph G'. Is there a vertex disjoint embedding ?

Proof.

It is difficult to credit the proofs to the right persons; the first result on the existence of embeddings is due to Rosenberg [22]; Schuster [23] proved a weaker version of this theorem.

a) and b) can be proved e.g. by reduction of 3-PARTITION, c) can be proved by reduction of HAMILTONIAN path for cubic graphs, see [12, GT39], and d) is the HAMILTONIAN path problem. The restriction to chains in a) and c) seems to be new.

In the literature there are many NP-completeness results on embeddings which optimize or bound aestetic parameters, such as area, dilation, etc. See e.g. [2, 3, 11-13, 15-17, 19, 22-24, 30, 31] and further references in these articles. We conjecture that further investigations on embeddings with new aestetic parameters generally will lead to NP-completeness. Thus we summarize known and expected results into a thesis saying that "the computation of optimal embeddings is intractable". By our identification of optimal embeddings and nice drawings this means that it is an intractable problem to draw graphs nicely. This meets our intuition that e.g. a nice drawing of a graph with a Hamiltonian path makes that path visible and thus the problem only polynomial.

Proposition:

For graphs G and G', where G' may be a grid, an integer K and for any of the aestetic parameter π defined for embeddings $f : G \longrightarrow G'$ with $\pi(f)$ denoting the size of π under f, the decision problem is NP-complete: Is there an embedding $f : G \longrightarrow G'$ such that $\pi(f) \leq K$?

3. Tree Layouts

Impressed by our "general and uniform" NP-completeness thesis we shall restrict ourselves to trees and their embeddings into the grids. We shall notice a fundamental difference between "good" drawings and "nice" drawings. A drawing is "good", if the lower and upper bounds of some formal parameter coincide up to some constant factor. A drawing is "nice", if it is sharp for the parameter, and is best possible. For example, any drawing of a tree of size n with area O(n) is a good drawing; a nice drawing with area K implies that there exists no drawing with area less than K. There are good layouts of trees and planar graphs obtained by the separator technique, see [30]. The upper bounds are based on the "divide and conquer" paradigm. This induces a hierarchical layout according to the recursive subdivision. However, this hierarchical layout may oppose our aestetics from visualization and does not give pleasing pictures. The separator technique dominates other layout strategies and takes flexibility away. Therefore we insist on nice drawings and on sharp bounds on aestetic parameters. However, we have to pay with high computational cost. There are fast algorithms for good drawings of trees; however, nice drawings of trees are intractable.

Trees can be defined as free trees, for example by their definition as connected, cycle-free graphs, or as rooted trees by the recursive definition that the empty graph is a tree and that k trees together with a root define a tree. These distinct views to trees induce completely different drawing strategies. Free trees are often drawn according to the H-tree layout, see Figure 3, or by a polar or radial heuristic [8]. In either case the root of a tree is placed into the center of the picture and the sons are on a circle round their father or the root. By our experience these strategies give pleasing pictures only for almost complete trees.

Rooted trees are usually drawn top down. The root is placed at the top level and the sons of each vertex are placed on the next lower level. This reflects the induced partial order and respects the distinction between left and right sons resp. subtrees. Rooted trees represent hierarchy; they visualize both a top-down order from the root to the leaves and a left-to-right order between sons and neighbors. The TR algorithm from [20] usually gives nice and tidy drawings of trees although it does not guarantee minimal width, as shown by a simple counterexample in [25].

In complexity theory one usually ignores linear factors and instead of a single function t(n) one considers the classes of functions O(t) or Ω(t) for upper and lower bounds. The notation Θ(t) is used, if upper and lower bounds coincide up to some constant factor. For many problems, the best one can do is analysing the complexity up to some constant factors and closing the gap between upper and lower bounds up to some constant factor. This is particularly true when speed-up theorems hold; they make constant factors disappear.

At first let us consider good layouts of complete binary trees. They are optimal up to a factor of 4. These results have appeared in [30].

Theorem 2

For complete binary trees, the H-tree layout is optimal and achieves the following upper and lower bounds:

area:	$\Theta(n)$
expansion:	$\Theta(n)$
total edge length:	$\Theta(n)$
maximal edge length:	$O(\sqrt{n})$
crossing number:	0
bends:	0

For layouts with maximal edge length a factor of log n can be saved by an iterated version of H-layouts. See [30, p. 85].

It is very pleasing that the conventional level by level tree layout is optimal, too. This is under the restriction that all leaves lie on the border. See [30].

Theorem 3

For complete binary trees with all leaves on the border, the standard layout as shown in Figure 2 is optimal and achieves the following lower and upper bounds:

area:	$\Theta(n \log n)$
expansion:	$\Theta(n \log n)$
width:	$\Theta(n)$
maximal edge length:	$\Theta(n)$
total edge length:	$\Theta(n \log n)$
crossing number:	0
bends:	$\Theta(n)$

Can we obtain good layouts for incomplete trees, too? Drawing arbitrary trees as subtrees of complete trees is obviously bad. This wastes resources, such as area, width, etc. However, the separator technique from VLSI theory saves area and gives optimal $O(n)$ bounds on the area for the layout of arbitrary trees, see [18, 30]. The separator technique is more general and for various classes of graphs it yields optimal bounds for the layout area. For example, every planar graph of degree 4 can be laid out in $O(n \log^2 n)$ area, see [18, 30].

Next we turn to nice drawings. Thus we ask for sharp bounds and we consider questions of the form: Given a graph G and a constant K: Is there an embedding or a layout, say into the grids, such that the cost of the layout is less or equal K? For the cost take any of the parameters from above. As claimed in our thesis, this is NP-complete, in general.

Our next theorem contributes to this area of research and improves NP-completeness results on area and dilation, e.g. from [11, 17, 24]. To this effect we exploit the construction of Bhatt and Cosmadakis [3]. They constructed a reduction from the NP-complete NOT-ALL-EQUAL 3SAT problem [12, LO3] to tree embeddings with unit edge length. Their proof also works for area, expansion and total edge length, so that we obtain:

Theorem 4

For (ternary) trees and a bound K the following are NP-complete:
   a) Is there a tree layout with area (expansion or width) ≤ K ?
   b) Is there a tree layout with maximal edge length = 1 ?
   c) Is there a tree layout with total edge length n -1, where n is the size of the tree?

Hence, it is intractable, i.e. NP-hard, to compute drawings of trees with minimal area, expansion, or edge lengths. The optimum can be achieved e.g. with log n queries to an NP oracle that answers the related decision problem.

Another interesting NP-complete tree layout problem are eumorphous layouts from [25]. See also [15, [8]]. Eumorphous layouts draw ordered binary trees level by level, with the fathers centered over their sons, with all vertices on grid points and isomorphic subtrees identical up to translation. Eumorphous layouts minimize width or equivalently area.

4.   Outlook

Is there a way to beat the NP-completeness of nice drawings? Are there tools for the description of interesting classes of graphs and problems which help mastering the layout problem? We propose graph grammars designed for the layout problem. Basically, a graph grammar consists of a finite set of graph replacement rules. These are applied repeatedly and so define usually infinite sets of graphs. Graph grammars can be seen as generalizations of context-free grammars used in formal language theory. However, there is a broad variety of different types of graph grammars, and it beyond the scope of this paper to go into details. Our optimism in the usefulness of graph grammars is based on a first result by Schuster [23], from which we can conclude:

Corollary:

There is a polynomial time algorithm for the embedding of rooted trees on the grid that minimizes the maximal edge length.

Hence, trees can be drawn nicely, if nice means maximal edge length and the trees are rooted. Conversely, nice drawings of trees are intractable, if the trees are rooted and nice means area or width and if the trees are free and nice means anything, e.g. area, maximal edge length etc.

References

[1] N. Ahuja, "Efficient planar embedding of trees for VLSI layouts"
Computer Vision, Graphics, and Image Processing 34 (1986), 189-203

[2] B. Becker, G. Hotz, "On the optimal layout of planar graphs with fixed boundary"
SIAM J. Comput . 5 (1987), 946-972

[3] S.N. Bhatt, St. S. Cosmadakis, "The complexity of minimizing wire lenghts in VLSI layouts"
Inform. Proc. Letters 25 (1987), 263-267

[4] S.N. Bhatt, F.T. Leighton, "A framework for solving VLSI graph layout problems"
J. Comput. System Sci. 28 (1984), 300-343

[5] N. Chiba, K. Onoguchi, T. Nishizeki, "Drawing plane graphs nicely"
Acta Informatica 22 (1985), 187-201

[6] H. De Freysseix, J. Pach, R. Pollack, "Small sets supporting Fáry embeddings of planar
graphs", Proc. 20 ACM STOC (1988), 426-433

[7] P. Eades, R. Tamassia, "Algorithms for Drawing Graphs: An Annotated Bibliography"
University of Queensland, St. Lucia, Australia or University of Illinois, Urbana, Illinois, USA

[8] C. Esposito, "Graph graphics: theory and practice", Comput. Math. Applic. 15 (1988), 247-253

[9] S. Even, "Graph Algorithms", Computer Science Press, Maryland (1979)

[10] I. Fary, "On straight lines representations of planar graphs"
Acta Sci. Math. Szeged 11 (1948), 229-233

[11] M.J. Fischer, M.S. Paterson, "Optimal tree layout", Proc. 12 ACM STOC (1980), 177-189

[12] M.R. Garey, D.S. Johnson, "Computers and Intractability: a Guide to the Theory of
NP-Completeness", Freeman and Company, San Francisco (1979)

[13] M.R. Garey, D.S. Johnson, "Crossing number is NP-Complete"
SIAM J. Alg. Disc. Meth. Vol. 4 (1983), 312-316

[14] B. Grünbaum, "Convex Polytopes", Interscience Publishers (1967)

[15] D. S. Johnson, "The NP-completeness column: An ongoing guide"
J. Algorithms 3 (1982), 89-99

[16] D. S. Johnson, "The NP-completeness column: An ongoing guide"
J. Algorithms 5 (1984), 147-160

[17] M. R. Kramer, J. van Leeuwen, "The complexity of wire-routing and finding minimum area
layouts for arbitrary VLSI circuits", Advances in Comput. Research 2 (1984), 129-146

[18] C. E. Leiserson, "Area efficient VLSI Computation"
MIT Press, Cambridge, Mass. 1983

[19] F. S. Makedon, I. H. Sudborough, "Graph Layout Problems"
Überblicke Informationsverarbeitung, B.I., Mannheim (1984), 145-183

[20] E. Reingold, J. Tilford, "Tidier drawing of trees",
IEEE Trans. Software Eng.SE-7 (1981), 223-228

[21] N. Robertson, P.D. Seymour, "Graph minors II, algorithmic aspects of tree width"
J. Algorithms 7 (1986), 309-322.

[22] A. L. Rosenberg, "Data Encodings and their Costs", Acta Informatica 9 (1978), 273-292

[23] R. Schuster, "Graphgrammatiken und Grapheinbettungen: Algorithmen und Komplexität"
Dissertation, Universität Passau (1987), MIP 8711

[24] J. A. Storer "On minimal-node-cost planar embeddings", Networks 14 (1984), 181-212

[25] K. J. Supowit, E. M. Reingold, "The complexity of drawing trees nicely"
Acta Informatica 18 (1983), 377-392

[26] R. Tamassia, "On embedding a graph in the grid with the minimum number of bends"
SIAM J. Comput. 16 (1987), 421-444

[27] R. Tamassia, G. di Battista, C. Batini, "Automatic graph drawing and readability of diagrams"
IEEE Trans. Systems, Man, and Cybernetics 18 (1988), 61-79

[28] C. Thomassen, "Planarity and duality of finite and infinite graphs"
J. Combinat. Theory B, 28-29 (1980), 244-271

[29] W. T. Tutte, "How to draw a graph", Proc. London Math. Soc. 13 (1963), 321-341

[30] J. D. Ullman, "Computational Aspects of VLSI"
Comput. Science Press, Rockville, Md. (1984)

[31] L. G. Valiant, "Universality considerations in VLSI circuits"
IEEE Trans. on Computers C-30 (1981), 135-140

[32] J. G. Vaucher, "Pretty-printing of trees"
Software-Practice and Experience 10 (1980), 553-561

[33] C. Wetherell, A. Shannon, "Tidy Drawings of Trees"
IEEE Trans. Software Eng. SE-5 (1979), 514-520

Figure 1:   grid   triangular tessalations   hexagonal tessalations

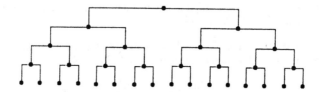

Figure 2:   standard tree layout

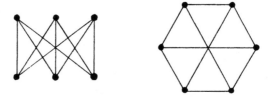

Figure 3:   H-tree

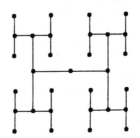

Figure 4:   Kuratowski graph $K_{3,3}$

Figure 5: Kuratowski graph K_5

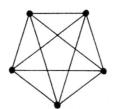

Beyond Visualization: Knowing and Understanding

Andreas Mahling, Jürgen Herczeg,
Michael Herczeg, Heinz-Dieter Böcker
Research Group INFORM, Institut für Informatik, Universität Stuttgart[1]

Abstract

Practical experience with several systems that heavily rely on the visualization paradigm has shown that visualization alone is not enough. The sheer existence of powerful visualization tools does not guarantee a successful human-computer-communication. Most visualization tools existing today lack semantic qualities in the communication process; they are not implemented in other than graphics terms. It is evident from our experience that the performance and success of visualization based systems can be greatly improved if these systems are built on top of deep representations of the knowledge underlying the relevant problem domain. The paper discusses two prototypical systems that combine knowledge representation and visualization techniques to reach a new level of human - problem-domain - communication.

1 Construction Kits and Knowledge

Recently, the paradigm of construction kits has become very popular as a conceptual base for building human computer interfaces. Bill Budge's original *pinball construction set* [Budge 83] has triggered a series of systems and design environments (e.g. [Boecker, Herczeg, Stenger 87; Fischer, Lemke 88]) that put the user into the active position of the designer within some problem domain.

D. Norman points out that the pinball construction set has some very special characteristics [Norman 86]: It is a world in which illegal operations are impossible. An operation may not achieve a desired result but there is no such thing as an illegal operation. Whether an action achieves the desired result is simply controlled by visual inspection. Experience shows, however, that even in the simple case of the pinball construction set relying on visual control alone is not enough to successfully construct an interesting pinball game.

What is needed to make a construction kit into a successful one is some kind of machinery that constrains the user's actions to meaningful ones. To apply constraints to actions is equivalent to the application of real world knowledge, i.e. application of domain knowledge to the communication process. Construction kits of whatever kind therefore have to be augmented by the knowledge of the application domain as well as by a considerable amount of design knowledge, e.g. of how to organize and conduct experiments, of how to combine the parts of a kit in meaningful ways.

---

[1] The work described herein was partly made possible by a grant of the *Deutsche Forschungsgemeinschaft (DFG)* to the last author.

2 Human - Problem-domain - Communication and Exploratory Environments

The *desktop metaphor* [Malone 83] is just a specific instance of the more general class of *human - problem-domain - communication (HPC)* situations. It summarizes some surface characteristics of typical office workers' problem-domains and is among the best understood HPCs. Following a proposal by G. Fischer [Fischer 87] we believe the term HPC in many situations to be more appropriate as a fundamental research paradigm than human-computer-interaction (HCI). A user interacting with a computer is primarily not interested in the interaction process. The interaction just serves purposes and goals. It is a goal-oriented problem solving activity addressing application dependent problems of specific problem domains. The ultimate goal of a user is to inspect and manipulate the objects of the application he is interested in. It is therefore the prime task of a system designer to disguise the fact that the symbolic objects displayed on a computer screen are not the real objects of interaction.

Working environments with characteristics slightly different from the office situation are laboratories of any kind (e.g. electronics, physics or music laboratories). Laboratories provide exploratory environments within which to study problems and pursue goals of learning and research. Laboratory environments simulated on a computer screen and software based construction kits share a lot of properties, especially when used for educational and tutorial purposes: standardized parts, defaults, some deliberately introduced inefficiency, protective shields to prevent disaster, to name just a few.

The two laboratory prototypes AMUSED and ELAB combine ideas from the construction kit as well as the HPC paradigm. Both are designed to serve as learning environments within which a student can explore a problem domain, the world of electrical circuits and the world of musical concepts and notations, respectively. Both systems make heavy use of visualization techniques to mimic real laboratories; however, they also employ deep and detailed knowledge representations of the relevant domains to decide when to use which techniques. The knowledge embodied in these systems parallels the student's understanding of the subject domain. It is the combination of knowledge and communicating abilities that makes a handsome system; either of it alone is not enough.

3 AMUSED: A Music Editor

Musical notation and its editors are interesting research topics for HPC for a very special reason. The problem of how to derive semantic categories from purely syntactical information is much easier within the musical domain than within, say, the natural language domain. Conventional musical notation (CMN) restricts possible interpretation to a larger degree because of its formal nature. Moreover, musical tradition and scholars of musical history have developed a fairly elaborate and reasonably systematic set of musical concepts that can serve as a starting point in representing musical knowledge. This body of knowledge is a superset of the musical concepts expressible by notational means.

Musical concepts may be organized into layers of structural information. A musician or a composer is mostly interested in the higher levels when performing or creating music.

When writing music he does not think of his piece in terms of *put this quarternote at that position, then put this eigthnote at that position and put a single flat left of it, etc.* A musician would rather like to express himself as: *I think of a melody that is accompanied by a turnaround of the harmonic functions Sp Tp D T of a major scale* (cf [Schmidt 87]). To enable this it is not enough to recognize the adequate pitches within the current scale (the enharmonically right spelling) and to qualify a chord as a tonic, disregarding its interrelationships with surrounding concepts as there are accent, basic tone, preceding and succeeding harmonic function etc.

Commercially available editors for musical scores all fall short in providing a conceptual level of musical concepts familiar to a musician or composer (cf [Yavelow 85]). In this respect they are very similar to the aforementioned pinball construction set; they are little more than plain graphics editors. Entering a note is little more than bitmap editing thus resembling the scratching of surfaces of copper plates. We claim that the precise and deep representation of musical concepts like note, interval, and chord is a necessity if a knowledge based editor for musical scores is ever to become a reality.

The music editor AMUSED (*a music ed*itor) [Boecker 88] is based on a deep representation of musical knowledge. There are at least two conceptually different types of knowledge that are to be represented explicitly:

1. Knowledge that determines the behavior of a musical symbol during an editing task. Among others, this class of knowledge contains constraints controlling the legal locations of symbols within the score as well as special behavioral aspects of symbols (e.g. dynamically generating ledger lines when moving a note below or above the staff). This knowledge is closely interwoven with the editing process. It is this kind of knowledge that makes a general graphic editor into a music editor.

2. Knowledge relating to those aspects of a musical object that are independent of any visual representation of the object, e.g. a tone fulfilling a certain role within a chord. This kind of knowledge is required to allow the musician to communicate in the language he got used to by musical tradition. Figure 1 displays a situation in which this kind of knowledge comes into play. The user questions the system for some musical properties of a chord by selecting and sending messages to its graphical representation. It is this kind of knowledge that is needed to develop a music editor into an instance of the HPC paradigm.

To give a second example of knowledge-based HPC: As a composer, it may come to your mind to transpose a chord to yield another mixture of two lines of chords. To do this you wouldn't want to be forced to change the key or to give the transposition factor in terms of half steps; you just would like to say "transpose this chord a major third upwards" and have all sharps and flats adjusted automatically. This is obviously rather different from moving the chord first and deleting and adding accidentals separately thereafter. Also, it is independent of the visual representation of the objects; the users communication is directed towards the underlying musical concept using the graphical object as the channel of communication.

Musical concepts may be naturally represented as objects of an object-oriented programming language and objects are well suited to be organized into taxonomies (cf [Krasner 80; Lieberman 82; Morris 85; Lenat, Prakash, Shepard 86]). Our current implementation

Asking a selected chord for its type

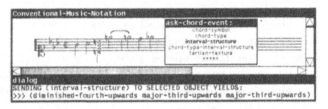

... its interval structure

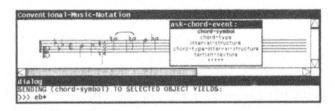

... and its chord symbol

Figure 1: The Editor AMUSED

(which is done in OBJTALK [Rathke C., Lemke 85]) is restricted to a subset of musical concepts; most of them relate to the pitch domain (e.g. tone, intervals, chords). The restriction is justifiable on the relative closedness of this subdomain. Figure 2 displays a selected portion of the hierarchy of a total of 21 concepts.

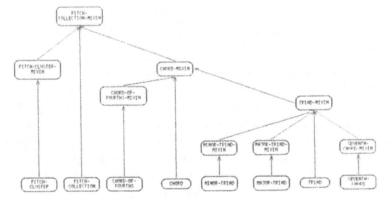

Figure 2: A class hierarchy of musical concepts

A considerable amount of musical knowledge is represented within the objects representing the concepts. The detailed structure of an instance of the class TONE is shown in Figure 3. A tone consists of a pitch, a duration etc. which are objects too. It responds to messages like *transpose yourself*, *what is your pitch?*, *what is your duration?*, *what is your pitches pitch class?*, *what is the size of an interval related to a second tone?*, etc.

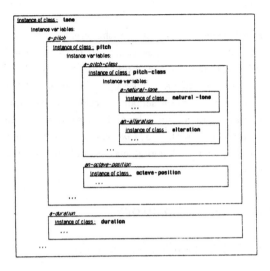

Figure 3: A template for a single tone

Implementational issues

To display (part of) a page of the entire score the editor traverses a hierarchically organized display list, (i.e. the structure of a staff is contained within the structure of the page on which this staff lives). To avoid the prohibitive computational costs of implementing each entity of the score as a single object and have it sent a *display* message be the editor, we stored all information of a music symbol that cannot be captured by a single object (e.g. its position) in a display list and accumulated all knowledge needed to manipulate (all) symbols of a symbol class (e.g. the class of all crotchets) into a reference-object. Thereby, the display method of the editor traverses the display list and delegates the display message to the reference objects supplying additional information from the display list.

However, it is not only for display that the editor delegates messages to the reference objects. Suppose for example creating a clef on a yet empty staff: After receiving the *create* message invoked by the user the editor asks the reference object of the current selected occurrence (which is the staff to hold the clef) for objects which legally can be placed on a staff; eventually the user gets prompted to select one of these. The *create* message will be delegated to the reference object for the selected staff object type, i.e. the instance *c-clef* of class *clef-class*. *c-clef* takes care that the occurrence will be placed accurately, e.g. that the hot spot of a c-clef always resides on a staff line and not in between. This is one of the constraints controlled by the instance *c-clef* which, upon creation of a c-clef, affects the semantics of the *create* command.

Semantic behavior upon receipt of a message can be altered by simply changing slot values or by enhancing or replacing existent methods. E.g., it may not be useful to allow notes with an unlimited number of ledger lines because of readability. Therefore we might want to restrict each staff object to have at most four ledger lines either above or below the staff. This can be done by changing the values of two slots namely *top-margin* and *bottom-margin*.

Introducing a new staff object type often leads to the creation of new classes. Initially there is only one class for all staff object types called *staff-object-class* which for example takes care that no staff object occurrence has more than 4 ledger lines on either side of the staff and implements the response to basic messages like *create*, *delete*, and *select*. The staff object type *note* however requires more semantic actions to be taken than are defined in *staff-object-class*, e.g. the above-mentioned dynamic, real time creation of ledger lines. This leads to a new class *note-class* with *staff-object-class* as its superclass and an extended *create* method. By adding and exchanging classes and instances the editor is highly redefinable.

4 ELAB: An Electronics Laboratory

4.1 Direct Manipulation Electronics Simulation

With ELAB, the analysis of electrical circuits may be performed on a computer in basically the same way as in a real laboratory. The user - e.g. an electronics expert - directly manipulates an experimentation field with most of the familiar working objects of an electronics laboratory (Figure 4):

- electrical devices (resistors, capacitors, coils)
- voltage source (function generator)
- measuring instruments (oscilloscope, frequency analyser, analog and digital gauges)

The user may interactively create a circuit out of the basic building blocks, "run" simulations of it and have the system display the results with the help of various instruments. The only thing the user has to learn in order to create a circuit and run a simulation is how to select, move, connect, and modify objects on the screen. The desktop metaphor has been transformed into a *lab metaphor*: the visualization and direct manipulation of a laboratory on a computer screen.

ELAB can handle the application domain of elementary four-poles consisting of resistors, capacitors or coils (Figure 5). The circuits that can be built out of these components quickly become complex enough that even a human electronics expert is unable to predict their behaviour qualitatively, let alone quantitatively. Some of the most interesting circuits are voltage dividers, filters (e.g. high-pass, low-pass, bandpass) and several resonant circuits. Diverse input signals (e.g. sine- or rectangle-shaped pulses) and initial states (e.g. a preloaded capacitor) of the devices may further increase the complexity of a circuit.

The various instruments to analyse the behaviour of the circuit look like real hardware instruments. There functionality however is increased. The oscilloscope, for example, may simultaneously protocol as many different signals as the user wishes to see. Its coordinate system is variable and it displays not only periodical signals like most hardware oscilloscopes do, but also arbitrarily short pulses and varying oscillations. The analog gauges

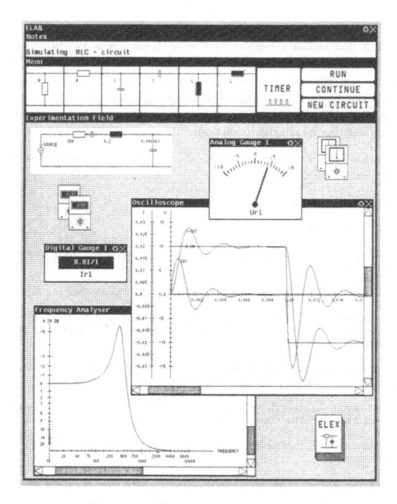

Figure 4: The experimentation field of ELAB

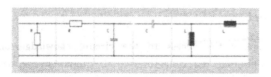

Figure 5: The elementary four-poles of ELAB

have interactively modifiable scales, hands and labels.

The actual creation of a circuit is done by using the mouse as a pointing and dragging device. *Pop-up-sheets* are used to change the attributes of the four-poles, *softbuttons* to start or continue the simulation. Before or after the simulation, the instruments may be connected to the components of the circuit to measure voltage and current of the devices.

4.2 ELEX

A system like ELAB that models a complex application domain turns out to be difficult to operate although it uses direct manipulation as its prime interaction technique. There are lots of details that are difficult to understand and even more difficult to adjust to appropriate values. Two kinds of knowledge are involved: knowledge about the very application domain, e.g. four-poles, and knowledge about how to operate a simulated laboratory, e.g. how to set up and run meaningful simulations.

To cope with the problems of the complex application domain we augmented ELAB by an expert component (called ELEX). ELEX

- "watches" the user's actions;

- controls simulation parameters;

- adjusts the displays of the measuring instruments to guarantee a good overview of the sampled information;

- simplifies complicated circuits to simpler, functionally equivalent ones;

- builds circuits and adjusts parameters of devices according to high level descriptions (e.g. the user specifies that he wants to build a resonant circuit with some predefined resonant frequency);

- explains electronics concepts and enables the user to browse through a network of concepts (e.g. the user asks for information about the concept low-pass);

- explains what would happen if some parameter of a device would be modified (e.g. what will happen if the resistance in a bandpass will be increased), and

- tells about characteristic parameters in a circuit and describes how they are effected by the devices.

Functionally, ELEX consists of three major parts that roughly correspond to the different kinds of knowledge utilized by the system: The simulation expert, the laboratory expert and the electronics expert.

The Simulation Expert

The *simulation expert* manages the access to the circuit knowledge base, sets up the simulation parameters appropriately and runs the actual simulation; we will not describe it in more detail since this knowledge is not directly accessible by the user.

The Laboratory Expert

The laboratory expert supports the ELAB user while setting up experiments and ensures that the system is always in a consistent and reliable state. It also directs the attention of the user to critical situations that are obviously not intended, e.g.: the user starts the simulation of a circuit without having connected any measuring instruments; no simulation data, except the final state of the circuit after the simulation, would be inspectable. In this case the laboratory expert proposes to abort the simulation, but leaves the decision to the user. To detect situations like these a continuous communication is required between the expert and the experimentation objects, e.g. the measuring instruments. The expert applies heuristics to decide whether and when the actions of the user are to be interrupted thus using techniques typically applied by active help systems and intelligent tutoring systems.

The Electronics Expert

The electronics expert (cf Figure 6) is an on-call system component that may be asked for help or assistance by the user. It is by far too large to be described in full detail. The range of assistance it can provide to the user may suffice to hint at the amount of knowledge required in sophisticated HPC applications (the knowledge itself is represented in declarative as well as procedural form). The assistance relates to:

- explanations about various electronics concepts or about specific electrical circuits either built by the user or by the expert.

- information on how to simplify the present circuit,

- statements about the qualitative dependencies between the device parameters and the specific circuit parameters, e.g. how the resistance of a specific resistor affects the circuit parameters, or how the 3dB-frequency is affected by the device parameters. This qualitative information is particularly useful to understand how a circuit works, and how its behaviour is influenced by the parameters of its components.

- the detection and elimination of redundancy in user built circuits (e.g. resistors arranged in series can be replaced by one resistor).

- the automatic or semi-automatic building of circuits with specific, user defined characteristics.

Each piece of information has to be requested by the user, e.g. by pointing to the item in the expert window he is interested in. Such sensitive items are printed in bold face and are explained when selected by the mouse. In addition, some explanations are augmented by visual feedback for a better understanding of the explained concept, e.g. the 3dB-frequency is drawn into the diagram of the transfer function when the user asks for its value.

5 Conclusions

Practical experience with several systems that heavily rely on the visualization paradigm has shown that visualization alone is not enough. The sheer existence of powerful visualization tools does not guarantee a successful computer utilization. Most visualization tools existing today lack semantic qualities in the communication process; they are not implemented in other than graphics‧terms. It is evident from our experience that the performance and success of visualization based systems can be greatly improved if they are augmented by deep representations of the knowledge underlying the relevant problem domain. We have built prototypical systems that combine knowledge representation and visualization techniques to reach a new level of human - problem-domain - communication.

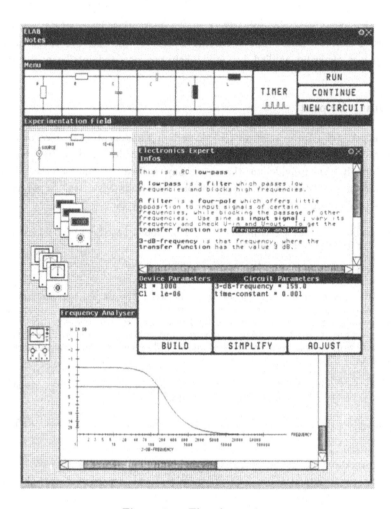

Figure 6:　The electronics expert

References

[Boecker 88]
　H.-D. Böcker: *"Objektorientierte Repräsentation musikalischen Wissens"*.
　Abschlußbericht DFG Projekt, Institut für Informatik, Universität Stuttgart, Januar,
　1988.

[Boecker, Herczeg, Stenger 87]
　H.-D. Böcker, M. Herczeg, H.-D. Stenger: *"ICKit: An Instrument Construction Kit
　for Software-Based Instruments"*. In G. Salvendy (Editor), *Abridged Proceedings of
　the HCI International '87. Second International Conference on Human-Computer* In-
　teraction, pp 31. Honolulu, Hawaii, August, 1987.

[Budge 83]
　B. Budge: *"Pinball construction set* (Computer Program)*"*. Electronic Arts, San
　Mateo, Ca., 1983.

[Fischer 87]
G. Fischer: *"Making Computers more useful and more usable"*. In G. Salvendy (Editor), *Cognitive Engineering in the Design of Human-Computer Interaction and Expert Systems. Proceedings of the Second International Conference on Human-Computer Interaction, Honolulu/Hawaii, August 1987, Vol. II*, pp 97-104. Amsterdam - Oxford - New York, 1987.

[Fischer, Lemke 88]
G. Fischer, A.C. Lemke: *"Construction Kits and Design Environments: Steps Toward Human Problem-Domain Communication"*. In *Human-Computer Interaction* 3(2), 1988.

[Hutchins et al. 86]
E.L. Hutchins, J.D. Hollan, D.A. Norman: *"Direct Manipulation Interfaces"*. In D.A. Norman, S. Draper (Editors), *User Centered System Design: New Perspectives on Human-Computer Interaction*. Lawrence Erlbaum Associates Ltd., 1986.

[Krasner 80]
Gl. Krasner: *"Machine Tongues VIII: The Design of a Smalltalk Music System"*. In *Computer Music Journal* 4(4), pp 4-14, Winter, 1980.

[Lenat, Prakash, Shepard 86]
D. Lenat, M. Prakash, M. Shepard: *"CYC: Using Common Sense Knowledge to Overcome Brittleness and Knowledge Acquisition Bottlenecks"*. In *AI Magazin* 6(4), pp 65-85, Winter, 1986.

[Lieberman 82]
H. Lieberman: *"Machine Tongues IX: Object-Oriented-Programming"*. In *Computer Music Journal* 6(3), pp 8-21, Autumn, 1982.

[Malone 83]
T.W. Malone: *"How do People Organize their Desks? Implications for the Design of Office Information Systems"*. In *ACM transactions on Office Information Systems* 1(1), pp 99-112, January, 1983.

[Morris 85]
St. Morris: *"A Personal Computer, Musical, Knowledge-Based System using Active Objects"*. In *Proceedings of the International Computer Music Conference 1985*, pp 237-242. Computer Music Association, San Francisco, 1985.

[Norman 86]
D.A. Norman: *"Cognitive Engineering"*. In D.A. Norman, S.W. Draper (Editors), *User Centered System Design. New Perspectives on Human-Computer Interaction*, Chapter 3, pp 31-61. Lawrence Erlbaum Ass., Hillsdale, N.J. - London, 1986.

[Rathke C., Lemke 85]
C. Rathke, A.C. Lemke: *"ObjTalk Primer"*. Translated Version by V.M. Patten and C.P. Morel, Dept. of Computer Science, University of Colorado, Boulder, Technical Report CU-CS-290-85, INFORM, Institut für Informatik, Universität Stuttgart, 1985.

[Schmidt 87]
B.L. Schmidt: *"A Natural Language System for Music"*. In *Computer Music Journal* 11(2), pp 25-34, Summer, 1987.

[Shneiderman 83]
B. Shneiderman: *"Direct Manipulation: A Step Beyond Programming Languages"*. In *IEEE Computer* 16(8), pp 57-69, August, 1983.

[Yavelow 85]
Chr. Yavelow: *"Music Software for the Apple Macintosh"*. In *Computer Music Journal* 9(3), pp 52-67, Autumn, 1985.

Generating Pictorial Presentations
for Advice-Giving Dialog Systems

Thomas Fehrle   Thomas Strothotte   Michael Szardenings

Institut für Informatik, Universität Stuttgart

Azenbergstr. 12, D-7000 Stuttgart 1, F. R. Germany

Abstract

Advice presented to the user of a dialog system should be in a form which is adapted to the domain of discourse. In some domains, pictures can be used very effectively to convey information in a way which is easy to understand. Thus if a dialog system is to provide effective advice, it must be able to present information in a pictorial manner.

We propose that pictorial representations of knowledge are a necessary part of knowledge-based systems. To illustrate the power of pictorial representations, we introduce the notion of a *picture generator*. This is a program which accepts as input a piece of information I from an application program and produces a pictorial presentation $S_v(I)$ to convey this information to the user of an advice-giving dialog system. We describe details of a picture generator which we implemented in Prolog. The generator can produce pictorial presentations concerning the installation and maintenance of micro-computers and is used as a front-end for a diagnosis system.

1 Introduction

An advice-giving dialog system presents information to its user so that he may solve a specific problem in a more effective manner[CM87]. The information which is presented should ideally be clear, concise and to-the-point. Due to their emphasis on graphical techniques, user interfaces with direct manipulation[Shn83] have enjoyed success in meeting these requirements. The visualization of objects sets the stage for the user; analogies and metaphors bridge the gap between the iconic representations on the screen and the user's task in the real world.

Missing from such user interfaces, however, is a theoretic basis for the presentation of information. Graphical presentations are typically hand-wired either into a user interface management system, the application program or both. Application programs can call up routines to present specific messages in a graphical form. However, more complex messages are typically formulated in natural language.

In this paper we show how graphical presentation techniques can be developed into a *general skill*[CM87] of such dialog systems. We describe a picture-lexicon with graphical symbols plus knowledge about their interactions and we show how a generator can build up pictures. In order to produce a graphical presentation, an application program computes an internal semantic representation of a message from which a picture generator produces a pictorial presentation which carries the intended meaning. The benefit to the end-user of advice-giving dialog systems is that the answers to his questions can be presented in a form which is usually easier to understand.

Section 2 of this paper discusses the role of language generators in user-interfaces for advice-giving systems. Section 3 lays a theoretical foundation for a graphical language. Algorithms and data structures for implementing a generator are surveyed in Section 4. Section 5 discusses a prototypical generator which has been implemented in Prolog. A discussion is found in Section 6.

2 The Human-Computer Interface of Advice-Giving Dialog Systems

2.1 A Model of Communication

Information stored in the computer is usually organized in a format which is unsuitable for the user to examine directly. To present a certain piece of information I to the user, the dialog system must thus encode it into a signal using some encoding function $S(I)$. The signal $S(I)$ may be multi-modal, i.e., it may, for example, have a visual $S_v(I)$ and an acoustic component $S_a(I)$. For his part, the user applies a decoding function S' to the signals which he receives. The function S' interprets the signal so as to assertain its meaning. We can state that a piece of information I has been *understood* when

$$S'(S(I)) = I,$$

i.e., when $S' = S^{-1}$.

2.2 Language Generators

A language generator has the task of producing the encoding of information, i.e., to compute $S(I)$. The resultant message may consist of text, graphics, speech or other acoustics or even a tactile component for a blind user. In choosing $S(I)$, care must be taken to use signals which the user can interpret. Thus if text is being produced and the user is a novice, jargon must be avoided, whereas if he is an expert in the area of application, jargon may provide a convenient, compact encoding of the information. In practice, several generators will be necessary, one to generate text, one for pictures and perhaps even one for speech. Text generators have been thoroughly studied (see Rösner[Ros86] and McDonald *et al.*[MPV87]). In this paper we shall concentrate on a picture generator.

2.3 A Picture Generator as Part of Advice-Giving Systems

When the domain of discourse deals with real-world objects, their inter-relationships, and how to put them together, graphics showing the parts are usually a better way of communicating information to the user than, say, texts. Thus, a language generator for encoding information for presentation to the user should have a strong graphical (picture-like) component.

The criteria for a graphical encoding of information are somewhat different than those for a natural language encoding of the same information. Whereas there exist strict rules and conventions governing natural language syntax and semantics, no hard and fast rules exist for graphical forms of communication. Many areas of application have certain conventions which are followed – for example, architectural drawings contain only symbols whose meanings are commonly agreed upon. However, the repertoire of graphical conventions which are common knowledge in our society is relatively small compared to the wealth of a natural language.

A graphical language can nonetheless make use of representations of objects as long as the untrained user can recognize the representation and can associate a real object with it. Thus in a graphical language, the semantic interpretation function relies on the user's ability to make associates with real-world objects, rather than on grammatical rules which were previously learned.

To be generally useful, a picture generator must be separate from the application, as illustrated in Figure 2.3. The picture generator accepts as input a semantic representation of an intended utterance within the domain of discourse of the application. The generator looks up in its picture-lexicon the semantic symbols used in this representation. Typical entries for nouns are icons and for verbs are descriptions of movements of icons on the screen. The generator assembles the icons retrieved and designs an appropriate graphical presentation.

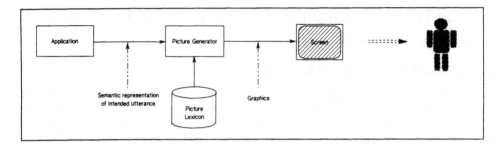

Figure 1: A picture generator as part of an advice-giving system.

3 Design of a Graphical Language

We shall now turn to the study of methods of graphically encoding information for presentation to a user. The first substantial problem is to define a graphical language. We develop a syntax for a language, and then show its relationship to the syntax of natural languages.

3.1 Structure of a Graphical Language

Our graphical language is built up on two basic building blocks:

- *primitive graphical symbols,* usually resembling real objects in appearance, and

- *graphical meta-level symbols*[BS88] such as arrows, lines and textual labels which are used to specify further details of an object.

One or more of these blocks may be combined to form a *composite graphical symbol (CGS)*. Such symbols are represented by the smallest rectangular bit-matrix containing all the basic building blocks of which it is composed. A CGS B has a reference point in the upper left corner. When the CGS is displayed, this reference point is associated with a location $B_{x,y}$ on the screen.

A picture is composed of a set of CGS's, with each B_i having a fixed position $(x_i(t), y_i(t))$ at a time t. A *sequence of pictures* is an ordered collection of pictures with monotomically increasing times.

3.2 Correspondence Between a Graphical Language and a Natural Language

A parallel can be drawn between the structure of the graphical language introduced in the last section and the structure of natural languages. Primitive graphical symbols and graphical meta-level symbols are like letters of the alphabet: they can consist of simple geometric shapes which by themselves carry no meaning or are ambiguous at best. A composite graphical symbol plays the role of a word, as an informed user can associate with it a meaning when it is used as a symbol in a message. Adjusting the relative sizes of the CGS corresponds to the morphology of a natural language. A picture is analogous to a sentence or sentence fragment: CGS's act together to provide a detailed specification of an object or to specify an action. A sequence of pictures corresponds to the discourse of a natural language. The techniques used in the graphics to cause the viewer to shift his attention from one part of the picture to another plays a role similar to the intonation of spoken language. Figure 3.2 summarizes this analogy.

Pictures	Text
primitive graphical symbols	letters
composite graphical symbols (CGS's)	words
size adjustment of CGS's	morphology
picture	sentence
sequence of pictures	discourse
shift of attention	intonation of spoken language

Figure 2: Correspondence between the graphical language and parts of speech of a natural language.

4 Algorithms and Data Structures for Generating a Graphical Language

The tools for graphically encoding information will now be applied to a picture generator. First we shall outline the major steps in the generation algorithm. Next we shall describe in detail the lexicon, which is the source of graphical symbols and the descriptions of their movements.

4.1 The Generator

The generator is responsible for choosing and organizing the sequence of events as they are to unroll on the screen. Given a semantic representation of a message, the following steps must be carried out:

1. *Determine, by looking up the necessary information in the lexicon, the sequence of CGS's and primitive actions which must be protrayed on the screen.*

2. *Ensure that the scale of the various CGS's is correct.*
   Should an important part of the object be too small for recognition by the viewer, the generator tries to find an enlargement in the lexicon and draws it as under a magnifying glass, showing clearly its relationship to the original object.

3. *Determine the layout of the entire presentation.*
   Here we use simple heuristics such as to place the object which is in the focus of the message in the center of the screen. All other objects are placed around the central object such that they do not overlap (insofar as this is possible).

A considerable amount of information is encoded implicitly in the graphical symbols used in the presentation. This information deals with the presence (or absence) of certain parts of a larger object, or the visibility of a part from a given angle. In order to generate a meaningful presentation, the objects in question must be shown such that the relevant parts can be seen. Furthermore, a user may not recognize the object if it is portrayed from an unusual viewpoint; thus if an unusual position must be shown, the usual view is presented first, then the object turned (or opened, etc.) to reveal the unusual position in a recognizable context.

The generator contains rules of inference which guide the process of displaying the objects. By applying these rules, the positions of the objects are calculated, some pictures are added to the sequence while redundant ones removed.

The picture generator produces a procedural representation of the presentation which consists of calls to primitive procedures. These calls are then interpreted by a graphics package to actually produce the graphics on the screen. The language for the procedural representation has the following primitives: The procedure *concat* builds up a CGS from primitive symbols; the procedures *show, erase, blink, move* and *rotate* display and manipulate objects on the screen. Finally the procedure *get_info* fetches the current position and status of an object on the screen. A list of the procedures and their parameters is given in Appendix A.

4.2 The Picture-Lexicon

The picture-lexicon contains all the graphical symbols which are needed for the picture generator to produce a graphical presentation. It consists of the following parts:

- descriptions of objects, stored in a declarative form, and
- descriptions of object movements, stored in a procedural form.

We shall describe each of these in turn.

4.2.1 Object Representations

Primitive graphical symbols are stored as bit-matrices; they represent two-dimensional views of prototypes of objects. Graphical meta-level symbols are stored either as bit-matrices, as a sequence of simple graphical primitives (for example, a line of a particular length and orientation) or in the case of textual labels, as ASCII-strings.

Associated with each of the primitive building blocks is an identifier. The primitives are organized in a hierarchy which describes more specific objects by adding details to the general ones. Combining one or more of the basic building blocks yields a CGS. The representation of CGS's is chosen so that if displayed on the screen, the knowledgeable user would recognize the objects being represented.

Associated with each graphical symbol or composite symbol is a set of markers which point to special locations in the representation. These are used for example to specify locations at which other graphical symbols can be overlaid or to identify points of rotation of the symbol. Such markers can also be used to organize enlargements of certain portions of the graphical symbols. Thus a region in one symbol can be marked and another, large symbol represent its enlargement.

4.2.2 Representations of Object Movements

Actions are stored in the lexicon in a procedural manner. The lexicon contains an entries for primitive actions describing the movements of the objects which are necessary in order to visualize the action. In encoding this information, it must be considered, however, that the visualization of an action is dependent on the object itself. For example, to "turn off" a switch is different for each kind of switch. In order to avoid a combinatorial explosion in the size of the lexicon, the objects are grouped together into classes such that for every member of a class, the action is visualized the same manner.

5 An Application

The construction and repair of devices, models and gadgets is a large domain in which pictures play an important role. Instructions accompanying kits for the amateur or novice routinely contain explosion diagrams or other pictorial presentations which show how to carry out an operation. Since such commercial products are often sold internationally, pictures sometimes even tend to be over-used in an effort to avoid translations of long text passages.

We have been studying the specific problem of an advice-giving dialog system to aid in the maintenance of IBM personal computers by casual users. A picture generator producing pictorial presentations of repair-plans encoded in semantic representations has been implemented[Sza87]. The generator was written in Prolog on an IBM PC-AT and can produce explanations for such tasks as opening up the computer to install printed circuit boards or to change the settings of internal hardware switches. Objects are moved around on the screen to illustrate the sequences of operations.

In this section we shall first show how a complex action is decomposed into several small ones. Then we shall describe how one such smaller action is visualized. So as to avoid the complex notation of the lexical entries, we shall describe the entries and algorithms in a textual form; the reader is reminded that these are actually made in terms of the primitives of Appendix A.

5.1 A Complex Action

If a user is involved in the maintenance of a PC, he will eventually have to open up the main system unit. An advice-giving dialog system wishing to instruct the user to carry out this operation can encode the message in the following manner:

(open 'IBM-PC' starting_with: 'normal_position')

This representation is then sent to the language generator. To a novice, the natural language message "Please open up the PC now" will be of little help; he may not realize that he should first turn off the power, unplug it and disconnect the peripheral devices. Further, he may not know how to open it up. However, such information can be encoded in a pictorial presentation in a clear manner.

The lexicon contains an entry for the action *open* as follows:

action *open* (IBM-PC)

1. turn off machine
2. unplug power and peripheral devices
3. unscrew casing
4. lift off casing.

The lexicon contains an entry for each of these primitive actions.

5.2 A Simple Operation

As an example, we shall now show in detail the lexicon entry for the primitive action *unscrew the casing of the IBM-PC.*; this is encoded as

unscrew('IBM-PC', 'casing-screws').

5.2.1 Graphical Symbols

The lexicon contains, among primitive graphical symbols, various views of the IBM-PC, a screwdriver and a hand (see Figure 5.2.1). The IBM-PC's back view has the annotation that the places where the casing may be unscrewed are in the four corners and the upper middle. Furthermore, the screwdriver has an annotation that if it is being used, a hand must hold it on its handle.

5.2.2 The Action *unscrew*

The following is the entry for the action *unscrew* in the lexicon:

action *unscrew* (<*object*>, <*what*>)

-- *this action generates a presentation showing*

-- *where to unscrew* <what> *on* <object>.

1. Construct a CGS consisting of a hand holding the screwdriver (call this "hand-holding-screwdriver").

2. Construct the CGS for <*object*>.

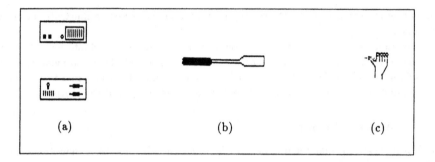

Figure 3: Graphical Symbols in the lexicon; (a) front and back views of an IBM-PC, (b)·
a screwdriver and (c) a hand.

3. Show the <*object*> from a viewpoint so that the position(s) of <*what*> on it are visible.

4. Show the "hand-holding-screwdriver" on the screen with the screwing-end of the screwdriver nearest to the object.

5. Highlight the positions of <*what*> on the <*object*>

5.3   Sample of Graphical Output

The generator assembles a presentation by merging the instructions for the four simple operations
and co-ordinating the transitions between the low-level primitives. The IBM-PC is considered the
most important object and is thus placed in the center of the screen. The sequence of pictures
which is generated is too long to show in its entirety here; instead we show two snapshots as
examples.

Initially the PC is shown from the front. The user must turn around the PC to switch it off;
Figure 5.3a shows the front view of the PC with the arrow (flashing in the actual presentation)
indicating that it is to be turned. After being shown how to switch off the machine and unplug
the peripheral devices, the user is shown where (on the back panel) he must unscrew the casing.
Figure 5.3b shows this "unscrew" action, generated from the primitive action above. The final
frames of the presentation show the casing being removed by the hand.

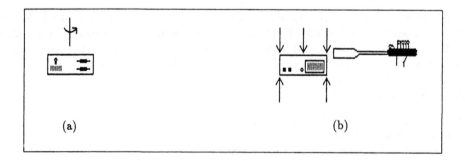

Figure 4: Two shapshots of the presentation of the action *unscrew('IBM-PC', 'casing-screws')*. Part (a) indicates that the PC must be turned around, while part (b) shows
where the screws must be opened.

6   Discussion

A picture generator such as we have implemented can be used as a front-end for a full diagnosis system. We developed such a diagnosis system[Dem87] which is used in conjunction with a larger dialog system about IBM-PC products[HEF*86]. The diagnosis system contains a problem-solving component capable of computing a solution to certain hardware and software problems which arise in daily use. The input to the diagnosis system is in the same notation as the input to the generator.

Our generator could equally well be used as a front end for other diagnosis systems, for example that of Mittal, Bobrow and de Kleer[MBdK88]. Currently their system has as output flowcharts and graph structures which outline a series of operations. In practice, however, a novice can benefit from the more detailed help provided by seeing the operations being carried out on the screen.

Our work opens up a number of areas for further research. The first deals with the design of a graphical language for presenting information to the user. We have structured our language in a manner similar to the way natural languages are structured. However, it is still unclear that this is the best way, since graphical and natural langauges are by their nature very different. A better way might be to structure the graphical language around the notion of the *attention* of a viewer. Language primitives might deal with shifting attention, narrowing down the scope of attention and attention in peripheral vision. Further work will be necessary to develop these ideas.

Another problem in the generator proved to be the calculations for where to place objects on the screen. We used simple heuristics which work for our application but which need to be formalized if they are to work in a more general context. Aesthetic aspects in the generation of pictures must also be considered; these are currently under investigation.

At the present time, the picture generator which we implemented is quite dependent on the domain of the application and is not yet a general tool. By contrast, text generation systems have achieved a higher degree of application independence. Such independence should be strived for in the case of picture generators also.

The prototypical system we have described in this paper generates purely graphical presentations from semantic representations. We are currently working on integrating synthetic speech output into the presentations. The spoken messages should be a significant enhancement to the visualization process as they can convey such information as can better be expressed in spoken natural language without distracting the user from the graphics. The difficult aspect, however, is finding algorithms for splitting up a semantic representation into those parts which will be expressed visually and those which will be expressed auditorially.

Finally, we see the need for algorithms for producing summaries of interactive sessions with advice-giving systems. Such summaries should contain important information of the sessions in a static form which is suitable for a hard-copy. Thus the graphical interpretations of primitive actions with moving parts must be presentable in a static form.

7   Acknowledgements

We would like to thank Prof.Dr.R.Gunzenhäuser for his support of our work. We would also like to thank Dr.Dietmar Rösner for several valuable discussions during the early phases of this work.

References

[BS88]   D. Böcke and Th. Strothotte. Technical diagrams in knowledge-based systems. In *Proc. 8èmes Journées Internationales sur les Systèmes Experts et leurs Applications*, pages 79–83, Avignon, June 1-3, 1988.

[CM87]   J. M. Carroll and J. McKendree. Interface design issues for advice-giving expert systems. *Communications of the ACM*, 30(1):14–31, January, 1987.

[Dem87]   J. Demmler. *Ein Regelinterpreter für ein wissensbasiertes Diagnosesystem*. Studienarbeit, Institut für Informatik, Universität Stuttgart, Oct. 1987.

[HEF*86]   E. Horlacher, A. Erben, Th. Fehrle, F. Mouta, M. Stauss, and W. Wernecke. *KEYSTONE 1.0*. Technical Report 1/86, IBM Deutschland GmbH, IS Informatik Zentrum, Sindelfingen, 1986.

[MBdK88] S. Mittal, D. G. Bobrow, and J. de Kleer. Darn: toward a community memory for diagnosis and repair tasks. In James A. Hendler, editor, *Expert Systems: The User Interface*, pages 57–79, Ablex, Norwood, N.J., 1988.

[MPV87]   D. D. McDonald, J. D. Pustejovsky, and M. M. Vaughan. Factors contributing to efficiency in natural language generation. In G. Kempen, editor, *Natural Language Generation: New Results in Artificial Intelligence, Psychology and Lingustics*, Kluwer Academic Publishers, Dordrecht/Boston, 1987.

[Ros86]   D. Rösner. *Ein System zur Generierung von deutschen Texten aus semantischen Repräsentationen*. Dissertation, Institut für Informatik, Universität Stuttgart, Sept. 1986.

[Shn83]   B. Shneiderman. Direct manipulation: a step beyond programming languages. *IEEE Computer*, 16(8):57–69, 1983.

[Sza87]   M. Szardenings. *Bildhafte Darstellung von Begriffen bei Dialogsystemen*. Diplomarbeit, Institut für Informatik, Universität Stuttgart, May, 1987.

Appendix A: Primitives for Procedural Entries in Lexicon

We present here a list if the language primitives used for encoding a graphical presentation. In general, the parameters have the following meanings:

- *<object>* is a primitive or composite graphical symbol.

- *<where>*, *<status>*, *<r_point>* are locations on an object or the screen, *<angle>* is an angle.

- *<how>* gives the mode in which bit-matrices representing objects are combined – for example, either by **and**-ing or **or**-ing them together.

The primitives are as follows:

- show(*<object>*, *<where>*, *<how>*) – displays an object on the screen

- erase(*<object>*, *<how>*) – erases an object from the screen

- blink(*<object>*, *<where>*, *<how>*) – makes an object on the screen blink

- concat(*<object_1>*, *<object_2>*, *<where>*, *<how>*, *<new_object>*) – merges two objects to form a new one called *<new_object>*

- move(*<object>*, *<where>*, *<how>*) – moves an object from its current location on the screen to another

- rotate(*<object>*, *<r_point>*, *<angle>*, *<how>*) – rotates an object

- get_info(*<object>*, *<status>*) – fetches the current status of an object

What Does Knowledge Look Like?
Presenting Knowledge Structures In A ZOO Of Objects.

Wolf-Fritz Riekert
Siemens AG, Otto-Hahn-Ring 6, D-8000 München 83

Software systems are usually defined by programs whose code cannot be understood by the average end user. Only a software specialist is able to understand and to modify the building schema of such a system. In opposition to this, a knowledge-based software architecture is presented where the facts and concepts of the application domain are represented in a network of data objects. For modifying a software system of this kind, it is often not necessary to write program code, instead it is sufficient to modify the network structure.

The ZOO knowledge editor [Riekert 1986, 1987] provides a graphic interface to the network structure which underlies a knowledge-based application system. ZOO is a user-oriented tool for visualizing the knowledge base as a network of icons. ZOO supports the modification of the knowledge base through direct manipulation of its visual representation. The name ZOO stands for a Zoo Of Objects.

An electronic communication system is given as an example. Suppose there is an electronic mail system where all the knowledge about letters, mailboxes, users etc. is represented in a network of objects. In the following scenario it is shown how the ZOO knowledge editor may be used to access the knowledge structures inside such a mail system. We will inspect the facts and the concepts in the mail knowledge base and we will modify both through direct manipulation of screen objects.

1. Visualizing Object-Level Knowledge

Object-level knowledge [Davies, Lenat 1982] deals with concrete facts from the application domain. It is knowledge about concrete objects and their mutual relations. In conventional systems, this knowledge is represented by data managed in a DBMS. Concerning the representation of facts, the network-oriented knowledge representation formalism is equivalent to the classical data base models. Moreover, it has the advantage of being very illustrative because it suggests a graphical interpretation. Figure 1 shows how the object-level knowledge of the mail system is displayed by the ZOO system.

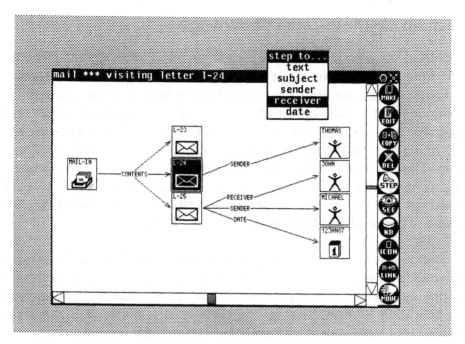

Figure 1: Object-Level Knowledge of a Mail System.

Objects, such as the mailbox *mail-in*, the letters in the *mailbox* and the senders and receivers of letters are represented by icons with a square shape. The relations between objects appear as labelled links between the objects.

Objects may be selected with the mouse. All object specific operations apply to the selected object. All functions of the ZOO system may be activated by pointing to the buttons on the border of the window.

- ZOO may be used as a graphical browser. By using the STEP function we may navigate to related objects and uncover new parts of the knowledge structure. A context sensitive menu of relationships guarantees that a relation originating from an object may be specified only if it is applicable to the object.

- ZOO may be used as a graphical editor. Relations between the objects may be established by drawing links between the icons. New objects may be created by copying existing ones. Finally, there are functions to delete a particular object and to cancel an existing relation between two objects. All these operations have an immediate effect on the underlying knowledge base.

2. Visualizing Meta-Level Knowledge

Object-level knowledge changes rapidly in an application system. Depending on the time and site of the mail system there are totally different instances of mail boxes, letters and users represented in the system. Nevertheless there is some permanent knowledge which usually does not change while the system is used. For instance, the function of the mail system is determined by which kinds of objects, relationships, and operations may be represented in the system. That is, the function of our system is limited by the number of concepts it is able to represent. Understanding these concepts requires knowledge of a higher level of abstraction than the object-level, therefore this kind of knowledge is called *meta-level knowledge*.

In conventional application systems, this meta-level knowledge is usually hardwired in programs. In our mail system, however, it is represented explicitly as a network of objects where each object stands for a concept of the application domain. That is, the meta-level knowledge is represented basically in the same way as the object-level knowledge is represented.

In most of our systems, we differentiate between three kinds of concepts: *classes*, *methods* and *slots*. Since concepts are represented themselves as objects they may be displayed by icons like any other object in the system (figure 2).

Classes are abstract objects representing the common properties of a set of similar concrete objects, which are called their instances. The class *letter*, for example, represents the structural and functional properties common to all letters. Without the existence of this class, it would be impossible to store and to process letters in our mail system. ZOO represents classes as square icons which are, opposed to ordinary objects, surrounded by a thick border. All classes form a specialization hierarchy which is established by a relationship with the name *superc*. The symbol within the icon of some class is transmitted by default to all of its subclasses and instances.

The operations applicable to a particular class of objects are represented by methods. Methods are displayed as arrow-shaped icons. The objects *send*, *delete*, and *edit* are methods of the mail system which are associated to the class *letter*. Classes and their associated methods are connected with one another by the relation *methods*.

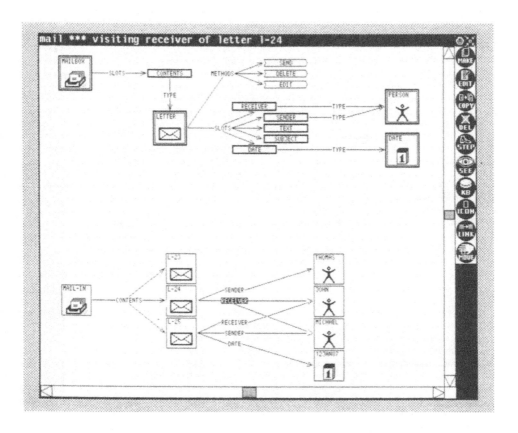

Figure 2: Meta-Level Knowledge and Object-Level Knowledge:
Both kinds of knowledge are presented as a network of icons.

A slot is an object which describes one structural property of a class. Each slot stands for a relation or an attribute defined on the instances of the class. Slots appear as flat rectangles enclosing the name of the slot. The relation *slots* connects slots to classes. Slots may have a type. Slot types are defined through the relation *type* between slots and classes. For instance, the slot *receiver* of the class *letter* is of type *person*.

Since the graphical presentation of concepts uses the same primitives as the presentation of facts, the concepts of the mail system may be modified in the same way as the facts are modified.

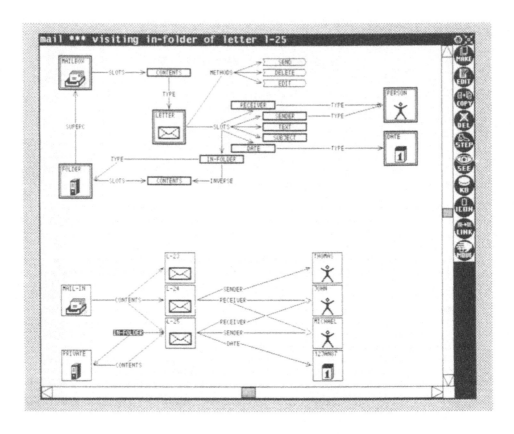

Figure 3: Creation of New Concepts and Facts:
The class *folder*, the slots *in-folder* and *contents*, and the folder *private* have been created and linked to the network of knowledge objects.

In order to introduce the new concept *folder*, we may create a subclass of the class *mailbox*. Later we may create an instance of *folder* and call it *private*. Slots may be created by copying existing ones. In figure 3 we declared the slot *in-folder* as an *inverse* to the slot *contents* of the class *folder*.

The definition of these new slots affects all instances of folders and letters, even those which already exist. So if we state that the letter *l-25* is *in-folder* of folder *private*, the inverse relation with the name *contents* will be established automatically by the system (figure 3 below).

3. External Representation vs. Communication

The representational aspect of knowledge is of crucial importance for the design of user interfaces. While the user and the computer interact there is knowledge represented on both sides: in the imagination of the user and in the storage of the computer. In both cases, the knowledge deals with the problem to be solved.

Interactive computer usage is an exchange of knowledge. The connection of the knowledge bases on both sides is performed by the user interface of the software system. In traditional software systems, the exchange of knowledge is done in a teletype-like fashion. The user inputs commands and queries. The computer outputs status reports or asks questions which the user answers in turn. The messages exchanged between the user and the computer usually concern changes of the knowledge base. The user interface is only a transit station for the informations: the screen contains a protocol of messages exchanged in the past, thus resembling the endless paper roll of a teletype. Although this kind of interaction is going out of fashion, it is the prototypical example of *human-computer communication.*

The situation changes if the screen is used for displaying the actual state of the knowledge base rather than for remembering a protocol of changes. The purpose of the user interface is now to generate an *external representation* of knowledge base objects. Besides in the brain of the user and in the storage of the computer, the screen of the terminal is a third place, where the knowledge about the problem space is represented. In this representation, the knowledge within the computer may be accessed and manipulated by the user. The representational aspect outweighs the communicational aspect: instead of telling the computer what to do, the user is directly exploring the problem space and is acting autonomously. The term *direct engagement* is used for this kind of interaction [Hutchins et al. 1986].

4. Design Principles Behind The ZOO User Interface

For the construction of the ZOO knowledge editor, we had to choose between various ways of representing knowledge on the screen of a computer terminal:

- The simplest way is to display the knowledge base objects in a textual representation. This textual representation may be presented in a screen-

```
(ask class renew: mailbox                    (ask slot remake: mail::sender_1 with:
    (slots    #.mail::contents_1))               (pname = sender)
                                                 (format = single)
(ask class renew: letter                         (type = #.person)))
    (methods  (edit: . #.edit)
              (delete: . #.delete)           (ask slot remake: mail::subject_1 with:
              (send: . #.send))                  (pname = subject) (format = single)))
    (slots    #.mail::subject_1
              #.mail::text_1                 (ask slot remake: mail::text_1 with:
              #.mail::date_1                     (pname = text) (format = single)))
              #.mail::sender_1
              #.mail::receiver_1))           (ask date remake: |11jan87| with:)

(ask class renew: person)                    (ask date remake: |12jan87| with:)

(ask class renew: date)                      (ask date remake: |5jan87| with:)

(ask method remake: delete with:             (ask person remake: thomas with:)
    (classes: = (#.letter))
    (body: = (mail::delete))                 (ask person remake: john with:)
    (filter: = nil))
                                             (ask person remake: michael with:)
(ask method remake: edit with:
    (classes: = (#.letter))                  (ask letter remake: l-23 with:
    (body: = (mail::edit))                       (text = "happy birthday john")
    (filter: = nil))                             (subject = "birthday")
                                                 (sender = #.michael)
(ask method remake: send with:                   (receiver = (#.john))
    (classes: = (#.letter))                      (date = #.5jan87))
    (body: = (mail::send))
    (filter: = nil))                         (ask letter remake: l-24 with:
                                                 (text = "Sorry this is a test")
(ask slot remake: mail::contents_1 with:         (subject = "test")
    (pname = contents)                           (sender = #.thomas)
    (format = list)                              (receiver = (#.michael #.john))
    (type = #.letter)                            (date = #.11jan87))
    (defaultvalue = nil))
                                             (ask letter remake: l-25 with:
(ask slot remake: mail::date_1 with:             (text =
    (pname = date)                                   "Dear John, wish you were here.")
    (format = single)                            (subject = "holidays")
    (type = #.date))                             (sender = #.michael)
                                                 (receiver = (#.john))
(ask slot remake: mail::receiver_1 with:         (date = #.12jan87))
    (pname = receiver)
    (format = list)                          (ask mailbox remake: mail-in with:
    (type = #.person))                           (contents = (#.l-23 #.l-24 #.l-25)))
```

Figure 4: The Textual Representation of the Mail Knowledge Base.

oriented program editor. Figure 4 shows what the mail knowledge base would look like in this kind of representation. Such a representation format is suited to a system programmer. It is still hard to understand for the end user.

- Another approach is to show an object in a form on the screen. The entry fields of such a form correspond to the attributes of the object. Filling in forms is easy compared with editing program code. The disadvantage of this approach is its local view onto the knowledge base. We can only look at one node in the network of knowledge objects at a time.

- The presentation of knowledge structures as a network of icons which was the solution finally chosen in the ZOO system offers a global view onto the problem domain. The usage of icons is very illustrative and comes close to the expectations of many users. This was shown by the success of the new graphic user interfaces which originated with the Xerox Star computer [Smith et al. 1982] and which are a standard now in a number of small computers.

Icons offer a set of graphic features which may be used for visualizing the internal state of an application system. The design of the ZOO display format for object-oriented knowledge bases was guided by a gestalt psychological approach. Some rules for icon-based interfaces were stated and tried to be considered in the ZOO system:

- The appearance of a visualization should correspond to the attributes of the visualized object. While an attribute with a large range of values requires a visualization of appropriate richness, a binary attribute should be reflected in a binary graphic feature. In ZOO, the identifier of an object is mapped to a wide range feature - the inscription of an icon. The binary property of being a class is reflected by a simple graphic attribute - a thick border around the icon.

- Categories of objects (such as the differentiation in classes, instances, methods, and slots) should be recognizable at first glance. ZOO uses the graphic features shape and border for this purpose.

- Common properties of objects, such as the structural similarity of a group of objects or the affinity between a class and its instances, should be implied via similar appearance. In ZOO, identical graphic symbols are used to show such similarities.

- A visualization feature should not be used twice: Each icon in ZOO has exactly one text field which always indicates the name of the object. Other properties (e.g. the class membership) are either mapped to other features of the icon or may be only displayed in a separate property sheet.

- Relations between objects require graphic elements for representing connections between icons. ZOO uses labelled links between the icons for this purpose. Another possible feature, which is not currently used for this purpose, is the position of an icon on the screen. The position could be used to indicate hierarchical relations or equivalence relations between objects.

Although it is possible to define precise semantics for the icon-based graphic representation of knowledge, graphic representation seems to be less formal than textual representation: the underlying syntax does not appear as strange as the syntax of a textual language. Often, graphic syntax is given by the laws of geometry or by aesthetic rules, being implicitly understood by the user. For instance, in ZOO, no one would try to connect two icons by any other graphic element than a labelled link. Whereas in a textual representation, there is no evidence where the name of an object is required and where the name of a relation.

5. Conclusions

The ZOO system demonstrates that it is possible to design a graphical language for representing both simple and conceptual objects of an application domain. The usage of icons makes this language easy to understand. Many people are already using graphic diagrams for the specification of technical systems. A ZOO diagram is more than a specification, it is a piece of executable software ready to run immediately after its construction. Moreover, ZOO processes active knowledge bases rather than passive text files, therefore the usage of the system may be supported by the knowledge already existing in the system.

Manipulating the concepts of an application system by using the ZOO knowledge editor corresponds to defining data in conventional data base models. Since meta-level knowledge and object-level knowledge are represented basically the same way, the processes of data manipulation and data definition are handled uniformly. The data manipulation language and the data definition language are identical and may both be represented in a graphical form. The conceptual model which defines the structure of the data is itself part of the data base and may be accessed by the user. The uniform representation of object-level knowledge and meta-level knowledge is therefore of high importance for the construction of user interfaces which help the user to understand and to modify the behavior of a software system.

Acknowledgements

ZOO has been developed by the author in the research group INFORM at the University of Stuttgart. ZOO was built on top of the object-oriented language ObjTalk [Rathke 1986], the Wlisp window system [Fabian, Lemke 1985], and the INFORM icon system [Herczeg 1986]. Thanks to the authors of these systems - Christian Rathke, Franz Fabian, Michael Herczeg - and to all other former colleages for their assistance. This research has been funded by the German Federal Ministery of Research and Technology (BMFT), and by the TA Triumph Adler AG, Nürnberg, as part of the joint project WISDOM.

References

[Davis, Lenat 1982] R. Davies, D.B. Lenat: *"Knowledge-Based Systems in Artificial Intelligence"*. McGraw-Hill, New York, 1982.

[Fabian, Lemke 1985] F. Fabian Jr., A.C. Lemke: *"Wlisp Manual"*. Technical Report CU-CS-302-85, University of Colorado, Boulder, February, 1985. Translated by V. Patten and C. Morel.

[Herczeg 1986] M. Herczeg: *"Eine objektorientierte Architektur für wissensbasierte Benutzerschnittstellen"*. Dissertation, Fakultät Mathematik und Informatik der Universität Stuttgart, Dezember 1986.

[Hutchins et al. 1986] E.L Hutchins, J.D. Hollan, D.A. Norman: *"Direct Manipulation Interfaces"*. In D.A. Norman, S. Draper (Eds.), *User Centered System Design*: New Perspectives on Human-Computer Interaction. Lawrence Erlbaum Associates Ltd., 1986.

[Rathke 1986] C. Rathke: *"ObjTalk. Repräsentation von Wissen in einer objektorientierten Sprache"*. Dissertation, Fakultät Mathematik und Informatik der Universität Stuttgart, Oktober 1986.

[Riekert 1986] W.F. Riekert: *"Werkzeuge und Systeme zur Unterstützung des Erwerbs und der objektorientierten Modellierung von Wissen"*. Dissertation, Fakultät Mathematik und Informatik der Universität Stuttgart, Oktober 1986.

[Riekert 1987] W.F. Riekert: *"The ZOO Metasystem: A Direct-Manipulation Interface to Object-Oriented Knowledge Bases"*. In J. Bezivin, J.-M. Hullot, P. Cointe, H. Lieberman (Eds.), *ECOOP '87 - European Conference on Object-Oriented Programming*, Paris, France, June 1987, Proceedings. Springer Verlag, Berlin - Heidelberg, 1987.

[Smith et al. 1982] D.C. Smith, Ch. Irby, R. Kimball, B. Verplank: *"Designing the Star User Interface"*. BYTE, April, 1982.

REPRESENTING SEMANTIC KNOWLEDGE WITH 2-DIMENSIONAL RULES IN THE DOMAIN OF FUNCTIONAL PROGRAMMING

Claus Möbus , Olaf Schröder

Project ABSYNT[1]
FB 10, Informatik
Unit on Tutoring and Learning Systems[2]
University of Oldenburg
D-2900 Oldenburg, FRG

Abstract

One of the many difficult problems in the development of intelligent computer aided instruction (ICAI) is the appropriate design of instructions and helps. This paper adresses the question of optimizing instructional and help material concerning the operational knowledge for the visual, functional programming language ABSYNT (ABstract SYNtax Trees). The ultimate goal of the project is to build a problem solving monitor (PSM) for this language and the corresponding programming environment. The PSM should analyse the blueprints of the students, give comments and proposals (SLEEMAN & HENDLEY, 1982). First, we will explain our motivation for choosing this domain of discourse. Second, we will shortly present the programming environment of ABSYNT. Third, we represent the development of two alternative 2-D-rulesets (appendix A, B), which describe the operational semantics of the ABSYNT interpreter. The development of the 2-D-rules was guided by cognitive psychology and cognitive engineering aspects and results of an empirical study. The study showed that the rules were comprehensible even for computer novices.

1. Introduction

The main research goal of ABSYNT is the construction of a PSM. We chose the domain of computer programming because the main activity of the programmer is problem solving, a very relevant research area from a cognitive science point of view. Because our PSM will have to analyse the planning processes of novices in depth, we decided to use a simple programming language, the syntax and semantics of which can be learned in a few hours. We propose a purely *functional* language. From the view of cognitive science functional languages have some beneficial characteristics. So less working memory load on the side of the programmer is obtainable by their properties, "referential transparency" and "modularity". Furthermore, there is some evidence that there is a strong correspondency between

[1]This research was sponsored by the Deutsche Forschungsgemeinschaft (DFG) in the SPP Psychology of Knowledge under Contract No. MO 293/3-2

[2]We are grateful that Gabriele Janke and Klaus Kohnert implemented ABSYNT in INTERLISP and LOOPS, that Heinz-Jürgen Thole did part of the rule-based programming in LPA-PROLOG and that Klaus-Dieter Frank assisted in empirical research and did the first implementation of the help system in HYPERCARD.

programmer's goals and use of functions (PENNINGTON, 1987; SOLOWAY, 1986; JOHNSON & SOLOWAY, 1985, 1987). This correspondence helps to avoid the difficult problem of interleaving plans in the code which shows up in imperative programming languages. SOLOWAY(1986) has argued that this kind of interleaving makes the diagnosis of programmer's plans rather difficult and time consuming. If we take for granted that a goal can be represented by a function, we can gain a great deal of flexibility in the PSM concerning the programming style of the student. We can offer him facilities to program in a bottom-up, top-down or middle-out style. The strategy of building up a goal hierarchy corresponds to the development of the functional program.

There are similar psychological reasons for the use of a *visual* programming language. There is some evidence that less working memory load is obtainable through the use of diagrams if they support encoding of information or if they can be used as an external memory (FITTER & GREEN, 1981; GREEN, SIME & FITTER, 1981; PAYNE, SIME & GREEN, 1984; LARKIN & SIMON, 1987). Especially if we demand the total visibility of control and data flow the diagrams can serve as external memories.

The diagrammatic structuring of information should also reduce the amount of verbal information, which is known to produce a higher cognitive processing load than "good" diagrams (LARKIN & SIMON, 1987). "Good" diagrams enable automatic control of attention with the help of the location of objects. These are in our case object icons of two sorts: straight connection lines and convex objects. Iconic objects of these types are known to control perceptual grouping and simultaneous visual information processing (POMERANTZ, 1985; CHASE, 1986).

A very crucial point concerning the "intelligence" of a PSM lies in the quality of the feedback system design. In this paper we are restricting ourselves to an instructional and feedback system based on 2-D-rules describing the operational semantics of ABSYNT. Other more formal approaches specifying the semantics of a language (ALBER & STRUCKMANN, 1988; PAGAN, 1981) are suited for computer scientists but not for programming novices.

When should an ICAI system administer feedback? Our tutorial strategy is guided by "repair theory" (BROWN & VanLEHN, 1980) and follows the "minimalist design philosophy" (CARROLL, 1984a,b). The latter means, that if the learner is given *less* (*less* to read, *less* overhead, *less* to get tangled in), the learner will achieve *more*. Explorative learning should be supported as long as there is preknowledge on the learner side. Only if an impasse occurs feedback becomes necessary and information should be given for error recovery.

According to repair theory an impasse occurs, when the student notices that his solution path shows no progress or is blocked. In that situation the person tries to make local patches in his problem solving strategy with general weak heuristics to "repair" the problem situation. In our tutorial strategy we plan to give feedback and helps only, when this repair leads to a follow-up error.

2. The Programming Environment of ABSYNT

The programming environment of ABSYNT was developed in our project, using ideas from the "calculation sheet machine" (BAUER & GOOS, 1982). The complete programming environment was implemented in INTERLISP and the object-orientated language LOOPS (JANKE & KOHNERT, 1988; KOHNERT & JANKE, 1988) to get a programming environment with direct manipulation capabilities. Following SHU's (1986) and CHANG's (1987) dimensional analysis, ABSYNT is a language with high visual extent, low scope and medium level. The ABSYNT-environment comprises three modes: a programming mode, a trace mode, and a prediction mode (KOHNERT & JANKE, 1988).

2.1 The Programming Mode

The programming mode is shown in FIGURE 1. The screen is split into several regions. On the right and below we have a menu bar for nodes. A typical node is divided into three stripes: an input stripe (top), a name stripe (middle) and an output stripe (bottom). These nodes can be specialised to constants or variables (with black input stripe) or are language supplied primitive operators or user defined functions.

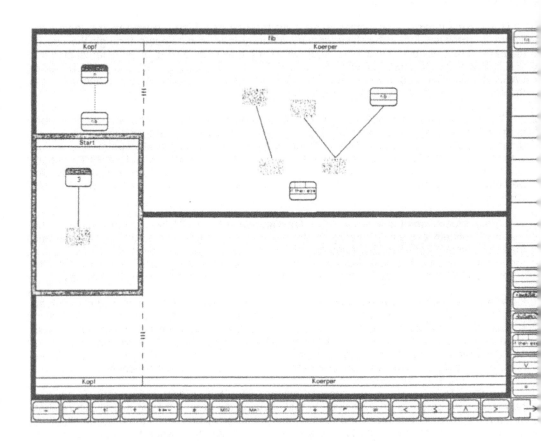

FIGURE 1: The programming mode of ABSYNT

In the upper half of the screen the programmer sees the main worksheet and in the lower half a subordinated one. Each worksheet is called frame. Frames are split into a left part "head" (in German: "Kopf") and into a right part "body" (in German: "Körper"). The head contains the local environment with parameter-value bindings and the function name. The body contains the body of the function.

Programming is done by making up trees from nodes and links. The programmer enters the menu bar with the mouse, chooses one node and drags the node to the desired position in the frame. Beneath the frame is a covered grid which orders the arrangements of the nodes so that everything looks tidy. Connections between the nodes are drawn with the mouse. The connection lines are the "pipelines" for the control and data flow. If a node is missed the programmer is reminded with a shaded grey node that there is something missing. The editor warns with flashes if unsyntactic programs are going to be constructed: crossing of connections, overlapping of nodes etc. The function name is entered by the programmer with the help of pop-up-menus in the root node of the head. Parameter names and values for constants are entered in the leaves of the head and the body by pop-up-menus, too.

If the function is syntactically correct, the name of the function appears in the frame title and in one of the nodes in the menu bar so that it can be used as a higher operator. When a problem has to be solved a computation is initialized by the call of a function. This call is programmed into the "Start"-Tree. Initial numbers are entered by pop-up-menus in constant nodes in the start tree. This tree has a frame without a name, so that the iconic bars are consistent.

The design of the programming mode is motivated by regarding the operational knowledge of ABSYNT as a necessary prerequisite for the development of planning and programming knowledge. That is, features which are necessary for the understanding of the computational process are visualized in the programming mode as well as in the other modes of the programming environment.

2.2 Trace Mode and Prediction Mode

If the user has programmed a start tree for his program, he can run the program and get a trace for it. FIGURE 2 (a to d) displays 8 different states of the trace for the Fibonacci function. The design of the trace is a result of our iterative specification cycle in the development of abstract rules and process icons (MÖBUS & THOLE, 1988; MÖBUS & SCHRÖDER, 1988). In the case of recursive programs, the frame actually computed is in the upper half of the screen. The lower half shows the frame one level deeper in the stack, so that the recursive call stays visible.

As an experimental tool of the ABSYNT environment, there is also a prediction mode. Here the user can predict the actions of the interpreter, that is, compute ABSYNT-programs by himself, so that he can smoothly acquire the operational knowledge for ABSYNT.

3. Preliminary Instructional Material and Semantic Bugs

Our starting point for developing a functional visual programming language was a paper-and-pencil study where we did some explorations without any computer implementations. Part of this feasability study was a verbal specification of the syntax and the operational knowledge, illustrated by simple programs and trees (MÖBUS & SCHRÖDER, 1988). The goals of the pilot study were:

- to get suggestions for the design of the language and the interface
- to collect syntactic and semantic bugs in order to find reasons for bugs and conditions under which they occur
- to study the memory representations of example programs

51

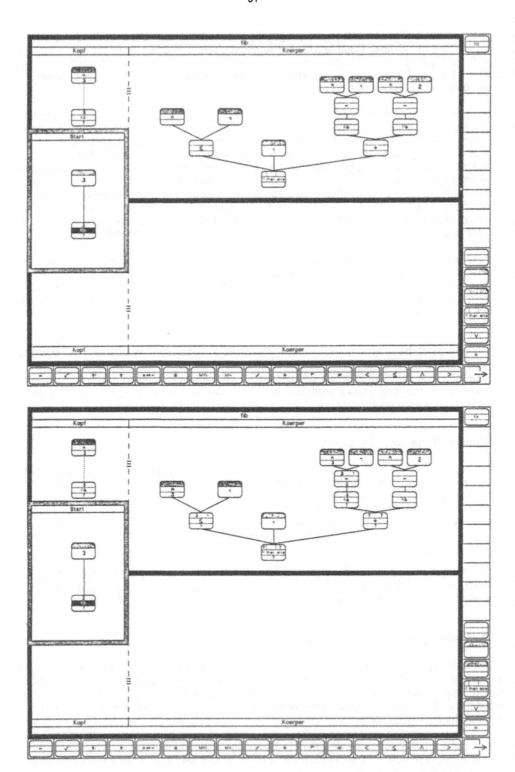

FIGURE 2a: The trace mode of ABSYNT

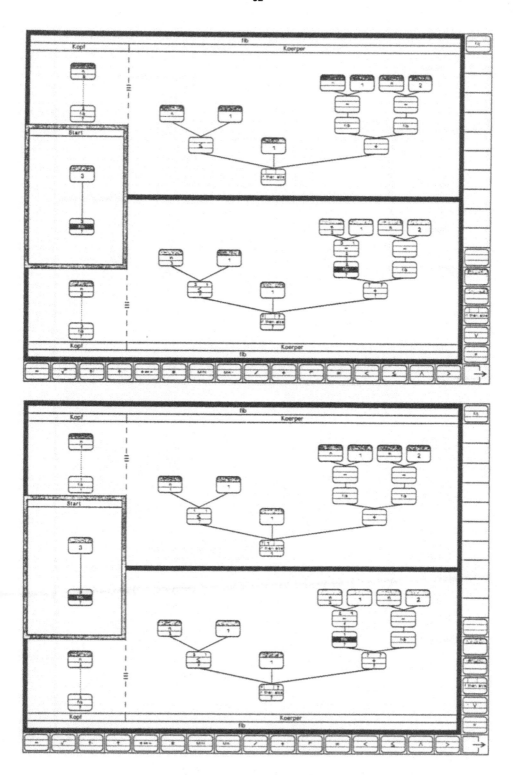

FIGURE 2b: The trace mode of ABSYNT (some computation steps later...)

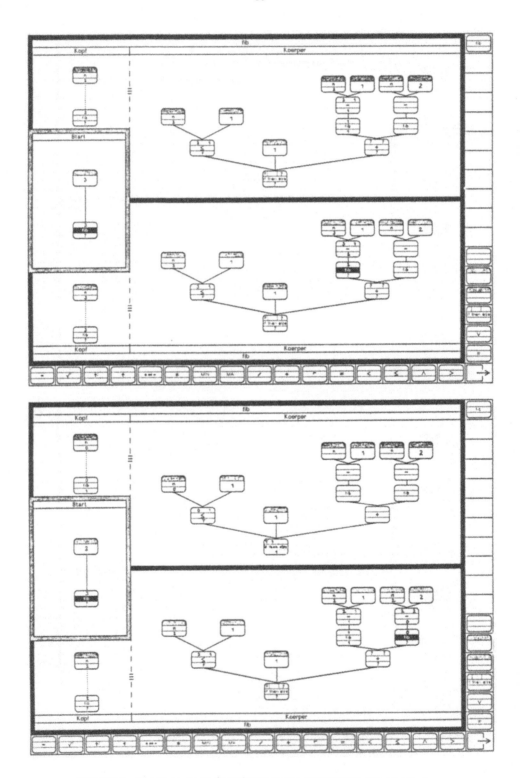

FIGURE 2c: The trace mode of ABSYNT (some computation steps later...)

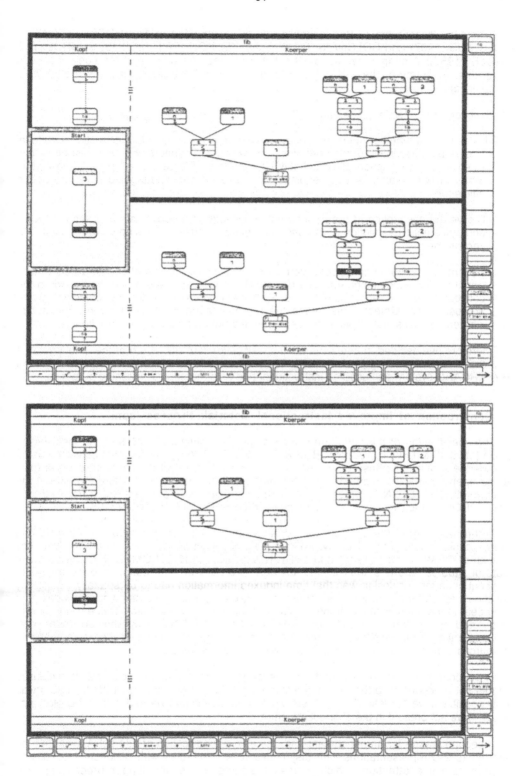

FIGURE 2d: The trace mode of ABSYNT (some computation steps later...)

A detailed description of the feasability study is provided in SCHRÖDER, FRANK & COLONIUS (1987) and COLONIUS, FRANK, JANKE, KOHNERT, MÖBUS, SCHRÖDER & THOLE (1987). Among other things the subjects had to compute the value of various programs, simulating the ABSYNT interpreter. Then we analysed the observable computational errors.

However, this collection of semantic bugs gave rise to the following problems:

- It was unclear whether the bugs arose because of ambiguities in the instructional material (the verbal description of the operational knowledge). Therefore, we could not be certain whether this description could actually be viewed as the semantic "expert" knowledge, which in our opinion is a prerequisite for a user of our language to plan and debug efficiently.

- The verbal description of the operational knowledge is a poor base for a more detailed and systematic description of the observed bugs in terms of missing or wrong pieces of knowledge.

- It seems unnatural to construct a verbal specification of the operational knowledge for a visual programming language. The design of a visual language has to be based on the concept of generalized icons (CHANG, 1987), which can be divided into object icons and process icons. Object icons define the representation of static language constructs, whereas process icons specify the representation of data flow and control flow.

Therefore, we decided to use a runnable specification (DAVIS, 1982) of the language as a foundation for constructing process icons. These process icons were then programmed in the HYPERCARD-system and used as instructional and help material for teaching purposes.

4. Construction of Improved Instructional Material: Process Icons

The specification of the operational knowledge was achieved in an iterative specification cycle (MÖBUS & THOLE, 1988; MÖBUS & SCHRÖDER, 1988). The first step consisted of the knowledge acquisition phase. The next step led to a rule set A of 9 main Horn clauses (plus some operator-specific rules). The set contained the minimal abstract knowledge about the interpretation of ABSYNT programs. The abstract structure of a program was formalized by a set of PROLOG facts similar to an approach of GENESERETH & NILSSON (1987, ch. 2.5).

In the next step of the specification cycle we tried a 2-D-representation of the facts and Horn clauses of rule set A. Thereby, we kept in mind design principles which are motivated by results of POMERANTZ (1985) and LARKIN & SIMON (1987). POMERANTZ made some careful studies about selective and divided attention in information processing. One consequence for our design was that time-indexed information had to be spatially indexed by locations, too. Information with the same time index should have the same spatial index, that is appear in the same location. In our design a location is a visual object. These insights were supported by the formal analysis of LARKIN & SIMON (1987). They showed under what circumstances a diagrammatic representation of information consumes less computational resources than an informational equivalent written representation.

In the course of time we realized that a visual representation of the facts and Horn clauses of rule set A according to the recommendations of POMERANTZ and LARKIN & SIMON was only possible if we "enriched" the 2-D structure. This means that we had to add 2-D elements which were not present in the abstract structure.

A second reason for an enrichment and, thereby, a modification of rule set A, was that the set led to 2-D-representations with disjunctive rules. 2-D-rules with disjunctive conditions require selective attention, which causes matching errors and longer processing time

(BOURNE, 1974; HAYGOOD & BOURNE, 1965; MEDIN, WATTENMAKER & MICHALSKI, 1987). Thus rule set A was modified in such a way such that

- any undesired perceptual grouping of information in operator nodes,
- 2-D-rules with disjunctive conditions,
  and
- visual hiding of dynamic successor frames already put on a stack.

was avoided.

We came up with a relaxed rule set B with 14 main rules (plus operator-specific rules)(MÖBUS & THOLE, 1988; MÖBUS & SCHRÖDER, 1988). The behavior of these rules led to a new visual trace. Time-indexed information was now location-indexed so that undesired perceptual grouping could not occur any longer.

But these rules still had some defects from a cognitive point of view. Computational goals and intermediate results are kept visible only as long as they are absolutely necessary for the ongoing computation. Intermediate results "die" before the corresponding frame "dies". This is not optimal for humans, because a programmer who wants to recapitulate the computation history has to reconstruct former computations mentally. This leads to higher working memory load for the programmer.

So we were forced to relax the minimum assumption a second time and introduce even more visual redundancy. This was i.e. in accordance with the third principle of FITTER & GREEN (1979).

Another reason for a further modification of the rule set was the recursiveness of the rules. Instructional and help material derived from such rules should enforce a higher mental working memory load because of the maintenance of a goal stack with return points.

The third rule set C with 29 (plus operator-specific) rules was motivated by the postulate, that the extent of the intermediate result should not end before the life of a frame ends. We have included examples for abstract rules of rule set C in FIGUREs 3 and 4. They are represented in visual 2-D-rules 8 and 9 in the state-specific rule set (appendix B).

Then the computational behavior of rule set C was "frozen" in our INTERLISP/LOOPS-Implementation (KOHNERT & JANKE, 1988). This completed the specification cycle.

```
output :-
    node(frame_name(Frame_name),frame_no(Frame_no),tree_type(Tree_type),
        instance_no(Instance_no),input_stripe(Input_stripe),name_stripe(Name_stripe),
        output_stripe(Output_stripe)),
    higher_operator(name(Name_stripe)),
    Tree_type = start,
    not(inverted_name_stripe(frame_name(Frame_name),frame_no(Frame_no),tree_type(Tree_type),
        instance_no(Any_instance_no))),
    Output_stripe = ? ,
    forall(on(Element,Input_stripe),value(Element)),
    copy_frame_on_top(frame_name(Name_stripe),top_frame_no(Top_frame_no)),

    assert(inverted_name_stripe(frame_name(Frame_name),frame_no(Frame_no),tree_type(Tree_type),
        instance_no(Instance_no))),
    root(frame_name(Name_stripe),frame_no(Top_frame_no),tree_type(head),
        instance_no(Instance_no_root_head)),
    modify(frame_name(Name_stripe),frame_no(Top_frame_no),tree_type(head),
    instance_no(Instance_no_root_head),output_stripe( ? )),
```

```
        modify(frame_name(Name_stripe),frame_no(Top_frame_no),tree_type(head),
        instance_no(Instance_no_root_head),input_stripe(Input_stripe)),
        bind_parameter_of_top_frame(input_stripe(Input_stripe)),
output.
```

```
/*  IF   there is a node which has the following features:
         (1) The node name is a higher operator.
         (2) The node is located in the start tree.
         (3) There is no node in the start tree with an inverted name stripe
         (4) The output_stripe of the node contains a "?".
         (5) The input_stripe of the node contains all input values.

    THEN create the frame with the operators name and place it on top of the frame stack.
         Invert the name stripe of the node.
         Determine it`s head root.
         Put a "?" into it`s output_stripe.
         Transfer the input_stripe of the node to the head root.
         Bind the parameters.  */
```

FIGURE 3:   Abstract Rule 8 of Rule Set C (First part of Call-by-Value, call in start tree ; corresponds to
2-D-rule 8 in the "state-specific" rule set in appendix B)

```
output :-
        node(frame_name(Frame_name),frame_no(Frame_no),tree_type(Tree_type),
        instance_no(Instance_no),input_stripe(Input_stripe),name_stripe(Name_stripe),
            output_stripe(Output_stripe)),
        higher_operator(name(Name_stripe)),
        Tree_type = start,
        inverted_name_stripe(frame_name(Frame_name),frame_no(Frame_no),tree_type(Tree_type),
            instance_no(Instance_no)),
        Output_stripe = ? ,
        forall(on(Element,Input_stripe),value(Element)),
        value_of_upper_visible_frame(Output_stripe_root_head),
        not_exist_lower_visible_frame,
        modify(frame(Frame_name),frame_no(Frame_no),tree_type(Tree_type),
            instance_no(Instance_no),output_stripe(Output_stripe_root_head)),
        delete_frame_from_top,

        retract(inverted_name_stripe(frame_name(Frame_name),frame_no(Frame_no),tree_type(Tree_type),
            instance_no(Instance_no))),
output.
```

```
/*  IF   there is a node which has the following features:
         (1) The node name is a higher operator.
         (2) The node is located in the start tree.
         (3) The name stripe of the node is inverted.
         (4) The output_stripe of the node contains a "?".
         (5) The input_stripe of the node contains all input values.
         (6) The head root of the upper visible frame contains a value.
         (7) There is no other visible frame

    THEN  transfer this value into the output_stripe of the node.
         Delete the upper visible frame.
         Undo the inversion of the name stripe of the node.   */
```

FIGURE 4:   Abstract rule 9 of Rule Set C (Second part of Call-by-Value, call in start tree; corresponds to
2-D-rule 9 in the "state-specific" rule set in appendix B)

In the visual trace, intermediate results now live as long as their frame. As with rule set B, there is no undesired perceptual grouping. Process icons derived from rule set C would not be applied recursively, and there would be no disjunctions.

On the basis of rule sets B and C we developed 2-D-rules to describe the operational behavior of the ABSYNT-interpreter so that it can be predicted by a student. We got two different 2-D-rule sets B and C with 8 respectively 16 2-D-rules. The 2-D-rules are visual representations of only the most important rules of the abstract rule sets. Additional rules of the abstract rule sets (i.e., for testing if a node is a root or a leaf) as well as the operator-specific rules are explained in a separate glossary. The glossary also contains a short introduction to the syntax of the 2-D-rules.

5. Empirical Evaluation of the Two 2-D-rule Sets

We did a study in which programming novices computed ABSYNT-programs with the aid of earlier versions (MÖBUS & THOLE, 1988) of the two 2-D-rule sets. One of the aims of the study was to evaluate the learnability of the 2-D-rules. We wanted to detect rules or parts of rules which led to misunderstandings and errors.

Procedure: 12 programming novices (6 subjects working with each rule set) computed ABSYNT-Programs of increasing difficulty. This was done in the prediction mode of the ABSYNT-Environment (section 2.2 and KOHNERT & JANKE, 1988). In this mode the user computed ABSYNT-Programs by himself without any help from the interpreter. The subjects worked in pairs (cf. MIYAKE, 1986). So three pairs of subjects worked with each rule set. Beside the 2-D-rule set, they were provided with the glossary, that is additional explanations of basic concepts mentioned in the rules. Therefore, complete instructional material was given.

Each pair of subjects computed 33 ABSYNT-programs. The sequence of programs was ordered by the number of 2-D-rules needed. So the most difficult program contained abstraction as well as recursion. The subjects computed each ABSYNT-Program once without being interrupted by the experimentator. In case of correct computation, the next program was presented. In case of a bug, the program was presented again. This time, if bugs occurred, the experimentator gave immediate feedback.

Preliminary results: The evaluation of the study is not completed as yet, but some results related to the aim of the study mentioned above will be presented.

First, some concepts are explained:

1. A "*computational step*" denotes the following actions:
    - changing the content of an input field or an output stripe
    - creating or deleting a frame (choosing the corresponding menu item)
    - typing a frame number

2. A "*rule-consistent computational step*" is any computational step which is part of a correct rule application. It is consistent with the part of an "action" description of a rule the "situation" description of which is satisfied. It is not regarded whether the computational step is made in the right context. So parts visible on the screen but not mentioned in the rule may be faulty.

3. A "*deviation*" is any computational step which is not part of a correct rule application. There are the following possibilities:

    3.1 *Faulty rule application:* The computational step is not consistent with any part of the action description of any rule.

3.2 *Omission:* The computational step is consistent with a part of an action description of a rule the situation description of which is not yet satisfied, but is satisfiable by intermediate computational steps.

3.3 *Interference:* The computational step is consistent with a part of an action description of a rule the situation description of which is not satisfied and not satisfiable.

3.4 *Shortcut:* This is an *optimizing deviation* since it leads to the same result (or the same intermediate result) as the correct sequence of computational steps, while simultaneously saving computational steps. Shortcuts may occur because of the visual redundancy on the screen. So the visible results of sequences of earlier computational steps may be used for handling later situations.

3.5 *Correction:* Recovering omissions, undoing computational steps, and replacing values by other values are corrections.

Faulty rule applications, interferences and omissions are *"bugs"*. Table 1 shows the absolute frequencies and percentages (in brackets) of types of computational steps for both rule sets:

		Computational steps			
		rule-consistent	bugs	shortcuts	corrections
Rule-set	operator-centered	7096 (97.82%)	71 (0.97%)	42 (0.58%)	45 (0.62%)
	state-centered	7815 (97.14%)	96 (1.19%)	38 (0.47%)	96 (1.19%)

Table 1: Absolute frequencies and percentages (in brackets) of types of computational steps for both rule sets

Within both rule sets, more than 97% of all computational steps were rule-consistent, and only about 1% were bugs. Although the subjects did not receive any feedback during the first computation of a program, the error rate was small. Moreover, there were no typical bugs. There are few examples of bugs for almost every 2-D-rule.

The results indicate that there is no need to redesign the 2-D-rule sets or to change specific rules. Moreover, the hypothesized differences between the two alternative 2-D-rule sets did not seem to show up in the behavior of the subjects. So they possibly used the rules to construct a mental representation which did not correspond to the different structure of the two 2-D-rule sets.

Some more observations should be mentioned though, which initiated some slight changes of the rules:

- 25 bugs altogether (= 15%) consisted of typing a wrong frame number. This supported the decision to drop the frame number, which was possible because the interpreter uses a linear stack, and there is at most one pending call in function bodies and in the start tree.

- 40 bugs altogether (= 24%) were omissions occurring with rules containing several computational steps in their action description, (i.e., rules for creating and deleting frames). This motivated a clarification of the structure and an improvement of the readability of the action descriptions of these rules.

- 37 more bugs (= 22%) were interferences occuring when the subjects worked in the head of a newly made frame. This caused us to clarify the structure and improve the readability of the situation descriptions of the rules for creating a new frame.

6. Representing Operational Semantic Knowledge of ABSYNT with 2-D-Rules

We tried to make the 2-D-rules as self-explaining as possible. Appendix A shows the rules from the *"operator-specific"* 2-D-rule set which is based on the abstract rule set B. Furthermore Appendix B shows the rules from the *"state-specific"* 2-D-rule set which is based on the abstract rule set C. Two examples of state-specific rules (rule 8 and 9) are shown in FIGUREs 3 and 4.

The operator-specific rules in appendix A are to be interpreted according to the following rough guidelines. The thick arrows on the left side of the rules indicate that this rule may be entered here. The thick arrows to the right side indicate that the rule may be left here. So, if the first situation description is true, the first action can be executed. Now the user may temporarily have to leave the rule in order to produce the computational state which satisfies the second situation description. He will have to do this with the help of other rules. If the second situation description is true, the second action can be performed. The same is true for a third situation-action pair.

In contrast to this, the state-specific rules (appendix B) are individual situation-action pairs. Like production rules they are not reentered a second time.

7. Summary

With the 2-D-rule sets at hand, we are now able to overcome the shortcomings of purely verbal or example based instructions. Now there is precise and unambiguous instructional and help material concerning the operational knowledge. We can be confident that the student acquires very easily and rapidly operational knowledge as a solid base for his programming and debugging activities which will be a further topic in our research.

References

ALBER, K., STRUCKMANN, W., Einführung in die Semantik von Programmiersprachen, Mannheim: BI-Wissenschaftsverlag, 1988
BAUER, F.L., GOOS, G.: Informatik, 1.Teil. Berlin, Springer, 1982 (3. Edition)
BOURNE, L.E.: An Inference Model of Conceptual Rule Learning. In: SOLSO, R. (ed): Theories in Cognitive Psychology. WASHINGTON, D.C.: ERLBAUM, 1974, 231-256
BROWN, J.S.; van LEHN, K.: Repair Theory: A Generative Theory of Bugs in Procedural Skills. Cognitive Science, 1980, 4, 379-426
CARROLL, J.M.: Minimalist Design for Active Users. In: SHACKLE, B. (ed): Interact 84, First IFIP Conference on Human-Computer-Interaction. Amsterdam: Elsevier/North Holland, 1984a
CARROLL, J.M.: Minimalist Training. Datamation, 1984b, 125-136
CHANG, S.K., Visual Languages: A Tutorial and Survey, in: P.GORNY & M.J.TAUBER (eds), Visualization in Programming, Lecture Notes in Computer Science, Heidelberg: Springer , 1987, 1- 23

CHASE, W. G., Visual Information Processing, in: K.R. BOFF, L. KAUFMAN, J.P. THOMAS (eds), Handbook of Perception and Human Performance, Vol. II, Cognitive Processes and Performance, New York: Wiley, 1986, 28-1 - 28-71

COLONIUS, H., FRANK, K.D., JANKE, G., KOHNERT, K., MÖBUS, C., SCHRÖDER, O., THOLE, H.J., Stand des DFG-Projekts "Entwicklung einer Wissensdiagnostik- und Fehlererklärungskomponente beim Erwerb von Programmierwissen für ABSYNT", in: R. GUNZENHÄUSER, H. MANDL (eds), "Intelligente Lernsysteme", Institut für Informatik der Universität Stuttgart, Deutsches Institut für Fernstudien an der Universität Tübingen, 1987, 80 - 90

COLONIUS, H., FRANK, K.D., JANKE, G., KOHNERT, K., MÖBUS, C., SCHRÖDER, O., THOLE, H.J., Syntaktische und semantische Fehler in funktionalen graphischen Programmen, ABSYNT Report 2/87, 1987

DAVIS, R.E., Runnable Specification as a Design Tool, in: K.L. CLARK, S.A. TÄRNLUND (eds), Logic Programming, New York: Academic Press, 1982, 141 - 149

FITTER, M; GREEN, T.R.G.: When Do Diagrams Make Good Computer Languages? Int. Journal of Man-Machine Studies, 1979, 11, 235-261, and in: COOMBS, M.J.; ALTY, J.L. (eds): Computing Skills and the User Interface. New York: Academic Press, 1981, 253-287

GENESERETH, M.R.; NILSSON, N..J.: Logical Foundations of Artificial Intelligence. Los Altos, California: Morgan Kaufman, 1987

GREEN, T.R.G.; SIME, M.E.; FITTER, M.J.: The Art of Notation. In: COOMBS, M.J.; ALTY, J.L. (eds): Computing Skills and the User Interface. New York: Academic Press, 1981, 221-251

HAYGOOD, R.C.; BOURNE, L.E.; Attribute- and Rule Learning Aspects of Conceptual Behaviour. Psychological Review, 1965, 72, 175-195

JANKE,G., KOHNERT,K., Interface Design of a Visual Programming Language: Evaluating Runnable Specifications, in: F.KLIX, H.WANDKE, N.A.STREITZ, Y.WAERN (eds), Man-Computer Interaction Research, MACINTER II, Amsterdam: North-Holland, 1989, 567-581

JOHNSON, W.L.; SOLOWAY, E: PROUST: An Automatic Debugger for PASCAL Programs. BYTE, 1985, April, 179-190, and in KEARSLEY, G.P. (ed): Artificial Intelligence and Instruction. Reading, Mass.: Addison Wesley, 1987, 49-67

KOHNERT, K., JANKE, G.: The Object-Oriented Inplementation of the ABSYNT-Environments. ABSYNT-Report 4/88, Project ABSYNT, FB 10, Unit on Tutoring and Learning Systems, University of Oldenburg, 1988

LARKIN, J.H.; SIMON, H.A.: Why a Diagram is (Sometimes) Worth More Than Ten Thousand Words. Cognitive Science, 1987, 11, 65-99

MEDIN, D.L.; WATTENMAKER, W.D.; MICHALSKI, R.S.: Constraints and Preferences in Inductive Learning: An Experimental Study of Human and Machine Performance. Cognitive Science, 1987, 11, 299-339

MIYAKE, N.: Constructive Interaction and the Iterative Process of Understanding. Cognitive Science, 10, 1986, 151-177

MÖBUS, C., Die Entwicklung zum Programmierexperten durch das Problemlösen mit Automaten, in: MANDL, FISCHER (Hrsgb), Lernen im Dialog mit dem Computer, München: Urban & Schwarzenberg, 1985, 140-154

MÖBUS, C., SCHRÖDER, O., Knowledge Specification and Instructions for a Visual Computer Language, in: F.KLIX, H.WANDKE, N.A.STREITZ, Y.WAERN (eds), Man-Computer Interaction Research, MACINTER II, Amsterdam: North-Holland, 1989, 535-565

MÖBUS, C., THOLE, H.J., Tutors, Instructions and Helps, in: CHRISTALLER, Th. (ed), Künstliche Intelligenz. KIFS87, Proceedings, Informatik-Fachberichte 202, Heidelberg: Springer, 1989, 336-385

PAGAN, F.G., Formal Specification of Programming Languages, Englewood Cliffs, N.J.: Prentice-Hall, 1981

PAYNE, S.J.; SIME, M.E.; GREEN, T.R.G.: Perceptual Structure Cueing in a Simple Command Language. Int. Journal of Man-Machine Studies, 1984, 21, 19-29

PENNINGTON, N.: Stimulus Structures and Mental Representations in Expert Comprehension of Computer Programs. Cognitive Psychology, 1987, 19, 295-341

POMERANTZ, J.R.: Perceptual Organization in Information Processing. In: AITKENHEAD, A.M.; SLACK, J.M. (eds): Issues in Cognitive Modeling. Hillsdale: Erlbaum, 1985, 127-158

SCHRÖDER, O., FRANK, K.D., COLONIUS, H., Gedächtnisrepräsentation funktionaler, graphischer Programme, ABSYNT-Report 1/87, Universität Oldenburg, 1987

SHU, N.C., Visual Programming Languages: A Perspective and a Dimensional Analysis, in: CHANG, T., ICHIKAWA, LIGOMENIDES, P.A.(eds), Visual Languages, New York: Plenum Press, 1986, 11-34

SLEEMAN, D.H., HENDLEY, R.J., ACE: A system which Analyses Complex Explanations, in: D.SLEEMAN, J.S.BROWN (eds), Intelligent Tutoring Systems, New York: Academic Press, 1982, 99 - 118

SOLOWAY, E.: Learning to Program = Learning to Construct Mechanisms and Explanations. Communications of the ACM, 29, 9, 1986, 850-858

Appendix A: Representing Computational Knowledge for ABSYNT with Operator Specific 2-D-ruleset

Rule 1: To compute the outputvalue of primitive operator nodes (except IF-THEN-ELSE-nodes !)

Rule 2: To fetch the input value for an operator node

Rule 3: To compute the outputvalue of the root of head

Rule 4: To fetch parameter bindings from the head for leafs in the body

Rule 5: To compute the outputvalue of a higher operator node (= user defined function) in the start tree

Rule 6: To compute the outputvalue of the IF-THEN-ELSE node in case of a true predicate

Rule 7: To compute the outputvalue of the IF-THEN-ELSE node in case of a false predicate

Rule 8: To compute the outputvalue of a higher operator node in a body tree

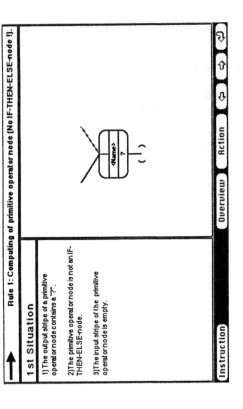

Rule 1: Computing of primitive operator node (No IF-THEN-ELSE-node !).

1st Situation

1) The output stripe of a primitive operator node contains a "?" .

2) The primitive operator node is not an IF-THEN-ELSE-node.

3) The input stripe of the primitive operator node is empty.

Instruction   Overview   Action

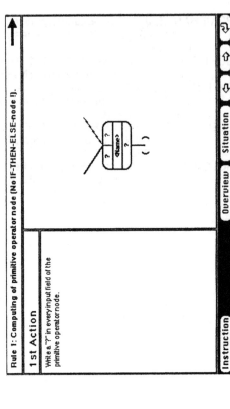

Rule 1: Computing of primitive operator node (No IF-THEN-ELSE-node !).

1st Action

Write a "?" in every input field of the primitive operator node.

Instruction   Overview   Situation

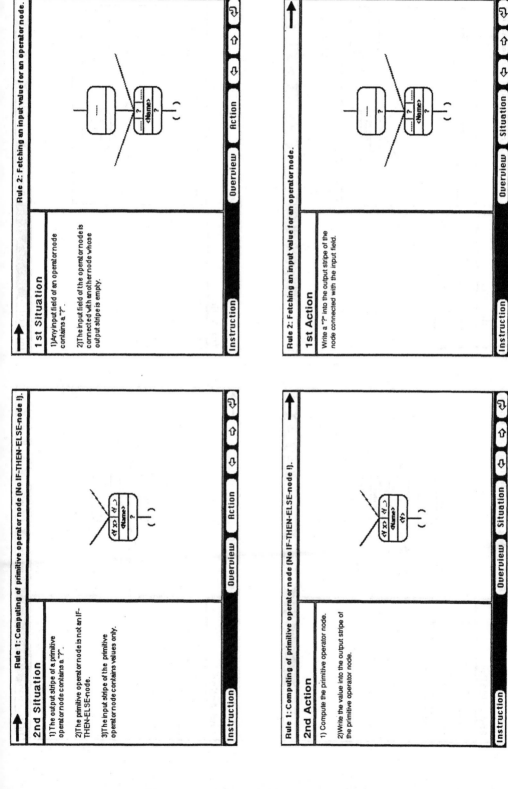

Rule 1: Computing of primitive operator node (No IF-THEN-ELSE-node).

2nd Situation

1) The output stripe of a primitive operator node contains a "?".

2) The primitive operator node is not an IF-THEN-ELSE-node.

3) The input stripe of the primitive operator node contains values only.

Instruction Overview Action

Rule 2: Fetching an input value for an operator node.

1st Situation

1) Any input field of an operator node contains a "?".

2) The input field of the operator node is connected with another node whose output stripe is empty.

Instruction Overview Action

Rule 1: Computing of primitive operator node (No IF-THEN-ELSE-node).

2nd Action

1) Compute the primitive operator node.

2) Write the value into the output stripe of the primitive operator node.

Instruction Overview Situation

Rule 2: Fetching an input value for an operator node.

1st Action

Write a "?" into the output stripe of the node connected with the input field.

Instruction Overview Situation

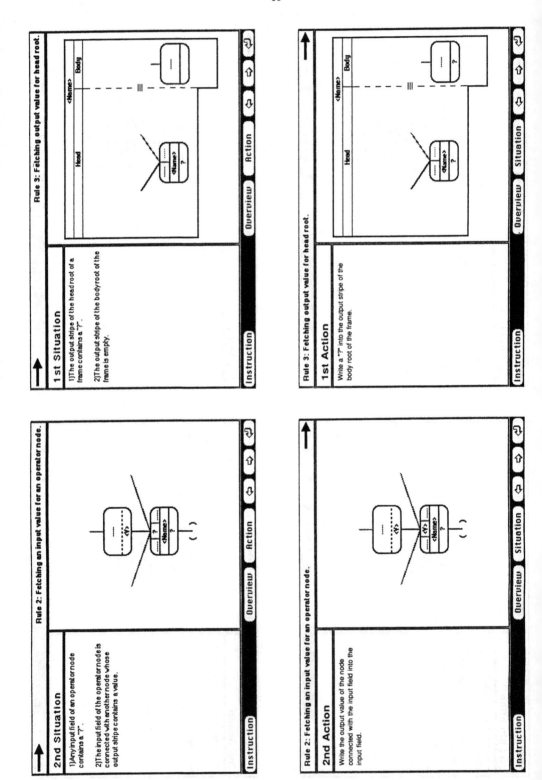

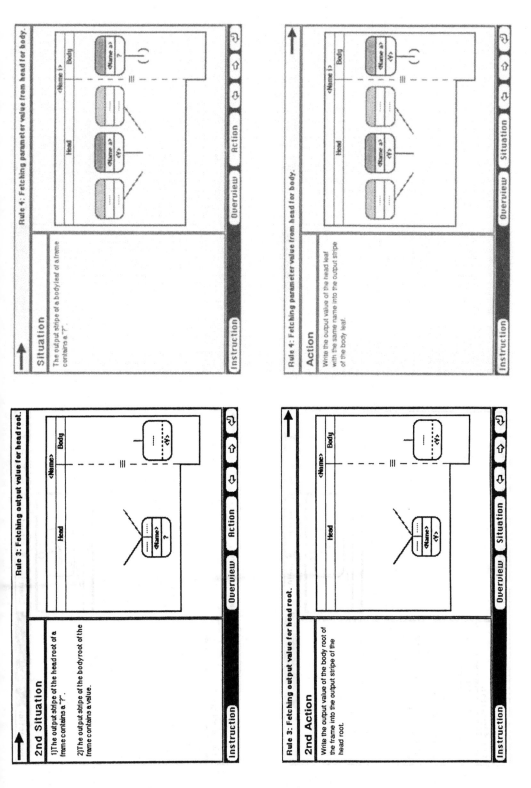

Rule 4: Fetching parameter value from head for body.

Situation

The output stripe of a body leaf of a frame contains a "?".

Overview | Action

Rule 4: Fetching parameter value from head for body.

Action

Write the output value of the head leaf with the same name into the output stripe of the body leaf.

Overview | Situation

Rule 3: Fetching output value for head root.

2nd Situation

1) The output stripe of the head root of a frame contains a "?".

2) The output stripe of the bodyroot of the frame contains a value.

Overview | Action

Rule 3: Fetching output value for head root.

2nd Action

Write the output value of the body root of the frame into the output stripe of the head root.

Overview | Situation

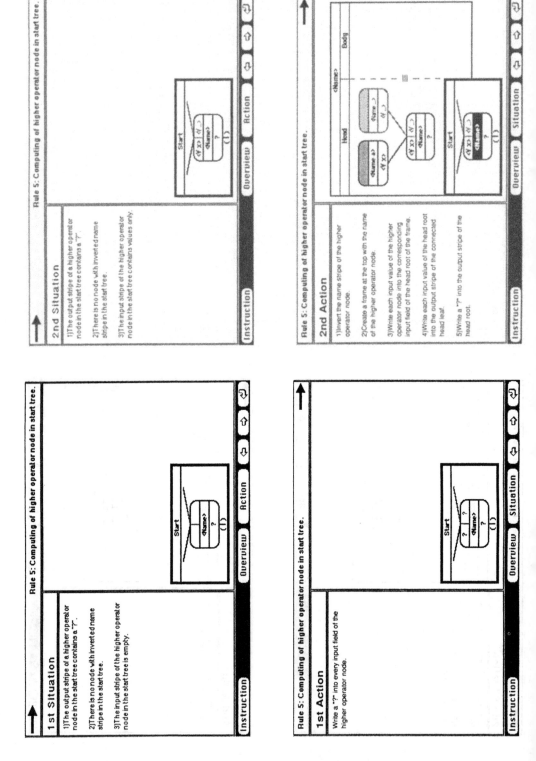

Rule 5: Computing of higher operator node in start tree.

Instruction

1st Situation

1) The output stripe of a higher operator node in the start tree contains a "?".

2) There is no node with inverted name stripe in the start tree.

3) The input stripe of the higher operator node in the start tree is empty.

Start
<Name>
(1)

Overview Action

Rule 5: Computing of higher operator node in start tree.

Instruction

1st Action

Write a "?" into every input field of the higher operator node.

Start
? ?
<Name>
(1)

Overview Situation

Rule 5: Computing of higher operator node in start tree.

Instruction

2nd Situation

1) The output stripe of a higher operator node in the start tree contains a "?".

2) There is no node with inverted name stripe in the start tree.

3) The input stripe of the higher operator node in the start tree contains values only.

Start
<X x> | <Y y>
?
<Name>
(1)

Overview Action

Rule 5: Computing of higher operator node in start tree.

Instruction

2nd Action

1) Invert the name stripe of the higher operator node.

2) Create a frame at the top with the name of the higher operator node.

3) Write each input value of the higher operator node into the corresponding input field of the head root of the frame.

4) Write each input value of the head root into the output stripe of the connected head leaf.

5) Write a "?" into the output stripe of the head root.

Head   <Name>
<Name a>   <Name _>
<Y x>   <Y _>

Body

Start
<X x> | <Y y>
?
<Name>
(1)

Overview Situation

Rule 5: Computing of higher operator node in start tree.

3rd Situation

1) The output stripe of a higher operator node in the start tree contains a "?".

2) The name stripe of the higher operator node is inverted.

3) The input stripe of the higher operator node contains values only.

4) There is a frame at the top with the name of the higher operator node.

5) The output stripe of the headroot contains a value.

Overview | Action

Instruction

Rule 6: Computing of IF-THEN-ELSE-node (1st rule).

1st Situation

1) The output stripe of an IF-THEN-ELSE-node contains a "?".

2) The input stripe of the IF-THEN-ELSE-node is empty.

Overview | Action

Instruction

Rule 5: Computing of higher operator node in start tree.

3rd Action

1) Write the output value of the head root of the frame into the output stripe of the higher operator node with the inverted name stripe.

3) Delete the upper frame.

2) Undo the inversion of the name stripe of the higher operator node.

Overview | Situation

Instruction

Rule 6: Computing of IF-THEN-ELSE-node (1st rule).

1st Action

Write a "?" into the 1st input field of the IF-THEN-ELSE-node.

Overview | Situation

Instruction

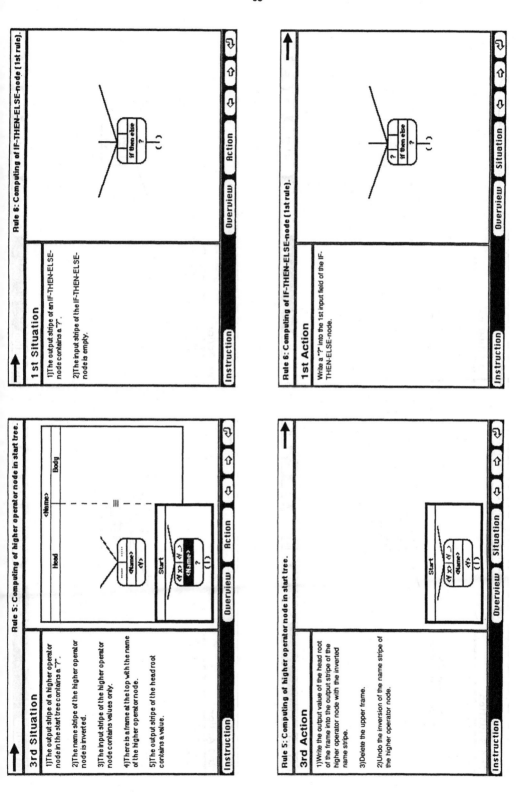

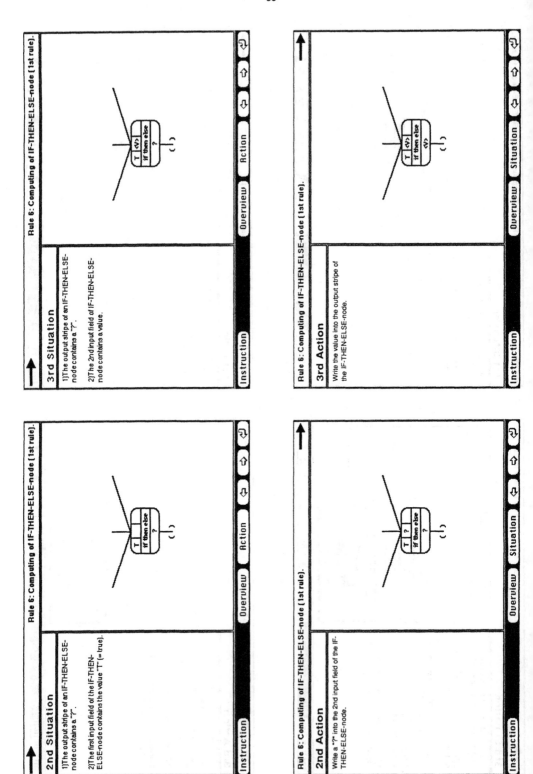

Rule 6: Computing of IF-THEN-ELSE-node (1st rule).

2nd Situation

1) The output stripe of an IF-THEN-ELSE-node contains a "?".

2) The first input field of the IF-THEN-ELSE-node contains the value "T" (= true).

Instruction   Overview   Action

Rule 6: Computing of IF-THEN-ELSE-node (1st rule).

3rd Situation

1) The output stripe of an IF-THEN-ELSE-node contains a "?".

2) The 2nd input field of IF-THEN-ELSE-node contains a value.

Instruction   Overview   Situation

Rule 6: Computing of IF-THEN-ELSE-node (1st rule).

2nd Action

Write a "?" into the 2nd input field of the IF-THEN-ELSE-node.

Instruction   Overview   Situation

Rule 6: Computing of IF-THEN-ELSE-node (1st rule).

3rd Action

Write the value into the output stripe of the IF-THEN-ELSE-node.

Instruction   Overview   Situation

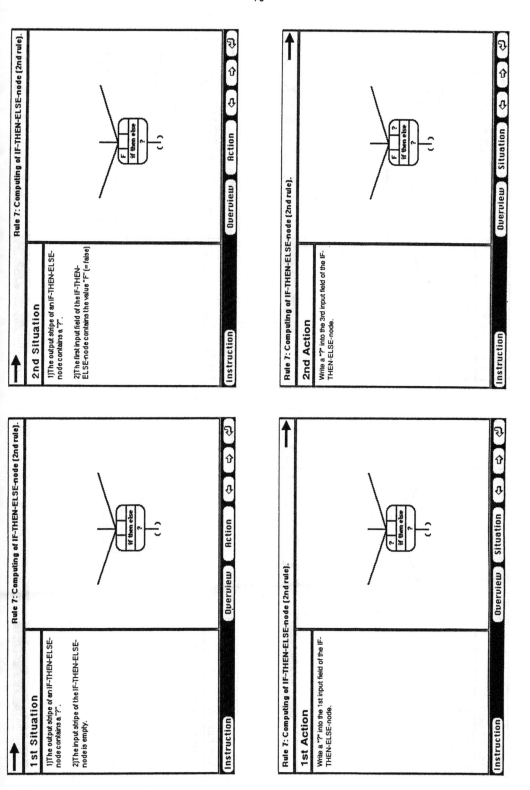

Rule 7: Computing of IF-THEN-ELSE-node [2nd rule].

1st Situation

1) The output stripe of an IF-THEN-ELSE-node contains a "?".

2) The input stripe of the IF-THEN-ELSE-node is empty.

Overview | Action

Instruction

Rule 7: Computing of IF-THEN-ELSE-node [2nd rule].

2nd Situation

1) The output stripe of an IF-THEN-ELSE-node contains a "?".

2) The first input field of the IF-THEN-ELSE-node contains the value "F" (= false)

Overview | Action

Instruction

Rule 7: Computing of IF-THEN-ELSE-node [2nd rule].

1st Action

Write a "?" into the 1st input field of the IF-THEN-ELSE-node.

Overview | Situation

Instruction

Rule 7: Computing of IF-THEN-ELSE-node [2nd rule].

2nd Action

Write a "?" into the 3rd input field of the IF-THEN-ELSE-node.

Overview | Situation

Instruction

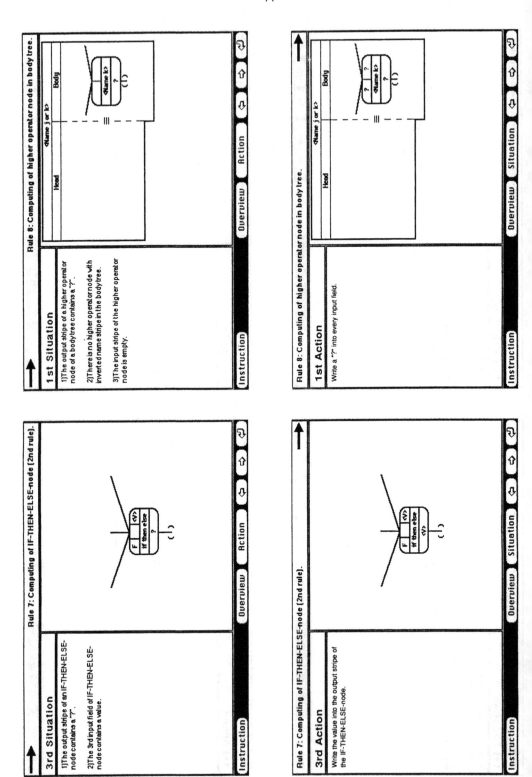

Rule 7: Computing of IF-THEN-ELSE-node (2nd rule).

3rd Situation

1) The output stripe of an IF-THEN-ELSE-node contains a "?".

2) The 3rd input field of IF-THEN-ELSE-node contains a value.

Overview Action Instruction

Rule 8: Computing of higher operator node in body tree.

Head | <Name j or k> | Body

1st Situation

1) The output stripe of a higher operator node of a bodytree contains a "?".

2) There is no higher operator node with inverted name stripe in the bodytree.

3) The input stripe of the higher operator node is empty.

Overview Action Instruction

Rule 7: Computing of IF-THEN-ELSE-node (2nd rule).

3rd Action

Write the value into the output stripe of the IF-THEN-ELSE-node.

Overview Situation Instruction

Rule 8: Computing of higher operator node in body tree.

Head | <Name j or k> | Body

1st Action

Write a "?" into every input field.

Overview Situation Instruction

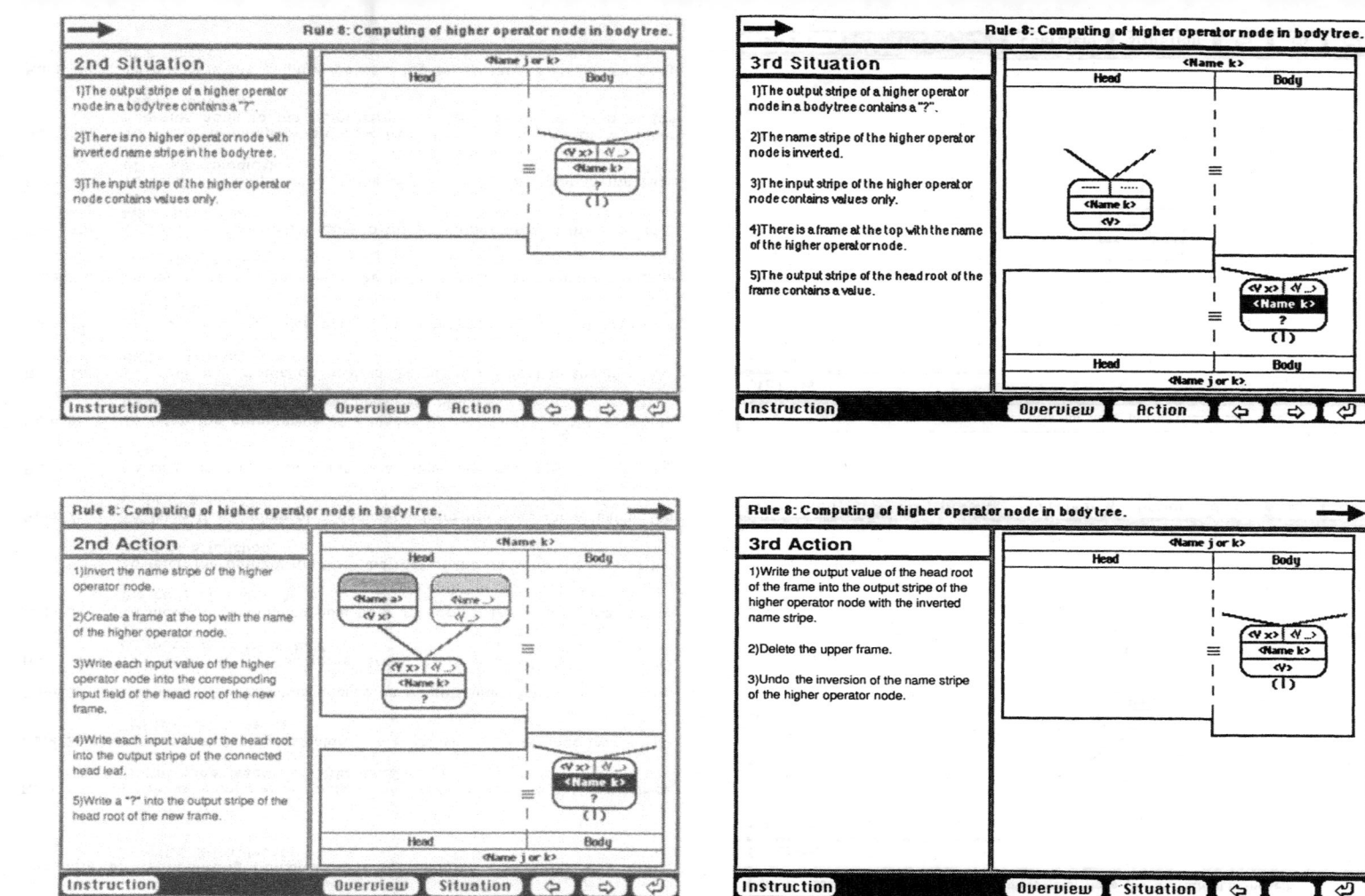

Panel 1 (top-left)

Rule 8: Computing of higher operator node in body tree.

2nd Situation

1) The output stripe of a higher operator node in a body tree contains a "?".

2) There is no higher operator node with inverted name stripe in the body tree.

3) The input stripe of the higher operator node contains values only.

Instruction · Overview · Action

Panel 2 (top-right)

Rule 8: Computing of higher operator node in body tree.

3rd Situation

1) The output stripe of a higher operator node in a body tree contains a "?".

2) The name stripe of the higher operator node is inverted.

3) The input stripe of the higher operator node contains values only.

4) There is a frame at the top with the name of the higher operator node.

5) The output stripe of the head root of the frame contains a value.

Instruction · Overview · Action

Panel 3 (bottom-left)

Rule 8: Computing of higher operator node in body tree.

2nd Action

1) Invert the name stripe of the higher operator node.

2) Create a frame at the top with the name of the higher operator node.

3) Write each input value of the higher operator node into the corresponding input field of the head root of the new frame.

4) Write each input value of the head root into the output stripe of the connected head leaf.

5) Write a "?" into the output stripe of the head root of the new frame.

Instruction · Overview · Situation

Panel 4 (bottom-right)

Rule 8: Computing of higher operator node in body tree.

3rd Action

1) Write the output value of the head root of the frame into the output stripe of the higher operator node with the inverted name stripe.

2) Delete the upper frame.

3) Undo the inversion of the name stripe of the higher operator node.

Instruction · Overview · Situation

Appendix B: Representing Computational Knowledge for ABSYNT with State-Specific 2-D-ruleset

Rule 1: To move computation goals in an operator node to the inputstripe of the node (except IF-THEN-ELSE-node !)

Rule 2: To compute the outputvalue of a primitive operator node (except IF-THEN-ELSE-node !)

Rule 3: To move a computation goal to an outputstripe of a connected node

Rule 4: To fetch an outputvalue from a connected node for the corresponding input field

Rule 5: To move a computation goal from the root of the head to the root of the body of a function

Rule 6: To fetch the outputvalue from the root of the body for the root of the head of a function

Rule 7: To fetch the binding of a parameter from the head for a leaf in the body of a function

Rule 8: To compute the outputvalue of a higher operator node in the start tree

Rule 9: To fetch the outputvalue of a higher operator node in the start tree from the root of the head of the called function

Rule 10: To move a computation goal to the predicate field in the IF-THEN-ELSE operator

Rule 11: To move a computation goal to the THEN-inputfield in the case of a true predicate

Rule 12: To fetch the outputvalue in the IF-THEN-ELSE operator in the case of a true predicate

Rule 13: To move a computation goal to the ELSE-inputfield in the case of a false predicate

Rule 14: To fetch the outputvalue in the IF-THEN-ELSE operator in the case of a false predicate

Rule 15: To move a computation goal from the outputstripe of a higher operator node to the outputstripe of the root in the head of the called function

Rule 16: To compute the outputvalue of a higher operator node in the body of a function

---

Rule 1: Passing goals to input stripe of operator node (No IF-THEN-ELSE-node!).

Situation

1) The output stripe of an operator node contains a "?".

2)The operator node is not an IF-THEN-ELSE-node.

3)The input stripe of the operator node is empty.

Overview   Action

Instruction

Rule 1: Passing goals to input stripe of operator node (No IF-THEN-ELSE-node!).

Action

Write a "?" in every input field of the operator node.

Overview   Situation

Instruction

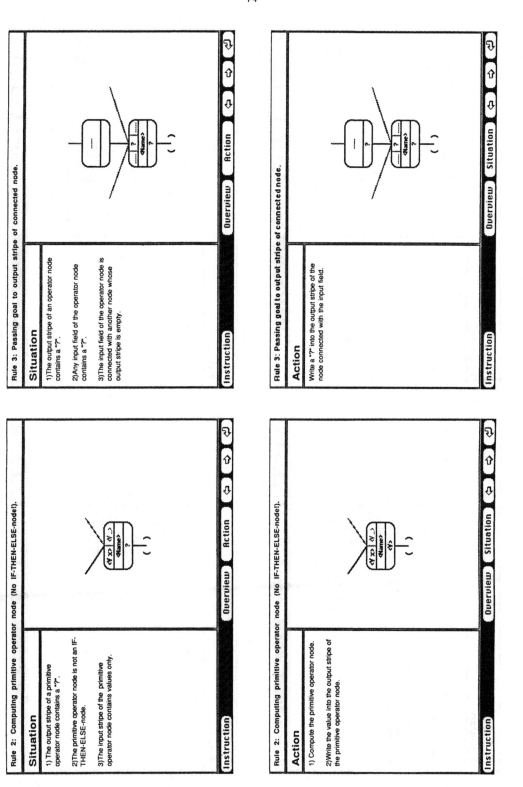

Rule 3: Passing goal to output stripe of connected node.

Situation

1) The output stripe of an operator node contains a "?".

2) Any input field of the operator node contains a "?".

3) The input field of the operator node is connected with another node whose output stripe is empty.

Instruction · Overview · Action

Rule 3: Passing goal to output stripe of connected node.

Action

Write a "?" into the output stripe of the node connected with the input field.

Instruction · Overview · Situation

Rule 2: Computing primitive operator node (No IF-THEN-ELSE-node).

Situation

1) The output stripe of a primitive operator node contains a "?".

2) The primitive operator node is not an IF-THEN-ELSE-node.

3) The input stripe of the primitive operator node contains values only.

Instruction · Overview · Action

Rule 2: Computing primitive operator node (No IF-THEN-ELSE-node).

Action

1) Compute the primitive operator node.

2) Write the value into the output stripe of the primitive operator node.

Instruction · Overview · Situation

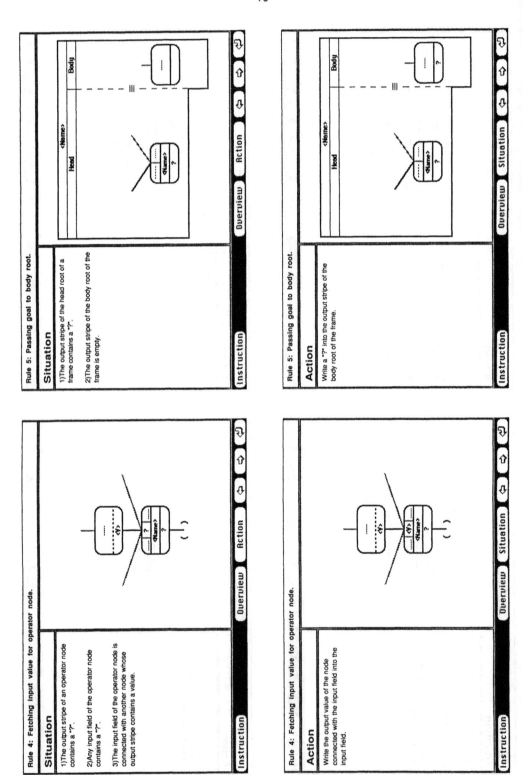

Rule 4: Fetching input value for operator node.

Situation

1)The output stripe of an operator node contains a "?".

2)Any input field of the operator node contains a "?".

3)The input field of the operator node is connected with another node whose output stripe contains a value.

Overview · Action · Instruction

Rule 5: Passing goal to body root.

Situation

1)The output stripe of the head root of a frame contains a "?".

2)The output stripe of the body root of the frame is empty.

Head   <Name>   Body

Overview · Action · Instruction

Rule 4: Fetching input value for operator node.

Action

Write the output value of the node connected with the input field into the input field.

Overview · Situation · Instruction

Rule 5: Passing goal to body root.

Action

Write a "?" into the output stripe of the body root of the frame.

Overview · Situation · Instruction

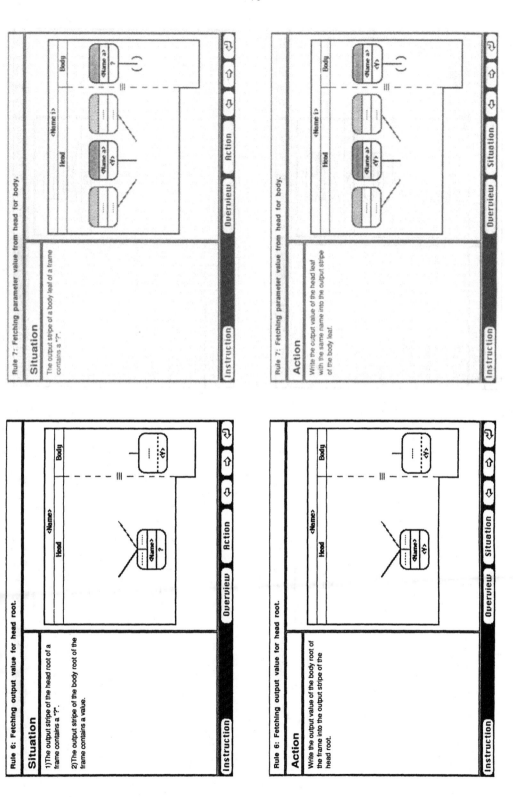

Rule 7: Fetching parameter value from head for body.

Situation

The output stripe of a body leaf of a frame contains a "?".

Overview | Action

Instruction

Rule 7: Fetching parameter value from head for body.

Action

Write the output value of the head leaf with the same name into the output stripe of the body leaf.

Overview | Situation

Instruction

Rule 6: Fetching output value for head root.

Situation

1) The output stripe of the head root of a frame contains a "?".

2) The output stripe of the body root of the frame contains a value.

Overview | Action

Instruction

Rule 6: Fetching output value for head root.

Action

Write the output value of the body root of the frame into the output stripe of the head root.

Overview | Situation

Instruction

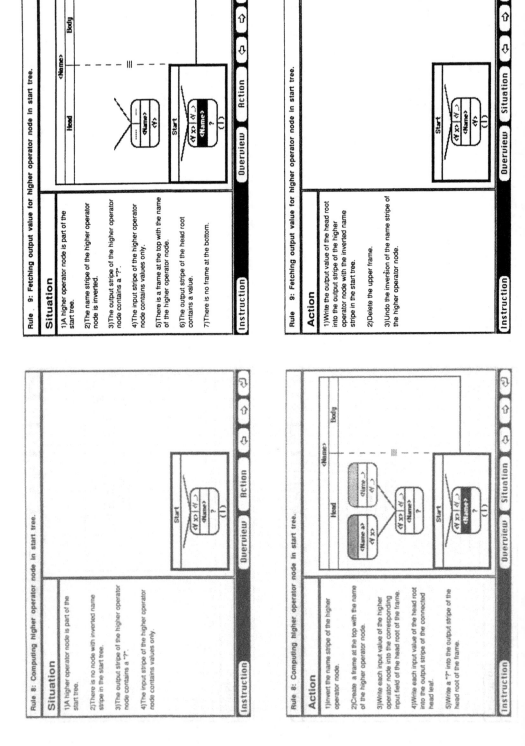

Rule 9: Fetching output value for higher operator node in start tree.

Situation

1) A higher operator node is part of the start tree.

2) The name stripe of the higher operator node is inverted.

3) The output stripe of the higher operator node contains a "?".

4) The input stripe of the higher operator node contains values only.

5) There is a frame at the top with the name of the higher operator node.

6) The output stripe of the head root contains a value.

7) There is no frame at the bottom.

Instruction | Overview | Action

Rule 9: Fetching output value for higher operator node in start tree.

Action

1) Write the output value of the head root into the output stripe of the higher operator node with the inverted name stripe in the start tree.

2) Delete the upper frame.

3) Undo the inversion of the name stripe of the higher operator node.

Instruction | Overview | Situation

Rule 8: Computing higher operator node in start tree.

Situation

1) A higher operator node is part of the start tree.

2) There is no node with inverted name stripe in the start tree.

3) The output stripe of the higher operator node contains a "?".

4) The input stripe of the higher operator node contains values only.

Instruction | Overview | Action

Rule 8: Computing higher operator node in start tree.

Action

1) Invert the name stripe of the higher operator node.

2) Create a frame at the top with the name of the higher operator node.

3) Write each input value of the higher operator node into the corresponding input field of the head root of the frame.

4) Write each input value of the head root into the output stripe of the connected head leaf.

5) Write a "?" into the output stripe of the head root of the frame.

Instruction | Overview | Situation

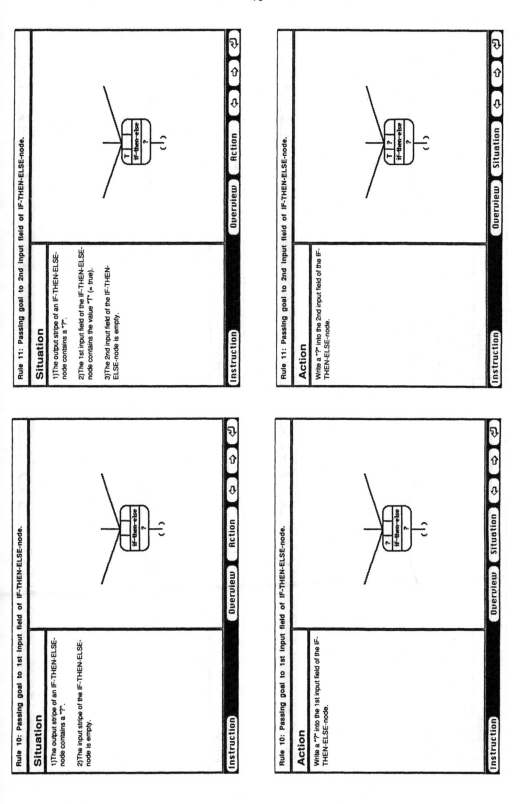

Rule 10: Passing goal to 1st Input field of IF-THEN-ELSE-node.

Situation

1) The output stripe of an IF-THEN-ELSE-node contains a "?".

2) The input stripe of the IF-THEN-ELSE-node is empty.

Overview   Action

Instruction

Rule 10: Passing goal to 1st Input field of IF-THEN-ELSE-node.

Action

Write a "?" into the 1st input field of the IF-THEN-ELSE-node.

Overview   Situation

Instruction

Rule 11: Passing goal to 2nd Input field of IF-THEN-ELSE-node.

Situation

1) The output stripe of an IF-THEN-ELSE-node contains a "?".

2) The 1st input field of the IF-THEN-ELSE-node contains the value "T" (= true).

3) The 2nd input field of the IF-THEN-ELSE-node is empty.

Overview   Action

Instruction

Rule 11: Passing goal to 2nd Input field of IF-THEN-ELSE-node.

Action

Write a "?" into the 2nd input field of the IF-THEN-ELSE-node.

Overview   Situation

Instruction

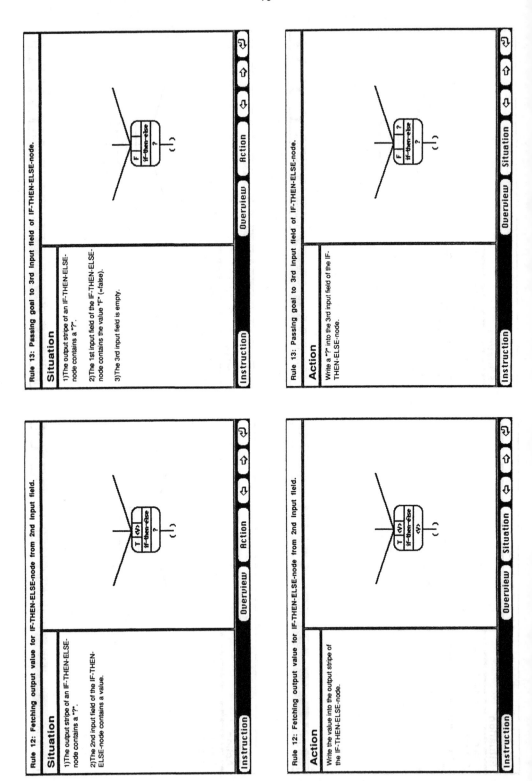

Rule 12:: Fetching output value for IF-THEN-ELSE-node from 2nd input field.

Situation

1)The output stripe of an IF-THEN-ELSE-node contains a "?".

2)The 2nd input field of the IF-THEN-ELSE-node contains a value.

Overview | Action

Instruction

Rule 12:: Fetching output value for IF-THEN-ELSE-node from 2nd input field.

Action

Write the value into the output stripe of the IF-THEN-ELSE-node.

Overview | Situation

Instruction

Rule 13: Passing goal to 3rd input field of IF-THEN-ELSE-node.

Situation

1)The output stripe of an IF-THEN-ELSE-node contains a "?".

2)The 1st input field of the IF-THEN-ELSE-node contains the value "F" (=false).

3)The 3rd input field is empty.

Overview | Action

Instruction

Rule 13: Passing goal to 3rd input field of IF-THEN-ELSE-node.

Action

Write a "?" into the 3rd input field of the IF-THEN-ELSE-node.

Overview | Situation

Instruction

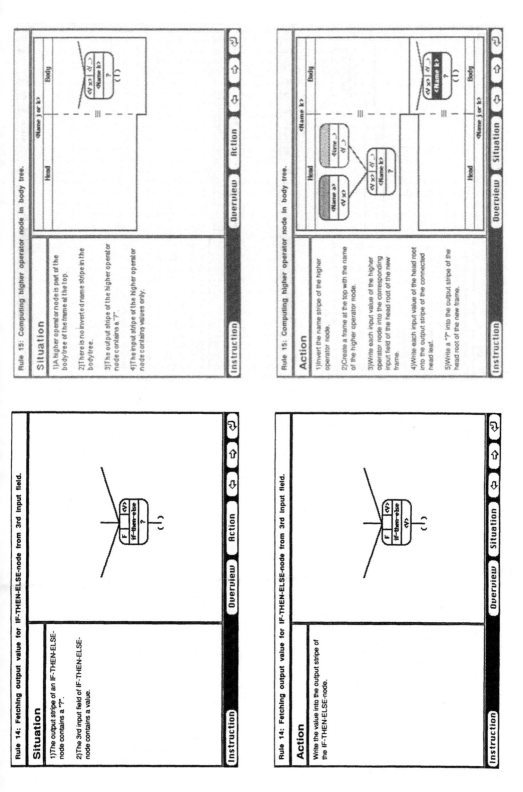

Rule 14: Fetching output value for IF-THEN-ELSE-node from 3rd input field.

Situation

1) The output stripe of an IF-THEN-ELSE-node contains a "?".

2) The 3rd input field of IF-THEN-ELSE-node contains a value.

Instruction | Overview | Action

Rule 14: Fetching output value for IF-THEN-ELSE-node from 3rd input field.

Action

Write the value into the output stripe of the IF-THEN-ELSE-node.

Instruction | Overview | Situation

Rule 15: Computing higher operator node in body tree.

Situation

1) A higher operator node is part of the body tree of the frame at the top.

2) There is no inverted name stripe in the body tree.

3) The output stripe of the higher operator node contains a "?".

4) The input stripe of the higher operator node contains values only.

Instruction | Overview | Action

Rule 15: Computing higher operator node in body tree.

Action

1) Invert the name stripe of the higher operator node.

2) Create a frame at the top with the name of the higher operator node.

3) Write each input value of the higher operator node into the corresponding input field of the head root of the new frame.

4) Write each input value of the head root into the output stripe of the connected head leaf.

5) Write a "?" into the output stripe of the head root of the new frame.

Instruction | Overview | Situation

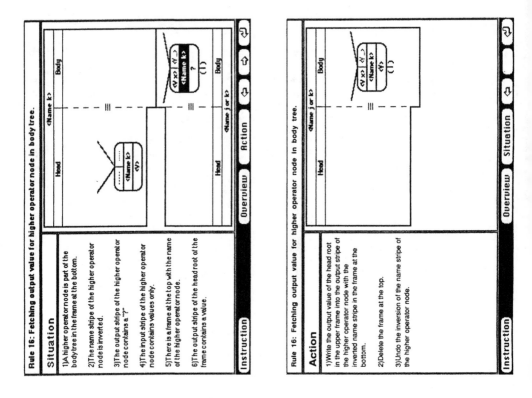

Rule 16: Fetching output value for higher operator node in body tree.

Situation

1) A higher operator node is part of the body tree in the frame at the bottom.

2) The name stripe of the higher operator node is inverted.

3) The output stripe of the higher operator node contains a "?"

4) The input stripe of the higher operator node contains values only.

5) There is a frame at the top with the name of the higher operator node.

6) The output stripe of the head root of the frame contains a value.

Overview | Action

Instruction

Rule 16: Fetching output value for higher operator node in body tree.

Action

1) Write the output value of the head root in the upper frame into the output stripe of the higher operator node with the inverted name stripe in the frame at the bottom.

2) Delete the frame at the top.

3) Undo the inversion of the name stripe of the higher operator node.

Overview | Situation

Instruction

A Graphical Representation of the Prolog Programmer's Knowledge

J. POLAK*   S.P. GUEST

Department of Computer Studies,
Loughborough University of Technology,
Loughborough LE11 3TU, United Kingdom.

*Visiting research fellow from the Department of Computers,
Czech University of Technology,
Karlovo n. 13, Prague, Czechoslovakia.

Abstract

This paper is concerned with the ability to provide the user of Prolog with a visual understanding of the language and its use. A graphical display is used to do this, based on the original 'box' model. The ideas presented here were initially derived from existing designs of Prolog database representations, but they are then linked in a real-time teaching and debugging environment. An introduction of the design and function of the tool is given, along with some examples of how the system appears to the user.

1.   Introduction

It has long been known that the learning of Prolog is not always an easy task. It can depend greatly on your previous knowledge. Initially the user needs to understand that the Prolog system simply searches its information base in an attempt to find the answer to a problem. The art, as some call it, of Prolog programming is to try and understand the steps through the search path and out again. Those who are experts in the use of top-down parsers may have a reasonable starting point to understand what Prolog is attempting to do when asked to evaluate some statement. We are concerned with those that do not.

For those who do not understand the theory of parsers then there must be some other way of learning the processes which Prolog uses in its attempts to answer problems. The first thing is to begin by forgetting most, if not all, of any procedural and list programming language knowledge that has been learnt over many hard years. Now if you can do that then you can now start to learn Prolog.

To begin with you must first understand that all Prolog uses are facts that are stored in its database. Next you must try and understand the path that a search for a solution to a problem will take within this database of facts. Now you understand these features you can begin to construct a simple Prolog program.

At this point most conventional programmers are either about to give up or are really dedicated. The simple task of trying to visualize what a Prolog program, and the structures within it, might do is very complex. It would be much simpler if the user could actually see the act of running the program. This would also be helped if a graphical approach was taken to display such a search path.

There are different approaches to the representation of Prolog programs. There are at least three ways in which Prolog tools could or are used. These are as follows:

1) Organizing textual information on paper/display to a more readable and understandable form. This is the common C-Prolog trace style of information.

2) A static graphical description of Prolog program, used mostly in text books.

3) A graphical tool for interactive programming and debugging.

As already stated this paper is interested in the third option. The use of a graphical tool is generally accepted as the best way of displaying complex knowledge.

As a general rule all programmers should develop their programs, whether these are written in Prolog or any other language, in an environment which should be very coherent and understandable. This will help to prevent errors, simplify the design process for the program and make the debugging as easy as possible.

Debugging is a difficult and time consuming problem solving task, so any graphical interactive (i.e. dynamic) tools that could help to overcome any problems easily should be useful. It must be emphasized that a graphical representation for any debugging system must have the same constructs as used in the program design process. This is a further problem in attempting to provide a lucid meaningful representation of a declarative programming language, such as Prolog. It would appear that this can only be solved by the procedural interpretation of Prolog program. The procedural interpretation of Prolog programs is very important for Prolog "machine" behaviour to be understood

There have been many different approaches to the visualization of Prolog computation rules. The very first "debugging box" model was not fully evaluated and used in its graphical form. The use of this lucid visualization format, as described in the first Prolog text book (Clocksin & Mellish, 1981), seems never to have been exploited.

2. The System

The system described here is based on the box model used initially for the Edinburgh Prolog trace information. This system introduces a graphical representation for all built-in predicates and for variable binding. There is also a style of graphical memory to support a clear representation for the backtracking process.

The system can be used to describe the knowledge that is built into a Prolog program, and thus help in both the comprehension and debugging of that program. Therefore this becomes more than a debugging aid. It is used to demonstrate and explain the workings of the Prolog machine.

Thus the implementation of this environment starts as a graphical tracer with an advanced user interface. Its next task is to be a graphical Prolog computation model for the design of program on the display. This means that the novice programmer can quickly visualize the state of a program and thus develop it. It also uses the Occam style of folding to allow expansion and reduction of the visual elements.

The graphical Prolog computation model should be the "story" for novice Prolog programmers, because all the ten points from the H. Pain and A. Bundy (Pain & Bundy, 1987) paper are satisfied by our graphical model. Pain refers to the box model, but unfortunately it is not presented in its graphical form. In this system it is proposed to use it for teaching purposes.

A uniform graphical story based on the Byrd box model (Byrd, 1980) for Prolog programs is presented. It seems to satisfy all the demands for such a story as described in Pain & Bundy's paper (Pain & Bundy, 1987). It is also very lucid because it uses only three graphical building units together with connecting lines.

3.   Introduction to Prolog Graphical Representation

Prolog should be understood to be an assistant, or friend. In this paper we will attempt to instil both the understanding needed to use Prolog and to make it appear friendly. To do this we will provide Prolog with a character, but do not wish to imply that we are correct in our assumptions on this point.

3.1.   Small bits of Prolog

Let us imagine that a Prolog system is a good friend who is able to remember perfectly any information we have told him. Then, when asked, he is able to answer our questions which relate to this information. So if we have initially given Prolog some information, *facts*: like these:

> **my_friend_is(prolog).**
> **my_friend_is(tom).**
> **my_friend_is(mary).**

Prolog can answer our *questions* according to this information. This information is really Prolog knowledge, which we put into the system. For example we can ask Prolog to decide who is my friend, or more accurately who "my_friend_is" (to understand this it should be stated that Prolog *variables* usually start with a capital letter, e.g. WHO):

> **?- my_friend_is(WHO).**

Prolog's answer is "prolog". Every question given to Prolog establishes some kind of a goal for it to reach, so we say that it has *satisfied* a given *goal* - which is **my_friend_is(WHO)** - and responds, quite rightly, with:

> **WHO = prolog**

It is a feature of Prolog that there may be further correct responses to the question. In this case it is not the only one right *answer* as we know. To ask Prolog check for more possible answers we have to say "is there anybody more known as my friend ?"; simply is there any other solution for the given goal? To do this Prolog we simply type a semi-colon ";" which always means *or* :

> **WHO = prolog ;**
> **WHO = tom**

We have obtained further answers to our question. When we try to ask Prolog to answer the same question, after a successful response, we say that we are asking it to *resatisfy* a goal, or simply *redo* it. The whole session dialogue follows:

?- my_friend_is(WHO).
WHO = prolog ;
WHO = tom ;
WHO = mary ;
no

So we can see Prolog answers: my friend is prolog, tom, mary and nobody more. Now if we were to ask if pascal is my friend:

?- my_friend_is(pascal).

And the answer understandably is simply no:

no

If we would simply like to discover if we have any friends then we would put the question slightly differently. We use the so called *anonymous variable,* symbol "_", because we are not actually interested in who the friend(s) is:

?- my_friend_is(_).

Here the answer is yes:

yes

Now we are able to introduce a graphical model of Prolog programmer's knowledge about the execution of Prolog programs.

3.2. Basic graphics units

For a lot of people any program, especially Prolog, is a black box. We start from the same point. What we do besides this is to add four arrows, which are connected to four possible Prolog experiences, or behaviours of the program, figure 1.

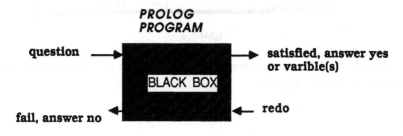

Figure 1

Hopefully it is clear that a program will consist of many parts, so there is normally something within the box. There can also be cases of empty programs, which would look like the program in figure 2.

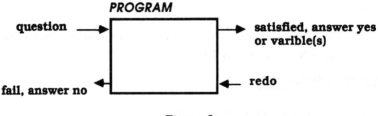

Figure 2

Our simple program in figure 3 contains three facts (please note that we will now only make brief comments on the arrows).

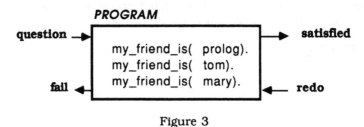

Figure 3

We shall show most elements of Prolog within the box model. It is assumed that every element of a Prolog program can be described using this box model. However, we need to make our box more abstract, see figure 4.

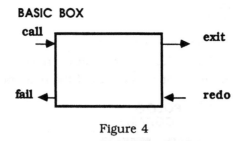

Figure 4

We can now put the facts to this box and our program is now represented by the graphical form shown in figure 5.

PROGRAM

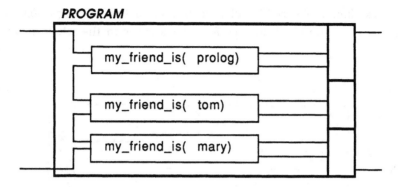

Figure 5

We can now ask this program a question, and watch the search path, figure 6.

?- my_friend_is(WHO).

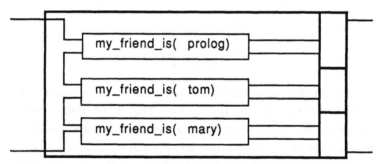

Figure 6

The Prolog system will start to search in its knowledge base for the answer to this question. To indicate this search path the computer uses a bold line to show the execution progress, figure 7.

?- my_friend_is(WHO).

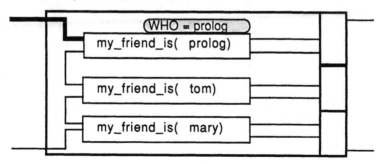

Figure 7

Using the first fact the variable WHO is bound to the value "prolog". It is the answer for this question and is therefore the answer to the whole program, see figure 8.

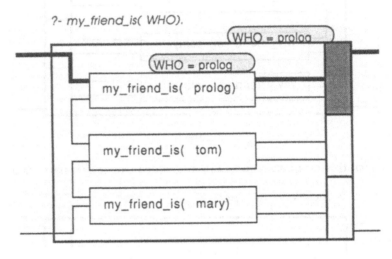

Figure 8

Note that the box on the right in figure 8 is shaded darker to indicate which way the search path came in obtaining the answer. This information will be needed for possible, and expected, redo. A redo is a demand for the continuation of the search for another answer to our question, see figure 9. This uses the technique known as backtracking through the knowledge base. The redo is requested by the user typing a semi-colon, ";".

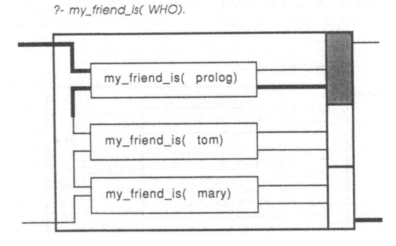

Figure 9

At this situation we can see in figure 9 that the previously bound variables are being unbound. This will happen whenever the search path comes back into the box through the entry path redo. The backtracking path is shown to the user via the dark shaded memory box. This helps to indicate which internal box should be reached next to continue the search. Figure 10 shows the second answer to this question.

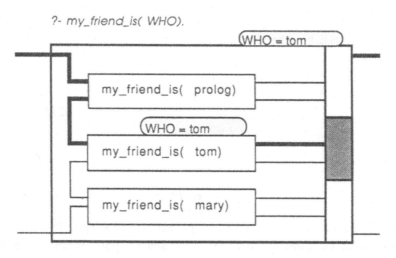

?- my_friend_is(WHO).

Figure 10

Note that in figure 10 the middle backtracking memory indicator is now shaded. This stresses the path used for this answer, and allows the user to remember which search path was used. Now for the next redo entry shown in figure 11.

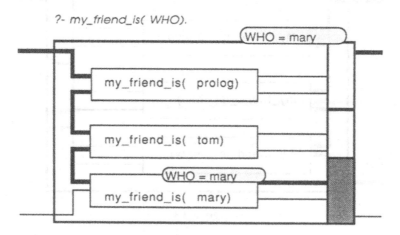

?- my_friend_is(WHO).

Figure 11

If we ask the system to redo this question a third time, it will present the answer no, see figure 12.

?- my_friend_is(WHO).

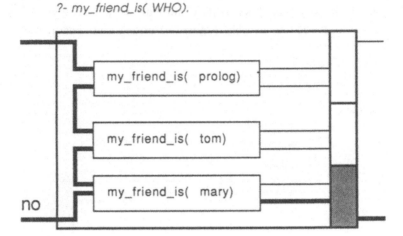

Figure 12

In the previous section we also asked if "pascal" is my friend. The next picture is only a repetition of known rules, with the search path failing each fact. The program will respond no and would appear in the Prolog graphical execution model as figure 13.

?- my_friend_is(pascal).

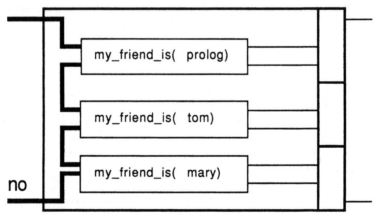

Figure 13

When we use the anonymous variable its scope is local, so its value is not shown on the higher box level. As we show in figure 14 the only response is yes.

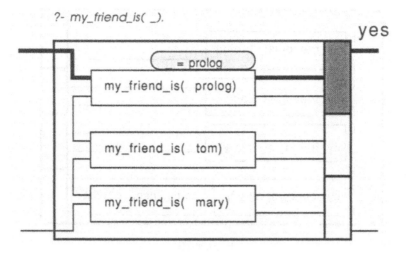

?- *my_friend_is(_).*

yes

Figure 14

We can make our simple program more complex by the introduction of a *rule*. A rule is a method of connecting facts from within the knowledge base. The fact that is added in figure 15 states that every known friend of Tom's is also my friend. Before we can make use of this rule we have to also add facts about Tom's friends.

```
my_friend_is( prolog).
my_friend_is( tom).
my_friend_is(mary).
my_friend_is( WHO) :-   toms_friend_is( WHO).


toms_friend_is(pascal).
toms_friend_is(john).
toms_friend_is(peggy).
```

Figure 15

In figure 16 we show only part of our program, facts about Tom's friends are hidden. How we can still use this representation shall be shown later. Note that a rule is easily expressed using the basic boxes.

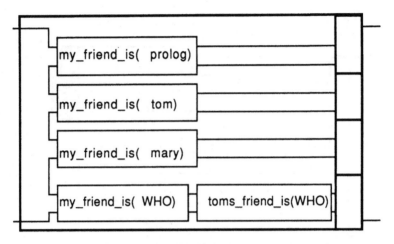

Figure 16

This is a totally new situation, so if we were to ask the same questions again we would obtain different answers. This is especially true of the query asking if "pascal" is my friend, see figure 17.

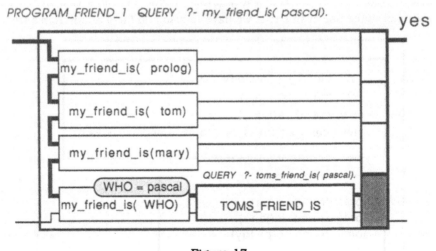

Figure 17

We have to find the reason for answer yes in *predicate/procedure* "toms_friend_is". Its contents are currently hidden in figure 17. This becomes clear in the figures 18 and 19 which show the different execution level details available in this representation.

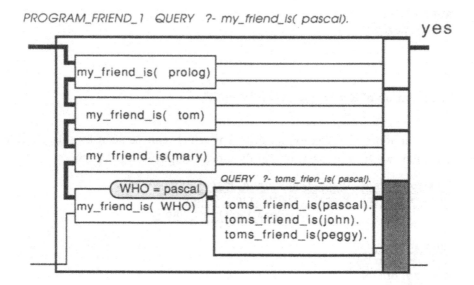

Figure 18

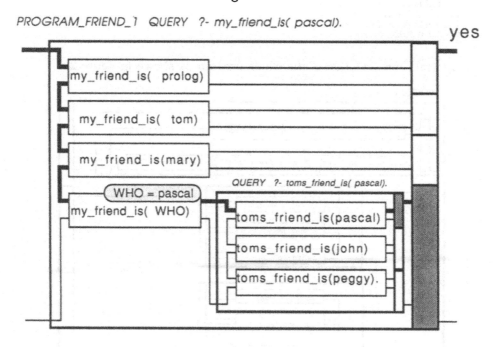

Figure 19

The others answers available to the original query are now clearly shown in this graphical representation. If the theory is understood then the system should obtain the further answers:

WHO = john ;
WHO = peggy ;
no

4. Visualization of Recursion and its "gestalt"

To indicate the more complex execution paths which can be seen by this graphical representation, we have chosen a slightly more complicated program:

<u>location(Person, Place) :- at(Person, Place).</u>
<u>location(Person, Place) :- visit(Person, Other),</u>
<u>   location(Other,Place).</u>

<u>at(alan, room19).</u>
<u>at(jane, room54).</u>
<u>at(betty, office).</u>

<u>visit(dave, alan).</u>
<u>visit(jane, betty).</u>
<u>visit(lincoln, dave).</u>

The graphical representation of the whole program is shown in figure 20.

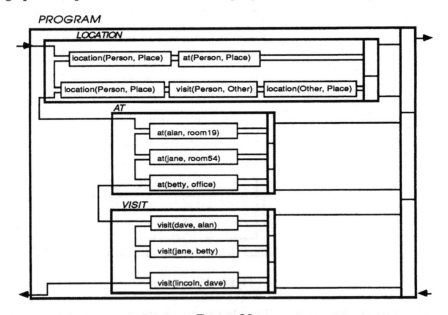

Figure 20

And the goal which we will set the Prolog to search for in figure 21 is to decide on the whereabouts of Lincoln. This is done by setting Prolog the question "location(lincoln, Where)".

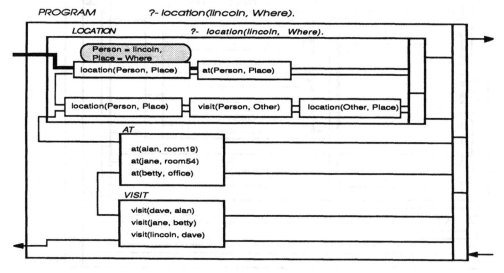

Figure 21

The first rule in the definition of location fails, because "at(lincoln, Where)" fails. The progress of the search to satisfy this goal can be seen in the figures 22 to 28.

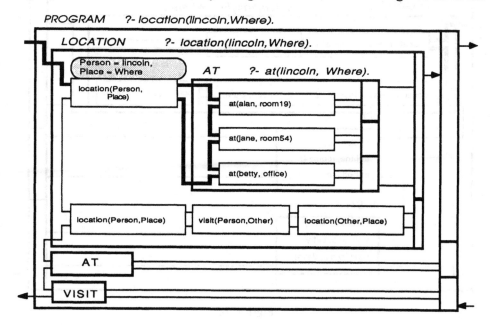

Figure 22

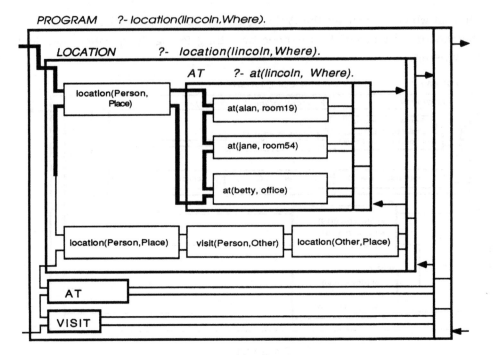

Figure 23

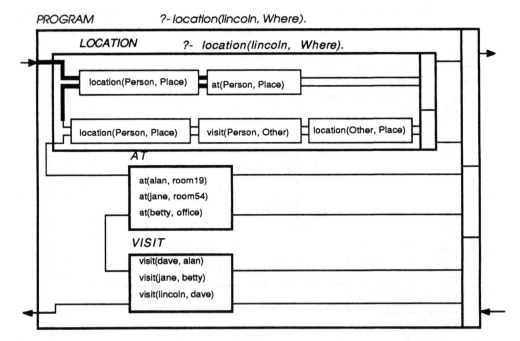

Figure 24

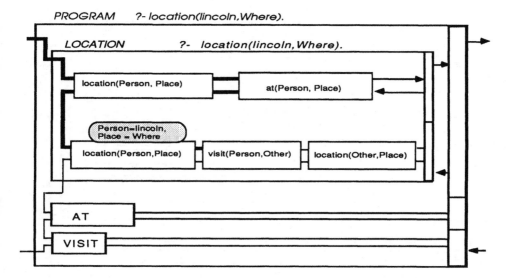

Figure 25

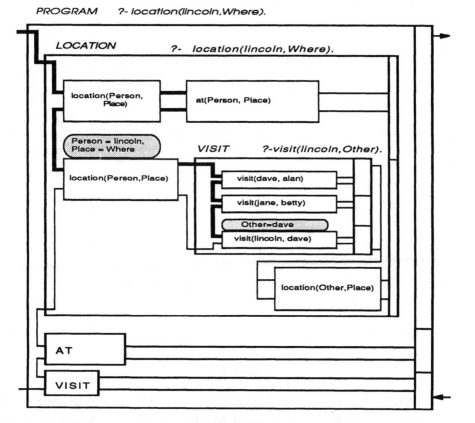

Figure 26

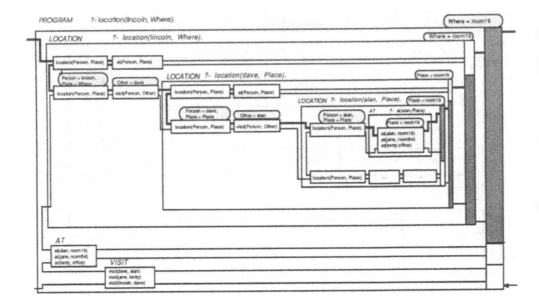

Figure 27

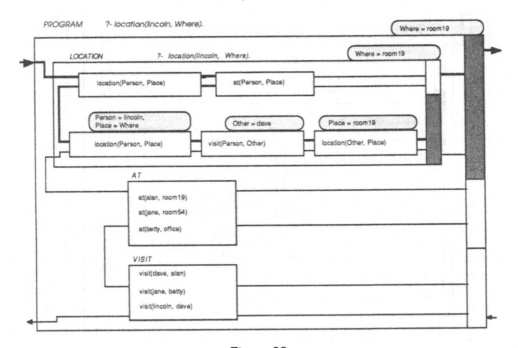

Figure 28

A very interesting feature within Prolog is the *cut*. The understanding of the function of the cut feature is very hard to explain, but is easily seen in this representation, see figure 29. To show the cut's behaviour the example program is changed by adding a cut to the first rule for predicate location. Now for the goal "location (betty, Where)" the search path is that shown in figures 30 and 31.

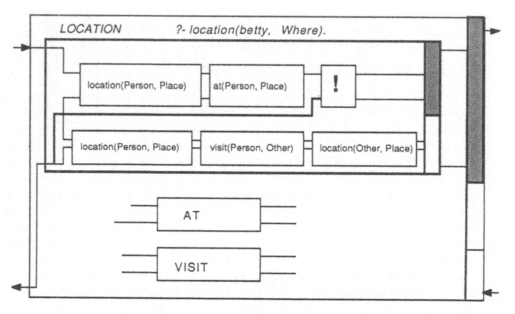

Figure 29

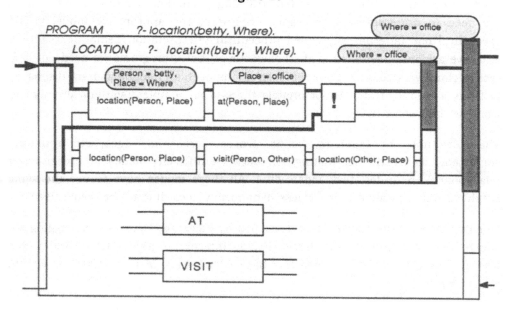

Figure 30

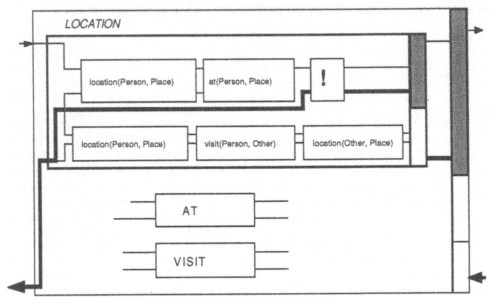

PROGRAM   ?- location(betty, Where).

Figure 31

A model for Prolog is required to understand the program's execution. Any story needs to explain such features as backtracking, recursion and unification. Due to the need to understand a program's execution, the appropriate model is the procedural one (alternatively called procedural interpretation/semantic/reading). Since we are only interested in the behaviour of Prolog programs we need not deal with declarative semantic. Four representations of this Prolog model are discussed in (Pain & Bundy, 1987). Unfortunately there is no complete solution given as to which is the best of these.

The story used by teachers, books, tracers, error messages, etc. must be consistent, so we do not distinguish between different modes of presentation (blackboard, computer, text, video, etc.). All these modes have to use the same graphical representation more or less dynamically according to the media used.

Our box model is based on a box developed by Lawrence Byrd as a debugging aid which he introduced for Edinburgh Prolog interpreter (Byrd, 1980) and which was also used in the first Prolog text book (Clocksin & Mellish, 1981) as well in many other publications.

5.   Related Works

There are two very good tree extensions used for graphical representation of Prolog programs and for their tracing and debugging (Eisenstadt & Brayshaw, 1988; Dewar & Clearly, 1986). However, they seem to introduce too many new graphical symbols and rules in comparison to our story.

A quite different graphical representation for logic programs was described in (Rusher et. al., 1986). This presents an attempt to represent a declarative interpretation of logic programs as it shows only relation and variable instantiations; the control flow is hidden. To establish a story from this representation could be a very interesting experiment.

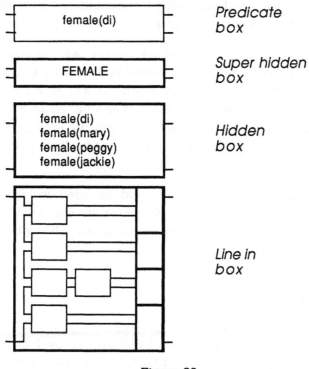

Figure 32

6.   Implementation Notes

To implement our graphical model one needs only to implement the four different graphical elements shown in figure 32. With these it should be possible to create a

Prolog program graphical representation picture on the screen. If they are then connected to a Prolog interpreter a very powerful debugger is obtained.

7. Conclusions

The conclusion of Pain & Bundy's paper (Pain & Bundy, 1987) was that "Presenting all this information (*i.e. story of the space, database of clauses and information for controlling search*) in one single story leads to a confusing complexity for all but the simplest examples." Our experience with the story described in this paper would suggest this is too strong a statement. We propose that any computer based implementation of our story would also include the options of allowing or suppressing detailed representation of each box level. This would be done by simply using the four graphical elements.

Our representation offers several distinct advantages over existing stories: (i) it serves as a uniform basis for text book material and all other teaching materials, and as an advanced user graphical environment as well as a user interface for Prolog; (ii) it tells the truth about unification, matching, variable instantiation & uninstantiation, and deals correctly with all built-in Prolog predicates; (iii) representation is based only on a few graphical units (box, line, variable and binding box).

The proposed graphical representation could be used widely for a Prolog Intelligent Tutoring System, the demands for which are discussed in Peter Ross's paper (Ross, 1987), and could improve the output of any existing box based tracer and debugger.

Acknowledgements

The authors wish to express their thanks to Professor Ernest Edmonds, the Head of the Department of Computer Studies at Loughborough University, who provided them the opportunity to finish this research. We would like to thank to Petr Novak (Department of Computers, Czech University of Technology), who firstly used such kind of a graphical presentation of Prolog programs and with whom we discussed a lot of details.

References

Byrd, L. (1980). Understanding the Control Flow of PROLOG Programs. Edinburgh DAI research paper 151, Edinburgh University.

Clocksin, W.F. & Mellish, C.S. (1981). Programming in Prolog. Berlin: Springer Verlag.

Dewar, A. D. & Clearly, J. G. (1986). Graphical display of complex information within a Prolog debugger. International Journal of Man-Machine Studies, 25, 503 - 521.

Eisenstadt, M. & Brayshaw, M. (1988). The Transparent Prolog Machine. Journal of Logic Programming, to appear.

Pain, H. & Bundy, A. (1987) What Stories Should We Tell Novice Prolog Programmers? In: Nawley, R. (ed): Artificial Intelligence Programming Environments, Ellis Horwood.

Ross, P. (1987). Some Thoughts on The Design of an Intelligent Teaching system for Prolog. Proceedings of AISQ 62, Autumn 1987.

Rusher, M., Thomas, M., Gubert, A. & Landret, D. (1986). A PROLOG Based Graphical Approach for Knowledge Expression. Microsoftware for Engineers 1986, 2, 4, 249 - 254.

FAST - A Stepper in an Object-oriented Programming Environment

Matthias Schneider[1]

Abstract

Steppers are important tools for debugging complex computer programs. The functionality of a stepper can be described as follows: before executing each program statement the user may inspect the statement in question and control the style of the evaluation to be performed. - This paper describes a stepper for the object-oriented programming language ObjTalk. During the development of this tool, special consideration has been paid to designing an appropriate user interface. - The first two chapters describe the two roots of our approach: first, our view of the software design process and second, object-oriented programming. In the following chapters we will show how these two roots affect the development of our programming tools and describe one of the tools in more detail.

1. Introduction

Rapid Prototyping becomes a more and more widely accepted programming style for the design of program systems, especially for designing man-computer interfaces. Instead of the linear order of design activities proposed in traditional programming models (Life Cycle Models) [Howden 82] these activities are highly repetitive in Rapid Prototyping Models. The result of each of these repetitions is a computer program which can be used as *input* for the following design cycles (see Fig. 1).

Designing software following the rapid prototyping methodology implies the writing of programs at a very early stage of the system design. Since at this time the program designer cannot know the necessary functionality of the emerging system in full, he is almost certain to produce both syntactic and logical errors in the code of his prototypes.

To find errors of this kind and to debug his prototypes, the program designer needs tools which help him analyze his code. The techniques for searching faulty code are very often language dependent.

Usually it is easier to find syntactic programming errors. If they are not discovered by a language interpreter or compiler during compile time then they will be found at the latest during the first evaluation of the faulty program statement. Sometimes, however, it is quite difficult to find the

---

[1]Forschungsgruppe INFORM, Institut für Informatik, Universität Stuttgart, Herdweg 51, 7000 Stuttgart 1

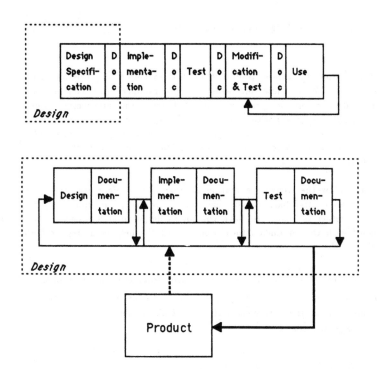

Figure 1: The process of software-design

While the so-called *Life Cycle Models* propose a strict separation and linear ordering of different design activities, in *Rapid Prototyping Models* the different stages of design are intermixed and change rapidly. During each cycle of the design the programmer creates versions of programs which are intended to solve his problems. These prototypes can be *analyzed* an *criticized* and thus enhance the designer's understanding of the problems he wants to solve and the pro's and con's of the solution he decided to develop. Finally, after many design cycles, he has acquired enough knowledge to create the final version of his product out of the prototypes which he developed earlier.

---

responsible statement in the source code of the system after having found a syntactic program error in the object code version. This task is especially difficult if the program designer uses different modules written by several other people and the bugs result from incorrect interface definitions between these modules. The results are very often error messages that are totally obscure and not understandable for a person not acquainted with all of the components.

Searching for logical errors in computer programs is a much harder task. Programs with logical errors can very often be executed[2] but the result is not the one expected by the programmer. One way of finding errors of this kind is to interpret the program *step by step* and to compare the actual state of the system with the expected state after each program expression. During this process the programmer must be in control of his tools on a very fine-grained level.

---

[2]A logic error that prevents code from being executed is, for example, *division by zero*, while selecting a wrong element from a matrix may cause faulty output without causing an execution error.

For this technique of searching programming errors two important types of tools have been developed:

- *Tracing tools* allow to create protocols of the execution of program structures (functions, procedures etc.). With these protocols the programmer may control the value of actual parameters and/or results of program parts. Usually the programmer can execute arbitrary statements at the program position where a trace-statement can be inserted. This allows him to interrupt his execution at these positions to inspect the environment of function calls, to change the state of his system *on the fly* and to continue with the evaluation of the statements in question.

- *Stepping tools* allow the stepwise execution of programs. Before executing a program statement the systems gives control back to the user. He may decide in which way the expression is to be executed, whether he wants to have control in deeper nested program structures or whether he is satisfied with the obtained information. With the help of a stepper faulty statements can be localized exactly.

The decision which of these tools to use is dependent from the specific problem, the usability and controlability of the tools and the specific environment of the system. Usually a trace suffices for an inexact localization of the erroneous statement while a stepper will be used to find the exact position of the program error.

2. Object-oriented programming

The object-oriented programming style is quite different from conventional procedural programming. Programs are no longer organized in terms of procedures and program statements but in terms of *objects* and *messages*.

Objects are active data-structures that are ordered in a hierarchical network of *classes* and *instances*[3]. Classes define the properties that are common to all of their instances. These properties include state variables (*slots*) and procedural information (*methods*). New classes are defined by refining and specializing existing classes. All of the properties of the *superclasses* of a class are inherited to all of its instances. For example, names, default values and value ranges of slots are defined in the different classes whereas the actual value of a state variable is defined at each instance.

Objects communicate with each other by sending *messages*. The properties of a class include *methods*; they describe whether and how an instance can react to an incoming message. This reaction can be to update the value of a state variable, to send new messages to other objects, to return a value to the sender, to cause an error message, or any combination thereof. It is important to note that the objects decide for themselves how to react to an incoming message. All that is known outside an object about the object itself are the messages that it will correctly interpret. Inside an object the state variables and their values and the existing message handlers (methods) are known. An object can only change the internal state of itself, changing the internal state of

---

[3]Actually the network is not necessarily restricted to a hierarchy but may support multiple inheritance as well.

other objects is only possible by sending messages to the object to be changed; the same is true for reading the value of slots of an object.

In an object-oriented programming environment[4] the execution of a program is no longer controlled by control structures like *while–loops, goto–statements, conditional branching* or *function calls* but by *sending* and *receiving* messages and by the reactions of objects defined in the message handlers of their classes. Tools for debugging object-oriented programs should therefore support the monitoring of this process of sending and receiving messages. Instead of controlling statements of procedural languages messages sent inside a system have to be considered.

There are several very well known object-oriented languages, the more important ones being SMALLTALK [Goldberg, Robson 83], LOOPS [Bobrow, Stefik 81; Stefik et al. 83], COMMON-LOOPS [Bobrow 85] and ACT-1 [Theriault 82]. The language used in our systems, ObjTalk [Laubsch, Rathke 83], is an object-oriented extension of the programming language LISP [Winston, Horn 81].

3. The functionality of a stepper in an object-oriented programming environment

A stepper for an object-oriented programming language should allow the programmer to control the *message passing* between the objects of his system. If an object receives a message, it reacts by returning the value of a state variable (*slot–values*) or by executing a message handler (*method*). During this execution new messages may be sent to other objects. In this case the current method will be interrupted until the answer to the new message is received. The interpretation of this answer is up to the sending object which continues executing its method.

In object-oriented languages there is a stack of suspended message handlers at each state of the execution of a program, which is initially empty (on toplevel). This stack is equivalent to the procedure stack of a procedural programming language. With a stepper at each message to be sent the programmer may choose between the following execution styles (see Figure 2):

1. He can decide to continue with the control of the execution of the *current message* (i.e. the message to be sent) on deeper levels of the message stack. In this case he will be informed about the next message to be sent independently of the depth of the message stack.

2. If he knows that the current message will be interpreted correctly by the receiving object he sends the message without controlling messages on deeper levels of the message stack. In this case he can only influence messages on a smaller or equal stack size compared to that of the current message.

3. He may decide that the message that is currently being interpreted will be handled properly and continue to the next level of the message stack. Eventually he wants to go up several

---

[4]This term denotes a programming environment that is designed especially for the support of writing programs in an object-oriented style and language.

levels of the message stack.

4. The pending messages in the message stack can be interpreted without further controlling the execution.

5. The sending of specific messages can be suppressed (the execution is skipped returning a specific value (nil)). Execution continues after the skipped message. The sender of this message must be able to handle the returned value.

6. The entire process can be aborted, returning a specific value (nil).

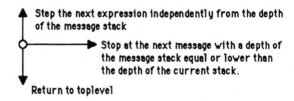

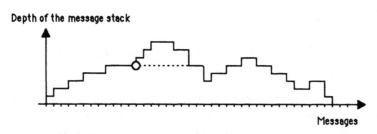

Figure 2: The message stack during the interpretation of a message

At each point during the execution of a method (i.e. handling of a message) the user decides whether he wants to have full control, control on lower levels of the message stack, control on the preceding level of the stack or return to the toplevel (empty stack).

These six control choices are a *minimum* of functionality necessary for a stepper for an object-oriented language. There is a strong analogy to steppers in functional or procedural environments.

Extensions to this functionality are dependent on the selected programming language and the desired man-machine interface. In addition to the functionality described above our stepper has the following features:

- The user can get a protocol of the message passing process if he selects one of the three possibilities 2, 3 or 4. This produces a kind of *complete trace* of all messages sent.

- He may decide whether he wants to see the answers to messages (results).

- He can obtain a printout of the entire message stack.

- He can see a graphically indented form of the *current message.*

- He may interrupt the execution process to evaluate arbitrary program statements.

In systems where different programming languages are used in parallel (as ObjTalk and LISP in our environment) one desirable feature is the possibility to step through programs independently from the programming language being used.

4. The man-machine interface

One important criterion for the usability of a software engineering tool is the design of the man-machine interface. During the development of FAST[5] a major amount of design work was dedicated to developing a good user interface.

4.1 Design criteria

Criteria for the design of the human-computer interface may be derived from the computer environment which is available, the expected user groups of a tool, the expected functionality of this tool and the complexity of input and output data necessary for communicating with the tool.

4.1.1 The hardware environment

The progress from teletype-interfaces to high-resolution raster-graphic display screens has changed the quality of human-computer dialogues entirely. While before this change commands and data had to be input with the keyboard, now it is possible to use pointing devices (mouse, graphic tablet etc.). With these devices the programmer can select objects on the screen directly. These objects represent arbitrary internal objects, for example commands which are activated by pointing on their external representation or devices like printers which can receive data or programs to be printed.

A similar change has occurred for the representation of output data. Data that had to be printed out textually can now be represented by graphical items on the screen if it is possible to design a representation that is intuitively understandable for the user. Examples of these representations are files shown as *icons* on the screen. Interfaces which stress this technique of object representation have been developed for the Xerox-Star [Smith et al. 82] or Apple's MacIntosh [Macintosh 83].

4.1.2 The software environment

For the design of the user interface it is important to know what kind of software support is available for the implementation. If the programming environment supports only a teletype-oriented interface, the interface of the tool has to be rather simple. If, however, there exists a window system in the environment that supports multiple windows and overlay techniques, one should be careful to design the user interface in a way that the tool will not effect the state of the rest of the system during its use. This can be achieved by creating separate windows for input and output of the tools. These windows may be overlaid with the system to be debugged.

---

[5]FAST- the Fred Astaire Stepper

4.1.3 User groups

The average user of a software engineering tool can be expected to be an experienced programmer who is well accustomed to the implementation language being used and who has a rather thorough understanding of the problems occurring during program design. Users without this knowledge will have great difficulties in debugging program code at all. The expected user will also know for which purpose he wants to use which tools and which tools are appropriate for specific problems.

There are, however, rather important differences between users concerning their familiarity with specific tools. Casual users of a tool are very often confused about the meaning of specific commands (Example: "What is the effect of typing 'G' at this place?") or they do not know how to reach a certain goal (Example: "Which command will interrupt the stepping process and return to toplevel?"). Quite often they do not even know how to load and start a tool because they do not remember the names of the files to be loaded and the functions to be called. Usually it will be sufficient for them to get some short situation-specific help if they are stuck with a problem. It is not necessary to give verbose explanations to them.

The user should be able to customize the input and output of the tool to his specific problem and working style. For example, the decision whether to use a mouse as the input device should not be made by the system but by the user. Even if there is a mouse in the hardware environment it is often more convenient for a programmer to use his keyboard, because he is working with the keyboard most of the time. Also, the output of the system should be customizable by the user (suppression of detail, graphical vs. textual output, etc.) A user interface which is designed to support this kind of customization has the additional advantage to be usable in environments lacking important hardware elements like pointing devices or graphic screens.

4.1.4 The functionality of the tool

The number of different functions to be supported by a tool influences the selection of the appropriate dialogue techniques and the style of interaction between the tool and the user. If there is a very limited number of different functions (like 2 or 3) it is possible simply to use the buttons of a mouse or another pointing device for the input. This technique does not seem to be very useful if there are many functions but usually only very few mouse buttons. In this case the input with menu selection, function buttons on the screen or the keyboard seem to be more appropriate.

4.1.5 Input and output data

The complexity of the necessary input and the expected output of a tool will influence the design of the interface. If complex data structures are to be input it is appropriate to implement a technique to save as much *typing work* as possible by menu selection or pointing to icons. If large amounts of output data are expected it is sensible to provide means for hiding the complexity of the data if the user does not want to see every detail.

A graphical representation of data is useful if, first, there is a representation that is intuitively obvious to the user and, second, the graphical representation shows relations that cannot be easily displayed in a textual form. The use of graphical representations of objects is especially valuable if these objects may be manipulated directly by means of a pointing device.

4.2 The user interface of FAST

Following the design criteria outlined in section 4.1 we will explain the design decisions taken during the development of the user interface of FAST.

FAST is a tool for ObjTalk programmers. ObjTalk has in its kernel version a teletype-oriented user interface. However, most of the programs written in ObjTalk were and are developed using a powerful window system with a high resolution raster display (BBN-Bitgraph) and a mouse. This window system WLISP [Fabian 84] is itself written in ObjTalk and allows multiple overlapping windows. The user interface of FAST was designed in such a way that FAST can be used with simple character oriented display terminals as well as with the WLISP window system taking advantage of many of its important features.

4.2.1 Possible input styles

Without the window system every input is given using the keyboard. Every command can be started with a single keystroke. There is some help available which describes the different commands and how to execute them. The output of the system will suppress large data so that it is possible to display each message on exactly one line.

With the window system the user may input data with exactly the same technique. In addition, he can use the mouse to input his commands. The output and help facilities are implemented similarly to the solution chosen without the window system. Since we can support scrolling windows and have the possibility to restore the contents of a window after it has been changed we need not suppress large amounts of data but simply display the data in a window and have the user select the contents he wants to see. In addition, all output of the stepper goes into one specific window and therefore the rest of the system is not affected by stepping through program parts.

FAST accepts 16 different commands which are listed in table 1, thus it is not possible to select commands by using different mouse buttons[6]. During the development we tested three different input techniques:

- Input with so-called pop-up-menus. Pushing a button on the mouse exposes a menu with the possible commands. The user selects one command, the menu disappears again and the command is executed.

- Input with permanently visible menus. These menus are separate windows which allow the selection of a command by simply clicking on an item displayed inside the window. The selected command is executed, the menu remains visible.

- Input with buttons. Buttons are mouse-sensitive regions on the screen or in a window. Clicking on a button activates this button which in turn executes a command. Usually buttons are displayed on the margins of a window and are permanently visible.

---

[6]The Bitgraph terminal comes with mice with either two or three buttons.

command name	Char	Description
next	n	Continue evaluation in stepping mode
continue	c	send current message without stepping, return to stepping mode afterwards.
up one level	u	Send current message and evaluate current method without stepping, return to stepping mode afterwards.
go	g	Return to toplevel without stepping, turn on stepping mode afterwards.
continue and show	C	Like "c" but show a protocol of the messages sent during the evaluation. of the current message.
up and show	U	Like "u" but show a protocol of the messages sent.
go and show	G	Like "g" but show a protocol.
skip	s	Do not send the current message, return "nil".
abort	a	Abort the execution, turn FAST off, return to toplevel.
break	b	Enter a breakpoint to evaluate arbitrary programs, turn off FAST during the break.
eval	e	Prompt the user for one expression and evaluate it, turn FAST off during the evaluation.
print message	p	Pretty Print the complete message inside the output window.
print message stack	P	Show all suspended and waiting messages.
help	?,h	Explain the possible commands.
toggle printing of results	r	Show/hide the answers to messages.
turn FAST off	t	turn FAST off, continue evaluation.

Table 1:   The possible commands of FAST

In the first case the selection has to be initiated[7], while selecting in permanent menus or with buttons is always possible. The latest version of FAST uses three different Menus for the command input. There were several reasons for this decision. First, pop-up-menus make the input process more complicated and usually more time consuming. Second, the entire programming environment depends heavily on the use of menus. Using buttons is a rather unusual style of interaction. Third, buttons can be used effectively if there exists a good graphical representation of the commands in question. This, however, was not the case for FAST. The commands are easier to find by their names which can be displayed (at least in part) in the items of a menu as well as on buttons.

The three menus and the output window of FAST are integrated in one *pane*, a superwindow which keeps all of its subwindows together. In addition, the pane does the reshaping of all its subwindows if this becomes necessary and does the entire layout planning.

---

[7]The menu has to be made visible.

The figures 4 to 6 show the use of FAST during a sample session. These figures show some properties of the user interface.

In these figures on the top right of the screen there is an area titled "identifier (assigns to 'me')". This is a so-called *softbar*, which can be activated by clicking on it. Clicking on this bar lets you select a window and have the variable *me* bound to this window.

The small window with the label *ObjTalk Stepper* (Fig. 3) is an *icon* representing the stepper pane. As soon as the stepper is started this icon will expand and display the entire stepper pane as shown in Fig. 5. It is possible to open this window without using the stepper by simply clicking on the icon.

On the right side of the stepper pane there are three menus designed for turning the stepper on and off, toggling the printing of results and selecting other stepper commands. The upper two menus display the last selection, which also is the state of the tool, with bold characters. This feature allows the programmer to always know the state of his tool.

The user can control the stepper either by selecting the appropriate item in these menus or by striking the equivalent keys on the keyboard.

4.2.2 The output of the stepper

For the output of the stepper we did not use many graphical components. There were some reasons for this decision:

1. The tool has been developed for programmers accustomed to the textual representation of their programs. They get much of the necessary information out of a textual form. Also, this is the form in which they wrote their program[8]. It may be easier for him to find the position of the actual message in his code by using a textual representation than by using some graphical representation that yet has to be transformed.

2. We could not find a graphical representation that was better suited to the needs of programmers than the textual representation.

3. Our hardware environment (a multiuser system) with rather slow terminal connections makes the creation and handling of graphical objects a rather time consuming task. Creating different graphical objects for the messages sent is to slow for all practical purposes. This may change entirely if we re-implement ObjTalk and FAST on powerful single user systems.

We have developed a version of an ObjTalk Trace with graphical output [Manz 86]. Although this tool is too slow to be used on a real programming task it shows how graphics may be integrated into programming environments (see Fig. 7). This tool could be considered as a prototype for the output of other tools.

---

[8]In our system there is currently no possibility of programming by direct manipulation on a graphical representation of the code.

It seems to be natural to represent the objects of an object-oriented program as graphical objects on the screen. The output of a stepper could then be a marker moving on this representation and displaying the current message while pending messages are displayed by labeled arrows. However, implementing such a solution causes some major problems:

1. There are several relations between different object which are of importance for the programmer and which should be made visible. The most important ones are the class-subclass relation and the class-instance relation. There might be more relations (part-of etc.) in other languages. In addition to these relations the relation created by sending messages should be displayed. It is unclear how to display these three relations without creating a rather messy screen.

2. In a system that is not used only for demonstration purposes there are usually very many objects[9]. There is no secure algorithm for positioning these objects and displaying their relations on the screen in a clear arrangement. On the other hand the programmer should not be bothered with positioning objects on his display because this is not his task.

3. For the same reason it is usually not possible to arrange all objects involved in the execution of a program on one screen. A graphical representation would either cause scrolling very often or necessitate switching between overlapping windows which show small areas out of the entire object world. Both solutions are not easy to understand and tend to mess up the entire display.

4. During the execution of a complex message handler it is often important to know about the time-relationships between different messages being sent. It is not straightforward how to integrate this time relation into the static class and instance relations. Either the representation of a message passing process stays on the screen after the message has been handled and the user has the problem of figuring out the time order of the messages or the messages being handled are erased from the display. This implies that after the entire message has been handled there is no information about the process left on the screen. On the other hand in a textual representation time relations are easy to figure out because they are represented by the order of the messages on the output stream.

There are, however, some graphical output techniques that can be used in our programming environment without slowing down the system too much. The depth of the stack of pending messages can be shown automatically and complete messages may be displayed using a graphical indenting printer. Some other ideas of integrating graphical tools are listed in section 5.

The visualization of the depth of the message stack is done by indenting the printed representation of a message. Example: A message with four pending messages on top is printed with four leading blanks. The answers to the messages are indented with the same amount of space. It is therefore quite easy to see the relationship between different messages. ("Which message is sent by which message handler?") Since the printed representation of each message fits into one line of the output window, the user gets an easy-to-read sequence of messages being passed in his system (see Fig. 5).

It is not necessary to shorten messages in order to have them fit into one line of the output window because the output window can scroll horizontally as well as vertically. Usually the user will see the beginning of a message, the tail of the message may be hidden. The user gets the entire current message printed inside the window with a pretty printer by selecting an appropriate command (see Fig. 4).

---

[9]The ObjTalk programming environment contains more than 1500 objects!

5. Concluding remarks ·

Our experience with FAST shows that the tool can be used effectively by programmers to search for errors in their programs. There is strong evidence that experienced programmers prefer to control FAST with the keyboard. There are advantages, however, in having the possibility of mouse-menu input. Programs that depend heavily on the use of the mouse in the man-machine dialog are easier to step using the mouse because the programmer does not have to switch back and forth between mouse input and keyboard input. For programming experts the menus at the right edge of the FAST output pane are a very easy but sufficient help facility; novices and casual users of FAST use these menus for input more often.

The output possibilities of FAST could be ameliorated in several ways, for example by integrating a graphical representation of the object world like the one being used by the KEE system [KEE 85]. In this representation the class-subclass and the class-instance relations are displayed statically in a tree-like manner. The representation of the message passing process would then have to be done in a separate window while the relevant parts of the object world may always be inspected.

Another possibility is the representation of the current message stack by using a separate output window in which the current stack is always visible. The size of the stack could then be easily deduced from the size of the output in this window. This update is certainly no major problem when using a more powerful hardware environment. It is important to note, however, that the usability of tools for programmers depends heavily on the response time of the system.

The functionality and the user interface of FAST is still being developed. We already implemented three different user interfaces for FAST, the last one being described here. The usability of FAST has been greatly improved during this development and FAST is now easier to use than other existing stepping tools that we use: with tools of this kind, programmers who always had to cope with very insufficient user interfaces can be offered much better support while doing their jobs.

References

[Bobrow 85]
    D.G. Bobrow, K. Kahn, G, Kiczales, L. Masinter, M. Stefik and F. Zdybel: *"Commonloops"*. Technical Report ISL-85-8, Xerox Palo Alto Research Center, August, 1985.

[Bobrow, Stefik 81]
    D.G. Bobrow, M. Stefik: *"The LOOPS Manual"*. Technical Report KB-VLSI-81-83, Knowledge Systems Area, Xerox Palo Alto Research Center (PARC), 1981.

[Böcker 84]
    H.-D. Böcker: *"Softwareerstellung als wissensbasierter Kommunikations- und Designprozeß"*. Dissertation, Universität Stuttgart, Fakultät für Mathematik und Informatik, April, 1984.

[Fabian 84]
    F. Fabian: *"Benutzungsanleitung für das Bitgraph-Fenstersystem"*. INFORM-Memo, Institut für Informatik, Universität Stuttgart, Februar, 1984.

[Goldberg, Robson 83]

A. Goldberg, D. Robson: *"SMALLTALK-80, The Language and its Implementation"*. Addison-Wesley, Reading, Ma., 1983.

[Howden 82]

W.E. Howden: *"Contemporary Software Development Environments"*. *Communications of the ACM* 25(5), pp 318-329, May, 1982.

[KEE 85]

"KEE Software Development System User's Manual". IntelliCorp, 1985.

[Laubsch, Rathke 83]

J. Laubsch, C. Rathke: *"OBJTALK: Eine Erweiterung von LISP zum objektorientierten Programmieren"*. In H.Stoyan, H.Wedekind (editors), *Objektorientierte Software- und Hardwarearchitekturen*, pp 60-75. Stuttgart, 1983.

[Macintosh 83]

C. Kaehler: *"MacIntosh Benutzerhandbuch"*. Apple Computer, California, 1983.

[Manz 86]

T. Manz: *"METRO - ein Methoden-Trace für ObjTalk"*. WISDOM-Forschungsbericht FB-INF-86-13, Forschungsgruppe INFORM, Universität Stuttgart, 1986.

[Schneider 86]

M. Schneider: *"INFORM-Manual: Object-sensitive Windows, Version 1.0"*. WISDOM-Forschungsbericht FB-INF-86-04, Institut für Informatik, Universität Stuttgart, Januar, 1986.

[Smith et al. 82]

D.C. Smith, Ch. Irby, R. Kimball, B. Verplank: *"Designing the Star User Interface"*. *BYTE* , April, 1982.

[Stefik et al. 83]

M. Stefik, D.G. Bobrow, S. Mittal, L. Conway: *"Knowledge Programming in LOOPS: Report on an Experimental Course"*. *The AI Magazine* , Fall, 1983.

[Theriault 82]

D. Theriault: *"A Primer for the Act-1 Language"*. AI Memo 672, MIT AI Laboratory, April, 1982.

[Winston, Horn 81]

P.H. Winston, B.K.P. Horn: *"LISP"*. Addison-Wesley, Reading, Ma., 1981.

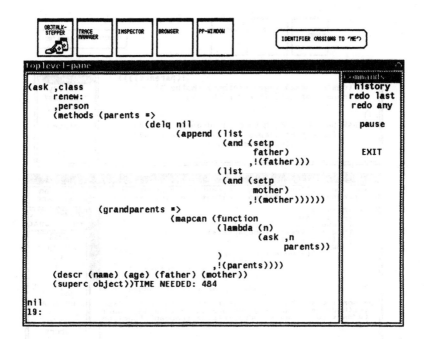

Figure 3: The ObjTalk programming environment

In an initial state the user has a toplevel window with some commands assembled in a menu attached to the output window. In addition he sees icons for different tools, from the left to the right the *stepper*, a *tree-browser* for visualizing class-subclass relations, an intrabrowser *inspector* to inspect the internal structure of objects, a window for pretty-printing arbitrary objects and a tool for setting up the *trace*. The long icon on the top left is a *softbar* used to bind the name of a visible window to a special variable.

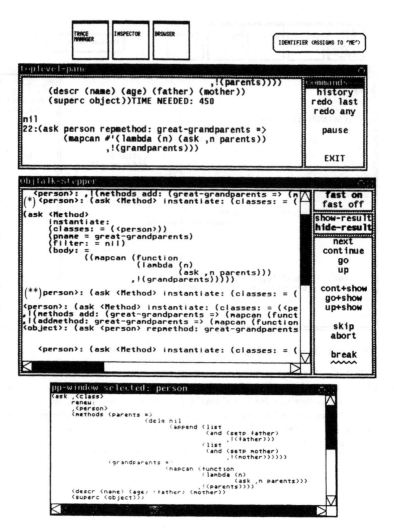

Figure 4: Definition of a method

In this figure the user defines a method with the stepper running. The leading blanks visualize the depth of the message stack. At (*) the command *pp msg* has been selected, at (**) the entire message stack was printed by selecting *pp stack*. In an additional window on the bottom of the screen the user obtained the definition of the class *person*. He can get this information at any time in the stepping process.

120

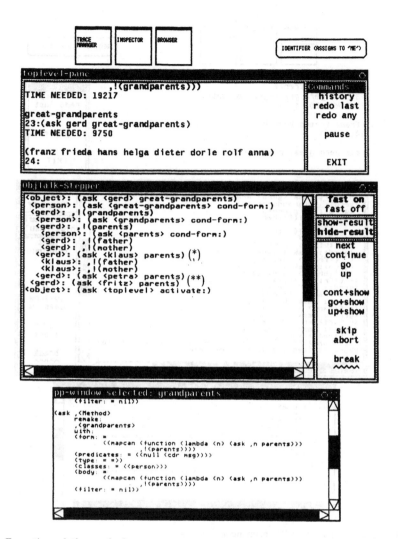

Figure 5: Execution of the method

The message defined in Fig. 4 is interpreted for the first time. At the position marked with a (*) the programmer realizes that the same message has been sent and answered before. Therefore he does not step the following *parents* messages, but continues the evaluation in each case with *cont*. Finally at the line marked with a (**) the user decided to go up one level. As there were no messages left to be sent, the system returned to toplevel. The ObjTalk objects visible in the output window are *mouse sensitive* [Schneider 86] and can be selected at any time for pretty-printing etc.

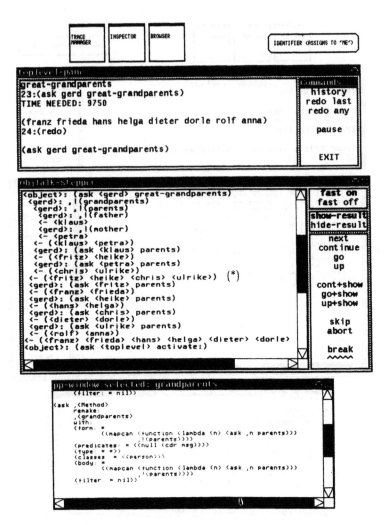

Figure 6: Message passing with printing of results

Additional information may be obtained by asking for a protocol of the results of the messages being sent.   From the result at (*) follows that the method handler first collects all the grandparents before sending a *parents* message to all of them.   The second menu on the right side of the stepper pane has changed its appearance.   Now the *show results* selection is highlighted to show both the state of the tool and the last selection of the menu.

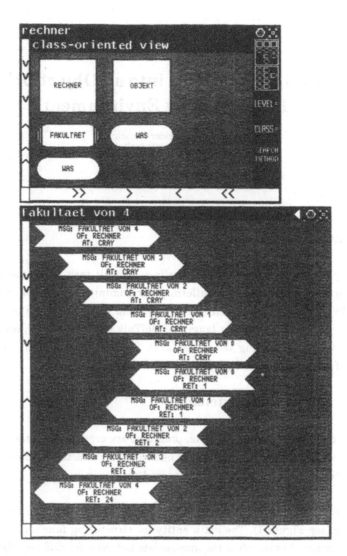

Figure 7: Graphical output from software engineering tools

METRO [Manz 86] uses graphical output for representing the information to the user. Although this system is too slow for everyday use it shows quite clearly what can be achieved with graphical methods. Each of the graphical objects on the screen is a small icon hiding more information from the user. He obtains this information by clicking on the icon.

Integrating Visual Aids into an Object Oriented Programming Environment

Matthias Schneider-Hufschmidt
SIEMENS ZT ZTI SOF 111
Otto-Hahn-Ring 6
D-8000 München 83
msch@ZTIVAX.UUCP

1 Abstract

Programming large object oriented systems is a difficult task. With the help of specific programming tools integrated in a uniform programming environment, this task can be facilitated. In this paper, we describe the design and implementation of a programming environment for the programming language ObjTalk [Rathke, C. 86], an object oriented extension to the programming language LISP. Special attention will be given to the integration of graphical and non-graphical visual aids.

2 Object Oriented Programming

In an object oriented programming style, programs are organized around objects which in turn can be ordered in some hierarchical or heterarchical structure of classes and instances (see [Cox 84] for an introduction to object oriented programming).

The object oriented style of programming can be compared with the functional style of programming (see Figure 1). The main entity for structuring functional programs is the *function*. A function has to define the appropriate behavior for different datatypes. Object oriented programs are organized around the data *object*. Each object supplies the necessary functionality, e.g. for accessing and changing internal variables of objects.

The object oriented programming style has shown several advantages over conventional (applicative) programming styles for the design of large program systems to solve ill-structured tasks.

1. Object oriented programming means programming by *specialization*. Instead of completely developing new functionalities the programmer creates new classes which specialize the inherited behavior of their super classes. This allows the fast development, testing, and modification of new program behavior which is typical for rapid prototyping environments.

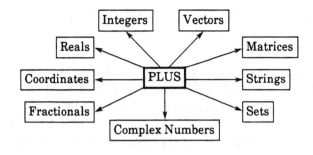

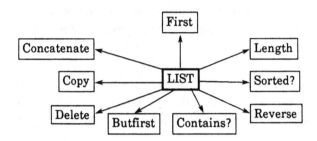

Figure 1: Functional and Object Oriented Styles of Programming

2. Object oriented programming supports the concept of *generic operations*. It is possible to define protocols which are understood by every object. Objects can change the generic behavior by redefining the generic methods defined at the root of the class hierarchy. This concepts facilitates the creation of uniform program code.

3. Objects are a means for *data abstraction*. Objects need no information about the internal structure of other objects. They only know the messages understood by other objects.

4. Object oriented programming *keeps related pieces of code together*. There is no separation between data (object) definition and algorithm (method) definition.

5. Object oriented languages facilitate the *division of complex algorithms in smaller parts*. Because objects can only affect their local state, algorithms are almost always split into small parts which are defined in different objects. The structuring of the data in a system becomes more important for understanding the system behavior.

6. Objects realize a *natural* representation of working environments. Users often view their working environments – independently from the use of a computer system – as a collection of related objects (documents, tools, devices etc.). Giving the user a similar

representation in his system reduces the necessary learning effort to understand and use a program.

7. In object oriented programming languages, the programmer himself defines a large part of the language syntax. Often, there is only a small predefined language kernel which can be enlarged by the programmer during the development of a system.

Another important aspect of object oriented programming concepts views objects as frame-like [Minsky 75] structures for the representation of knowledge. Objects contain explicitly represented knowledge about the environment and the system being developed. This knowledge can be used by tools which support the programmer during the implementation of his systems.

ObjTalk allows the *representation of knowledge* in a frame-like manner [Minsky 75]. Programs written in ObjTalk contain explicitly represented knowledge about the objects used in these programs. The design and implementation of ObjTalk is described in [Rathke, C. 86].

The kernel of ObjTalk is itself represented in ObjTalk. Therefore each ObjTalk system contains explicit knowledge about the programming language itself. Changing the representation of the language kernel means changing the behavior of the system. This technique was used as often as possible in implementing the ObjTalk programming environment *ObjEnv*. The explicit representation and changeability of a programming language is a powerful tool for developing programming environments. Tools for languages with explicit representations of the language to be worked on can be considered as *knowledge based programming tools* [Schneider 86]. Tools written in ObjTalk can easily be adapted to specific styles of programmers, or ported to other hardware.

3   A Programming Environment for ObjTalk

It is widely accepted that a programming language should have an environment to support programmers using the language. This is true both for conventional programming languages (like PASCAL) and AI-languages (like Lisp or ObjTalk). However, the environment becomes even more important when we move from compiler languages to interpreted programming languages which allow the interactive development of code [Barstow et al. 84].

From the analysis of the software engineering process, one can deduce a list of tasks for which it is desirable to have knowledge based software tools:

1. Support of the dialog between programmer and computer (undo/redo-facilities, spelling correction etc.),

2. Support for debugging tasks (trace, step, backtrace etc.),

3. Support for program creation (syntax directed editors, etc.),

4. Analysis of program data structures,

5. Analysis of runtime behavior,

6. Version control,

7. Test facilities,

8. Compilation and preprocessing to get more efficient programs,

9. Disassemblers.

This list is by no means complete and may change for different programming languages.

A system which contains tools to support some or all of these tasks is called a *programming environment*. Usually, the tools in a programming environment have a similar user interface and are integrated in a single common environment (as opposed to conventional systems with separate editor, compiler, debugger, etc.). The programmer never has to leave his environment to perform a task on his program.

The components of a programming environment for ObjTalk

The programming environment ObjEnv consists of the programming tools for analysis and debugging of existing programs, for creation and modification of program structures and for handling of large numbers of objects.

Tools for the analysis of the runtime behavior and for the debugging of ObjTalk code.

To understand the runtime behavior of an ObjTalk program and for tracking errors in its code, the user has two tools available: the *ObjTalk Trace* and the *ObjTalk Stepper*.

The *ObjTalk Trace* offers two different possibilities to trace the execution of methods as response to messages being received. *Message Tracing* (Inter-Trace) allows protocols of (specific) messages being sent to specific objects or members of a class, whereas *Method Tracing* (Intra-Trace) monitors the execution of specific methods being executed. The difference between these two techniques is subtle but important: the first possibility allows the tracing of messages which are not understood by the receiver while using the method trace the system would signal an error in such a case.

A second difference between method trace and message trace lies in the implementation technique. When executing a method which is to be traced, we have an ObjTalk object representing the method in question. Changing the execution behavior of this method object is a simple way of implementing a method trace by using ObjTalk itself. Message tracing is not that easy to implement in ObjTalk since at the time of its execution we do not know the method being executed. Moreover, messages are no ObjTalk objects. The desired behavior can be implemented within ObjTalk by adding new extended methods to the objects in question which display the trace information before or after resending the same message to the object. (An extended method is a method that can only be executed once during the processing of a top-level-message. Extended methods are invisible on higher levels of the message passing stack for messages matching the same syntactic pattern [Schneider 86].)

Neither the setup nor the output of the ObjTalk-Trace use graphical means to display necessary information. The setup is done by selecting method headers in a menu. The user can select between class-specific and method-name-specific selections. Traced methods are highlighted to display their different behavior.

The output of the trace tools is also done by using textual display. One important reason for this is the fact, that time dependencies are highly relevant when analyzing trace output. Textual output shows these dependencies quite clearly, while it is difficult to visualize them in graphical representations since these representations have to show other relations of the object world as well. However, simple techniques like indenting can be used to visualize different states of the message passing stack.

For the setup of the ObjTalk Trace, other display possibilities can be imagined. Using a system like ZOO (see the paper by W.-F. Riekert in these proceedings) one could set up a trace specification by placing 'hurdles' in the object world. Whenever a message tries to pass one of these hurdles, the hurdle gets highlighted and the user can inspect the information of the trace by clicking on the hurdle with the mouse.

The second tool is the *ObjTalk Stepper* which allows the interactive control of the message passing process. At each point of the process the user can select one of the following possibilities:

- to get a complete trace of the execution with or without keeping control of the process,
- to process the current message without further interruption,
- to finish the entire message passing process,
- to abort this process, or
- to inhibit the passing of the current message.

The design decisions taken when implementing the ObjTalk Stepper and its user interface have been described in detail in [Schneider 86a].

Tools for the analysis of data structures

For the analysis of data structures in object oriented systems, *browsers* are the most commonly used tools. We can differentiate between two types of browsers, *Inter-Browsers* to inspect the structure of class-networks and *Intra-Browsers* to analyze the internal structures of objects.

Each ObjTalk object is a member of a class. Classes are, in turn, objects of a class called "class". Classes are organized in a subclass-superclass-relation. This relation can be represented by a directed, non-circular graph, the topmost element being the class "object". Parts of this graph can be visualized using the *ObjTalk browser*, a tool comparable to the SMALL-TALK browser [Goldberg 84].

The internal structure of ObjTalk objects, i.e. the values of object slots and the definition of methods within ObjTalk classes can be visualized using the *ObjTalk Inspector* [von der Herberg 86].

The *ObjTalk Prettyprinter* is a tool which represents ObjTalk objects in a form which is understandable to the user, i.e. in a textual form which could be loaded into the system to redefine an already existing object.

While it seems obvious that the class dependency graph should be displayed by graphical means (see Figure 2 as an example), the internal structure of objects does not lend itself as nicely to graphical display. We have selected textual representations of internal object properties because they seem to be the most convenient representation for the programmer (see Figure 3).

Tools for the creation and modification of objects

The *ObjTalk Editor* is a self-modifying, syntax-driven editor for object structures. It combines the advantages of free text input with those of a template oriented editor. This is quite useful for object oriented languages since objects have a clear and unique structure. With the ObjTalk Editor, the user can input free text. However, when trying to replace data structures with this text the editor will only accept syntactically correct structures.

This syntax control is achieved with the help of language patterns which are matched against the structure typed by the user. These patterns are coded by hand for the definition of classes because of their complexity. For simple objects the patterns can be created on the

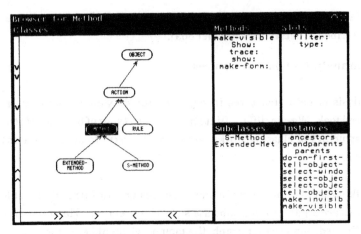

Figure 2: The ObjTalk Browser

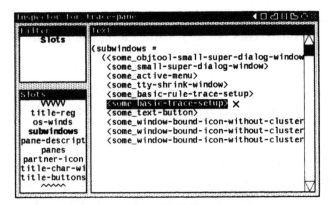

Figure 3: The ObjTalk Inspector

fly by sending an appropriate message to the class to which the object belongs. (See [Specht 86] for more details on the editor.)

Tools for the administration of large systems

Systems with many objects, possibly developed by a number of programmers, are difficult to organize. We need tools for version control and for the partition of large systems into smaller independent subsystems. Obviously, we have structures in large systems in addition to the usual class-subclass-object relation. These structures are important for the programmer trying to handle a large system. Examples are modules or packages defining different functionality.

Within the ObjTalk environment we developed a kind of *knowledge base,* which organizes the objects belonging to it, their different versions, the handling of copies on remote memory, etc. Technically a knowledge base is an object which *knows* details about its objects and classes.

Since we may have many knowledge bases in a system there is a unique object called the *knowledge base manager,* which incorporates the necessary information about the existing knowledge bases in the object world [Bauer 85].

Organizing the user dialog

For the organization of the user dialog ObjEnv uses the tools of the surrounding LISP-Environment [Foderaro, Sklower 82], the *LISP-Toplevel* and the *LISP-Break.* These tools have been adapted to support the use of ObjTalk as a programming language. In addition to this, we integrated these tools into the overall user interface using menus to select parts of the dialog history for modification or reuse (see Figure 4).

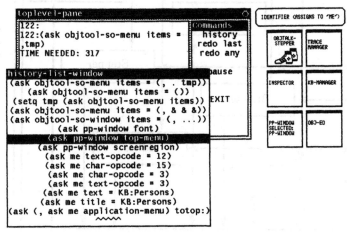

Figure 4: The integration of the Lisp-Toplevel

Figure 5 shows the different components of the ObjEnv programming environment with their logical relations. The tool interface on the left side of the figure is a simple interface to pass on pointers to objects from one tool to another. This is initiated by selection of a message within a menu which will be sent to the receiving object.

Usually the user interacts with the environment through a user interface component. The user interface of all components was kept as uniform as possible. If the functionality of the tools didn't allow this, at least the overall appearance was kept uniform. The screen organization of the environment is shown in Figure 6.

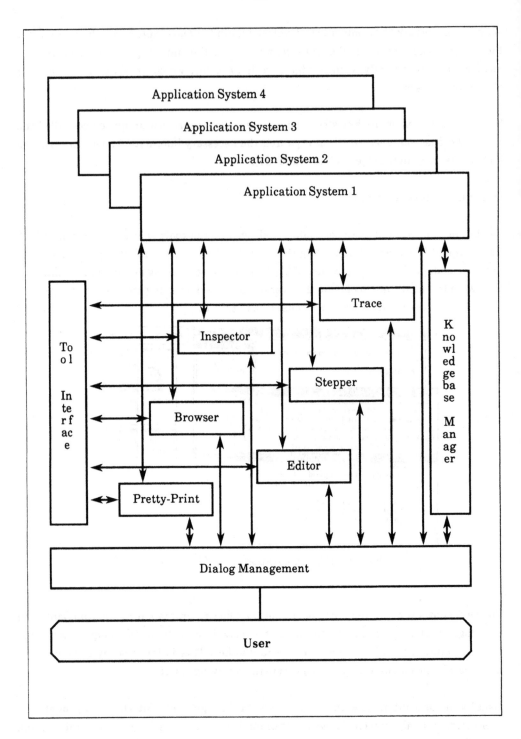

Figure 5: Schematic Representation of the ObjEnv environment

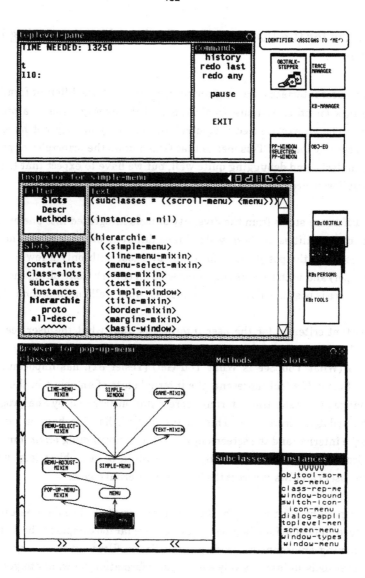

Figure 6: The screen layout of the ObjEnv environment. In the upper right hand corner, icons are visible which represent the tools of the environment currently not in use. The icons below represent knowledge bases loaded into the system. Each icon represents a window which contains all the necessary information about one knowledge base.

4 Criteria for the User Interface Design of Programming Environments

Designing a user interface for a programming environment is different from accomplishing the same task for other systems. One can expect the average user of a programming environment to be an experienced computer user who may or may not have difficulties in using this specific tool set. This means that (s)he knows the principles of programming, of program analysis, and debugging quite well, but we have to expect that (s)he lacks knowledge about how to accomplish a task.

Another difference stems from the diversity of tools integrated into one environment. The different functionalities of these tools makes different user interfaces necessary. As ·an example, consider the possibilities for input to a tool with only a few possible selections (like a stepper) and with free text input (as with an editor). Controlling the first tool with a pointing device is possible, however, this does not work well for the second kind.

One important criterion for the user interface is, that what the user sees on the screen should reflect the internal state of his system as well as possible. This principle, called *WYSIWYG* (What You See Is What You Get) [Tesler 81], has important effects on the interface of tools. If a tool represents the internal state of an object in the system and this object changes its state, the external representation (created by the programming tool) should be updated accordingly. This means that we have to have a logical connection between the internal and the screen objects in the programming environment. WYSIWYG allows also the reverse operation. By referencing a screen object (e.g. with a pointing device) the user can always access the matching internal object.

Another important point is the ability to *hide information*. The data necessary to describe the structure and behavior of a program system are far too complex to be displayed entirely. A programming environment needs possibilities to filter out necessary information and give the user tools to interactively select the information he wants to get from a specific tool.

The large amount of data produced by some of the tools in an environment creates the problem of *preemption*. Data that are necessary for the user are scrolled off the screen and irretrievably lost. A programming environment should prevent this kind of data loss in any case.

Users of a programming environment who are not totally familiar with the tool they use need information about the state of their environment, the possibilities they have to continue their work, and about how they can select one of these possibilities [Stelovsky 84]. There are several ways to show this information e.g. by displaying information in mode-lines, or by changing the appearance of the windows or icons representing tools or internal objects.

The user should have the possibility of selecting his favorite *style of interaction*. There is no need to force a programmer to one specific input style. With today's computer systems we can offer the programmer a range of input devices (keyboard, menu selection, picking with a pointing device, in the future perhaps voice input) and have him choose the one he wants.

The programmer wants to *communicate with the programming environment in the language of the program*. This is a very important aspect of the interface design. By this, we mean that the tools of the environment should present information in terms of the programming language being used. It does not make sense to display data in the form created by, e.g., a compiler. Code should be displayed in the form the user has written it in his editor, runtime information should only show information about the language specific code, not about the environment, interpreter status etc.

The programming environment must never mix the in- and output of the system to be worked on with the output of the tools of the environment. (This was a serious problem with teletype interfaces!)

Data objects represented on the screen should be accessible by *pointing* to their external representation. This saves the programmer much typing effort he would otherwise have to do. Transfer of objects from one tool of the programming environment to another should be possible via a tool interface, not only by entering the name by hand. The input done by the user should also be reusable. For this purpose the environment should keep a history of the dialog and allow the selective reuse and editing of earlier dialog steps.

However, the most important point for designing the user interface of a programming environment is the *consistency of the interface* over all integrated tools. To accomplish this consistency, it is necessary to select a standard set of interaction facilities (like pointing devices, icons on the screen, selection from menus, a window technique, etc.) and to use this set throughout the interface design.

5 The User Interface of ObjEnv

To organize the user interface of ObjEnv we used the following facilities (see Figure 6 for an example):

1. *Windows* organize the in- and output to different tools and keep the information of the environment separate from the system to be worked on.

2. Windows of tools not used at the moment are represented by *icons*.
3. *Window panes* organize different windows attached to one tool.
4. *Icon clusters* visualize the relationship between tools and the environment.
5. *Menus* are used for selection wherever this is possible.
6. *Buttons* can be used to start tools and to send predefined messages to system objects.

The *ObjEnv* environment consists of a set of loosely coupled tools. Most tools can exist several times in the environment. From each tool there is a default version which can be copied and adapted to specific situations. Each tool has a simple program interface which allows the transfer of object pointers to other tools. The user can initialize such a transfer by selecting the appropriate items in the menus of the tools in question.

Concluding Remarks

Our experiences with the ObjTalk Environment show that the use of integrated tools with a common user interface make the work of programmers more efficient. Programmers can cope with larger programs and are able to develop sufficiently correct programs faster. The possibility to select different interaction styles seems to be very important if a programming environment should be used by both casual and experienced programmers.

Acknowledgements

The work reported here was done at the University of Stuttgart, Project INFORM, (Fed. Rep. of Germany) and funded in part by the German Ministery for Research and Technology (BMFT). Many students and colleagues helped me to create this system by supplying code and tools and giving me important new ideas in discussions. [Schneider 1986] describes this work in much more detail.

References

[Barstow et al. 84]
  D.R. Barstow, H.E. Shrobe, E. Sandewall: "Interactive Programming Environments". McGraw-Hill, New York, 1984.

[Bauer 85]
  D. Bauer: "Wissensbank für Objekte". Diplomarbeit Nr. 518, Institut für Informatik, Universität Stuttgart, 1985.

[Cox 84]
  B.J. Cox: "Object Oriented Programming: An Evolutionary Approach". Addison-Wesley, Reading, Ma., 1986.

[Foderaro, Sklower 82]
  J.K. Foderaro, K.L. Sklower: "The FranzLisp Manual". Technical Report, University of California, Berkeley, 1982.

[Goldberg 84]
   A. Goldberg: "SMALLTALK-80, The Interactive Programming Environment". Addison-Wesley, Reading, Ma., 1984.

[Minsky 75]
   M. Minsky: "A Framework for Representing Knowledge". In P.H. Winston (editor), The Psychology of Computer Vision, pp 211-277. New York, 1975.

[Rathke, C. 86]
   C. Rathke: "ObjTalk. Repräsentation von Wissen in einer objektorientierten Sprache". Dissertation, Universität Stuttgart, 1986.

[Schneider 86]
   M. Schneider-Hufschmidt: "Methoden und Werkzeuge zur Software-Entwicklung in einer objektorientierten Programmierumgebung". Dissertation, Universität Stuttgart, 1986.

[Schneider 86a]
   M. Schneider: "FAST - A Stepper in an Object-Oriented Programming Environment". In M. Tauber (editor), Proceedings of the 5th Interdisciplinary Workshop Informatics and Psychology: Visual Aids in Programming. German Chapter of the ACM, ÖG, Schärding, May, 1986, reprinted in this volume.

[Specht 86]
   C. Specht: "Obj-Ed, ein objektorientierter Struktureditor für ObjTalk". Studienarbeit Nr. 554, Institut für Informatik, Universität Stuttgart, 1986.

[Stelovsky 84]
   J. Stelovsky: "XS-2: The User Interface of an Interactive System". Dissertation 7425, ETH Zürich, 1984.

[Tesler 81]
   L. Tesler: "The Smalltalk Environment". BYTE 6(8), pp 90-147, August, 1981.

[von der Herberg 86]
   H. von der Herberg: "Visualisierung von ObjTalk-Strukturen". Diplomarbeit Nr. 524, Institut für Informatik, Universität Stuttgart, 1986.

A Context-Oriented Approach for Decision Support

Angehrn Albert *, Arnoldi Massimo*, Lüthi Hans-Jakob*, Ackermann David **

*Swiss Federal Institute of Technology, Institut für Operations Research ETHZ,
**Swiss Federal Institute of Technology, Lehrstuhl für Arbeits- und Organisationspsychologie,
CH - 8092, Zürich, Switzerland

Abstract

In this paper we address the question, how to design a DSS-generator, such that the effort for building a specific DSS is small but at the same time the user-interface reflects the individual semantic structuring of the scope of actions. A conceptual answer to the question raised above is proposed in the rest of the paper. Through the a-priori specification of a context underlying a DSS-generator a mental frame is defined for 1. confining the problem-domain, 2. integrating harmonically the various components of a DSS-generator, 3. defining, representing and manipulating objects, relations and operations compatible to the user's mental processes and hence 4. facilitating the design of specific DSS reflecting the individual scope of actions.

Keywords : decision support systems, man-machine interaction, modelling, mental models, user-centered system.

1. Introduction

The development of software for supporting decisions (in contrast to automate decisions) requires the integration of skills from two different domains: The technical world of information processing (technical perspective) has to be carefully matched with the individual approach for problem solving (human perspective). Almost inevitably the different qualities of these worlds generate a dilemma: Whereas the technical world is based on precise, often axiomatic structures and constructs and hence a problem and its solution method (algorithms) have to be described using these rigid concepts, the mental world of humans is characterized by fuzzy, vague qualitative concepts where in particular problems and solutions are often tightly interrelated notions. Accordingly, system developers view the human-machine interaction as system-centered i.e. tend to perceive a problem in well structured terms whereas psychologists tend to focus on mental processes such as perception, cognition, motivation and action for describing a problem solving process (human-centered perspective). The technical processes can be observed, identified and described by a rigid methodology (hard science). Human actions, in contrary, can only be understood in the specific context of 'this self-interpreting system' [Dre 83]. Following Dreyfus a theory of human actions is only possible if we can refer to a theory of the context wherein an action takes place.

These considerations should suffice to motivate the content of this paper : aiming at a pragmatic synthesis of the technical and psychological perspective we will outline a methodology for the system-design process for decision-support, integrating some useful descriptive concepts due to Ulich [Uli 85] about human organization of activities into the DSS-design.

In section 2 we will first summarize the design principles for a specific DSS, where we based the dialog-grammar on the concept of a semantic structuring of the scope of action [Ack 87]. Starting from a critical appraisal of the presented specific DSS we will work out analogous design principles for DSS-generators. In section 3 we argue that for constructing a DSS-generator, in accordance with the principles specified in section 2 an underlying 'context' as a substitute for a mental model must be defined. We discuss the influence of the context on the design of the three major components of a DSS as an 'integrating agent'. Finally we will discuss examples of such DSS-generators which have been realized or are under development.

2. Design principles for decision support

2.1 Paradigm for DSS

Historically the DSS approach was a reaction to the MIS-movement in the early seventies. Ten years ago DSS represented a radical concept in the use of information systems and analytic tools; now it is part of the mainstream [Kee 87]. Although there is no commonly accepted definition of a DSS, it is generally recognized that the issues central to DSS are [PL 87]:

> *Decision Processes*, encompassing the nontechnical and analytic aspects of decision-making including criteria for selecting domain of applications for DSS ('semistructured problems').
>
> *Support* focuses on understanding of human actions and how to help them ('implementation and usage modality').
>
> *Systems* emphasizes design and development strategies ('adaptive design') and technological tools ('Document-based systems, Expert Systems, etc.').

The early work in DSS began from a discussion of decision making, moved on to the issue of effective support and ended up with a system. By contrast, Sprague and Carlson's book [SC 82] entitled "Building Effective DSS" moves in the reverse direction: How do we build *systems*? Within this technical view, DSS-generators became the technical vehicle for delivering support systems for a specific situation ('Specific DSS').

But the central issue still remains to be investigated: How can we deliver useful systems to support the intuition of the manager, i.e while respecting the primacy of judgement to complement it by adequate modelling tools (including nontrivial analytic tools). Towards that end the basic question to ask is: Why is decision making so hard? Understanding this question would give us a clue as to *what sort of support might be useful* for managers facing complex decision situations.

In the following paragraphs we present and illustrate some basic concepts for structuring and designing the support function relying on principles of work psychology. The approach was motivated by the successful development of a specific DSS where we based the dialog-grammar on the concept of a semantic structuring of the scope of action to be described in the next paragraph. Its empirically tested good performance and acceptance stimulated further research within this framework. The resulting design principles called *context-approach for decision support* will be presented in section 3 using a 'design-oriented view'.

2.2 Structuring of support for a specific DSS

According to the principles of differential and dynamic work design [Uli 78] (An optimal development of personality in working life is only possible if (1) individual differences in action-regulation are taken into account and if (2) possibilities exist to adapt existing worksystems or to create new worksystems) the 'support system' has to be tailored for and *by* the individual to his or her own individual demands and abilities in order to improve efficiency and to give optimal chances of task orientation and achievement motivation.

How can we match these requirements in the system design ? Many examples show that it is very puzzling to understand the prospective user's way of thinking and it is almost impossible to predict it without a profound analysis of the user's thinking. Difficulties in human-computer interactions during task solving processes are mainly due to the discrepancy between *individual mental representations* and goal setting on the one hand and the *scope of action* prescribed by the dialog on the other hand [Ack 87].

The *scope of actions* denotes the "*degree of freedom for various problem-oriented actions with regard to procedures, means and tools and temporal organization of subtasks*" [Hac 78]. Immediately we observe that with regard to the user two scopes of actions need to be distinguished:

The *system-oriented* scope of actions as described by the dialog-grammar (the vocabulary of commands and its corresponding rules) and the *task-oriented* scope of actions comprising procedures, means and tools to structure and handle the 'problem' based on the user´s underlying mental model. Therefore the central design question becomes how to derive the *conceptual design-structure of the support system* from the anticipated task-oriented scope of actions [Hol 83].

One way to solve this problem is by a *structured process of user participation* in the development and design phase with the intention to become acquainted with the user's specific knowledge about his task and by observing his way of working. The main result is what we will call a *semantic structuring of the scope of actions* best explained by a paradigmatic example.

Based on the above ideas we started out to develop a specific decision support system for evacuation planning in emergency cases for the Swiss Defense Organization in Zurich. **EPILOG** (Evacuation Planning in Dialogue) is an interactive system *supporting the planning* of reallocation of people already in atomic-shelters to other shelters for emergency reasons (fire, flooding, etc.). The task of evacuation planning is adhoc, depends on the actual situation and allocations and should be simple to organize by militiamen.

The (semantic) *structuring* of the scope of actions is grounded in the cycle of problem solving due to Simon [Sim 60]. The *semantic* is extracted by collecting documents and data about the problem solving process using 'pencil and paper'. In particular we used a chart with abbreviations, a map of the city with special marks of the organization, etc. In addition we got some instructions about how the regulations in shelter allocation should be applied. The result of this analytical process is depicted in Table 1.

Phase	Problem solving process	Semantic structuring
Intelligence	Problem instance	- region to be evacuated - prohibited areas
	Objectives	- shelter quality - walking distance - optimal protection
Design	Generation of alternatives	- gathering places - accessibility - availability
	Analysis of alternatives	- enough shelters - allocation pattern
Choice	Evaluation Decision and implementation	- comparison of alternatives with regard to objectives

Table 1

Proceeding from this outline of the scope of actions, the outline of the dialog including screen layout was assessed using comic-strips.

The problem representation was based on a graphical map containing the relevant organizational and geographical information.

All dialog-components such as problem definition, search for available shelters, alternative organization of the evacuation and allocation of new shelters were represented in this map but complemented with other representation aids such as tables and graphical charts.(Fig.1)

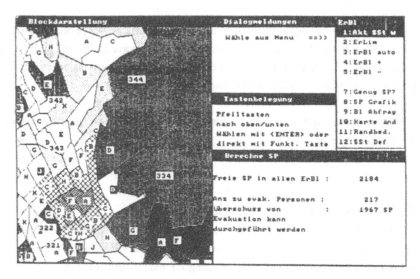

Figure 1

The system was experimentally tested and evaluated by members of the Civil Defense organization. A detailed description of the experimental design and performance analysis is contained in [Ack 87].Two results are remarkable: The system was well accepted even by computer novices and in theirs terms the quality of solutions increased remarkably with the time spent on the system (effect of learning). We also analyzed the 'Menu-navigation Diagram' showing individual differences in using the dialog and apparently the system *supports* different ways in solving the same task.

We attribute both phenomena to the correspondence of the individual mental problem-representation and processes (user-centered view) with the *semantic structuring of the scope of actions* (design-centered view) as reflected in the dialog-component of the support system (system-centered view).

2.3 Critical appraisal

We started out to investigate the question how individual differences in the task-oriented scope of actions ought to be reflected in a specific support system. Synthesizing, the described design-centered view for delivering support aims to meet the following design objectives:

(1) compatibility with regard to the user's mental processes

(2) support of the user's qualifications

(3) user's control

The first objective comprises the idea that the notions, concepts and operations used must be familiar to the user. Furthermore the representations, the language and the conceptual complexity of the dialog should be compatible to the user's knowledge [Uli 85].The second objective refers to the user's competence: The *supporting system* should not only help in finding solutions but in improving the user's skill for approaching such tasks. As a consequence the system should support elementary operations instead of strongly integrated (automated) functions in order to increase the user's understanding of the available methods and tools.

EPILOG meets the above design requirements but within a confined task and scope of decisions.In general specific DSS only allow to explore an a priori defined space of alternatives. Although in some cases this kind of freedom suffices, we strongly believe that the critical part of problem solving lies in formulating the problem. Hence the scope of actions should be variable.

Even if a variety of problems could be supported similarly, EPILOG is by its tailored conception not flexible enough for such accommodations.
In technical terms we lacked a DSS-generator permitting us to develop applications like EPILOG within a reasonable time frame.

2.4 Structuring Support for DSS-Generators

Referring to 2.3. the challenging question arises how to design a DSS-development environment (DSS-generator) wherein a specific DSS can be designed based on a semantic structuring of the scope of actions *most preferably by the user himself* and hence meeting the requirements (1)-(3).
Following Ulich [Uli 84], in work psychology the scope of actions is embedded in the broader concept of the scope of activities encompassing two more constructs: *The scope of variability and the scope of decisions* (Figure 2).

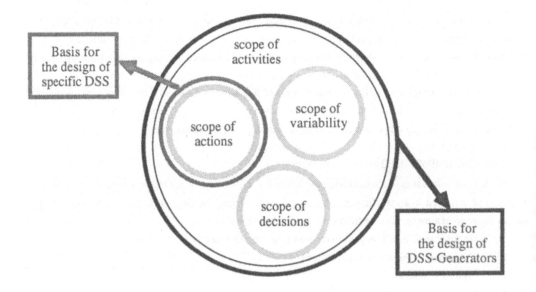

Figure 2 : Scope of activities

The *scope of variability* ('Gestaltungsspielraum') is defined by the possibilities to create own procedures and hence determines the variability of an activity. By the *scope of decisions* ('Entscheidungsspielraum') we mean the competence delegated to a person (or group) related to a task or organizational measure.

With regard to EPILOG we noticed already the absence of the scope of variability: New procedures can not be integrated easily into the system, i.e. the system can not 'grow' with the user's competence. Starting from our demand to individualize work activities and worksystems we will present in the next section a design-methodology such that the user can build applications himself encompassing all dimensions of the scope of activities.

3. The Context Approach

3.1 What is a Context ?

The term context as a colloquialisms refers to a text revealing the precise meaning of a word or a phrase contained in it. Generalizing this colloquial definition we can state : 'Context' refers to an environment revealing the precise meaning of an object or action specified in it. An appealing attempt to explain the concept of context from a phenomenological point of view has been proposed by Winograd and Flores in the interesting book "Understanding Computers and Cognition" [WF 86].

Starting from an analysis of language they focus on the crucial role of 'breakdowns', as "... the interrupted moment of our habitual, standard, comfortable 'being-in-the-world'. Breakdowns serve an extremely important cognitive function revealing to us the nature of our practices and equipment, making them 'present-to-hand' to us .... The analysis of a human context of activity can begin with an analysis of the domains of breakdown, and that can in turn be used to generate the objects, properties, and actions that make up the domain".

In the context-approach for decision support we deliberately associate the scope of variability of a DSS to a context with its generic notions and concepts. This context shall provide a conceptual basis for the semantic structuring of the scope of variability, finally leading to design a consistent DSS-generator .

Certainly by the a priori specification of a 'context' only a restricted domain of discourse can be accommodated. But, within this domain the interpretation of the contemplated objects or actions is implicitly given. More precisely we propose a systematic context analysis through the investigation of the following set of questions :

- What distinguishes a typical context-element and what are its characteristic attributes ?
- What are meaningful relationships among this elements ?
- Do exist generic notions for classifying them ?
- Which actions (operations on objects respectively) are meaningful and what are typical questions (problems, breakdowns) posed within this context ?

3.2 The context and its influence on the DSS-components

Figure 3 schematically represents the relationship among the main DSS-components (dialog, data/knowledge-base, model-base) and the underlying context.

How does the context influence the design of a DSS-generator ? This question will be investigated in the next sections.

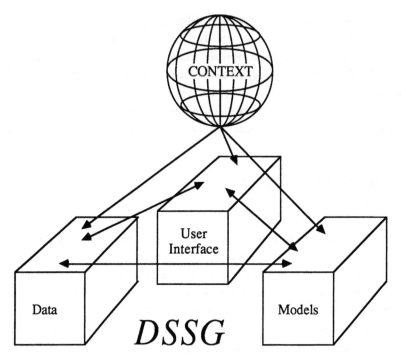

Figure 3

3.2.1. The influence on the user interface

"On working with people, we establish domains of conversations in which our pre-understanding lets us communicate with a minimum of words and conscious effort. We become explicitly aware of the structure of conversation only when there is some kind of breakdown calling for corrective action. If machines could understand in the same way people do, interactions with computers would be equally transparent" [WF 86].

The context-oriented design process emphasizes the identification of those elements (see section 3.1.) concurring to make pre-understanding and communication-ease possible.
In fact, these elements play a crucial role in the user-interface design for a decision support system. Their integration into a technical environment should be performed taking care of

(1) not losing their original, context-inherent semantic (conceptual view)
(2) preserving as far as possible their context-specific representations (practical view)

The key objective of point (1) is to support the user allowing him to work with familiar concepts, unlike using context-independent abstractions such as first-order logic, programming or command languages.
Point (2) is directly concerned with the design of the user-interface and the interaction with it : In terms of end results - what the user sees - context-specific representations (visualizations) enhance a feeling of directness. As noted by [HHN 85] [Hud 87] this feeling is characterized by following three aspects :

Engagement	the feeling of communicating with the objects of interest directly.
Articulatory distance	the degree to which the form of communication with the system reflects the application objects and tasks involved.
Semantic distance	the degree to which the semantic concepts used by the system are compatible with those of the user and can be used to easily accomplish the user's goals.

The resulting interface is transparent to the user, so that he can concentrate himself <u>directly</u> into his task (see for example the 'invisible' user-interface of Apple MacIntosh in the context of files- , text- and graphic manipulation).

The relationship between the technical aspects of an user interface and the psychological requirements of chapter 2 are depicted in figure 4.

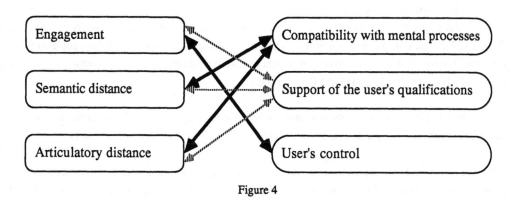

Figure 4

Supporting many representations not only facilitates the man-machine communication. It has been recognized [Sim 81] that switching between different representations also plays a central role in the problem solving process. For example theorem proving in mathematics can be interpreted as throwing light on a problem (the theorem assertion) by changing stepwise its representation.

As noted in [Fis 87] "whenever the user of a system can directly manipulate the concepts of an application, systems become more understandable and the distinction between programmers and non-programmers vanishes." We are convinced that the early consideration of the underlying context into the design is a fundamental prerequisite for developing useful and usable DSS generators.

3.2.2. The influence on the other components : data and models

Early Decision Support Systems were labeled as data- or model-centered, depending on whether their kernel was rooted in a data base or a mathematical package.

In this technical-based approach the user interface was build a posteriori, resulting in a lack of flexibility and in a difficult cooperation and communication between the different system- components.

In our approach, through the analysis of the context, we define already in an initial stage a conceptual frame for identifying and embedding the needed functionality.

Furthermore, by the context-approach those rules are specified which govern the 'use of data' and 'use of models' within the system and hence imprint the variability of the system :

Under the term 'use of data' we subsume the way an object of the context is addressed, selected and manipulated. Particularly, the context determines the distinguished attributes and what type of questions a useful system should support.

The term 'use of models' means the way models are defined, used and manipulated within the underlying context. In particular we include herein a supporting component (modelling by example, context-dependent explanation of the methods available in the model base, semantic and syntactic support within this instance) with context-dependent input / output options.

3.3. User´s and Builder´s view in the Context-Approach

3.3.1. The Builder´s view

From the designer's view the main task is to 'model' the context in terms of the variability perceived as necessary. The result should be a semantic structuring of the scope of variability of the associated DSS-generator. The focus on an a priori specified context and hence on a confined problem domain results in a number of advantages for the design of a DSS-generator:

1.The different components of a DSS-generator can be smoothly integrated (in a balanced manner) and the dialog-component is no longer designed 'adhoc' but reflects the inherent structure of the context.

2. Instead of posing the question "how to add a good interface to a system with high functionality" the context-approach explicitly focuses on the scope of variability for deducing the necessary functionality and semantic from the context.

3.3.2. The End-User´s view

From the user's view context means the mental model wherein the man-machine interaction takes place. The more this mental model corresponds to his own way of thinking , the better he will be able to use the system for his support.

The context-approach is based on the semantic structuring of the scope of variability resulting in a user-interface compatible to the user's mental processes. Therefore, the user should be capable, by using his semantic knowledge, to model the conceived scope of actions himself. This corresponds to the psychological requirements discussed in chapter 2 and eliminates the communication problems encountered in the classical DSS-design.

4. Examples

It may be helpful to illustrate the context-approach described in section 3, analyzing the following two familiar contexts :

- the geographical context, pointing out the influence on the user interface
- the accounting context, pointing out the influence on working with models

4.1 Geographical context

Centuries ago human invented the 'map' as a well accepted model for representing geographical objects, state of affairs and events of geographical nature.

A deep analysis of the geographical context in conjunction with an investigation of what kind of decisions can be effectively supported in such an environment is the subject of a project at the author's institute. Nowadays we are developing a decision support generator, which supports end-user in formulating, structuring and analyzing different decision situations in a geographical context [AA 86].

Starting from a class of atomic objects and using structuring concepts analogous to object oriented systems the user can model specific problems using direct manipulation techniques.

He has the possibility to model his problem using objects of the geographical context like points, regions, links or paths, associating to these objects the relevant information in form of simple data (if necessary retrieved from a database) or through the specification of methods for their retrieval (e.g. describing through formulas quantitative relationships between the attributes of the modeled objects). All the supported activities are embedded in a highly visual environment, permitting the end-user to perform complex operations (data-retrieval, structuring, using mathematical methods...) simply working on the map. For example the end-user can integrate in the modelling process some predefined ('formal') models supporting the generation and choice between alternatives through the use of algorithms for routing problems, location and distribution problems, districting, logistical problems ..., just by drawing an example of the desired result ('modelling by example').

The context represents herein the key-element for allowing the user the utilization of highly sophisticated tools without beingbothered with task-independent technical details.

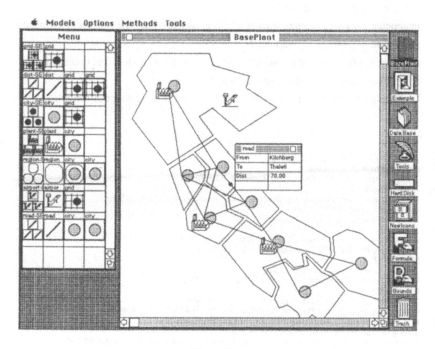

Figure 5

4.2 Accounting Context

Every accounting program, payroll program and billing program operates within a systematic domain of bookkeeping that has evolved over centuries of commercial experience [WF 86].

In our perspective we interpret for example spreadsheets as limited DSS-generators in an accounting context. The objects are cells (ranges respectively) characterized by their locations on a grid and their contents (text , data or formulas). Again, the intimacy with the underlying mental model and its corresponding interface enables the user to model and to analyze decision-problems. Methodically, spreadsheet-programs only support the recalculation of the model after changes in the content of cells, which is sufficient for generating, evaluating and comparing alternatives (what-if analysis). There is now a tendency to support what's best analysis, risk analysis, and other sophisticated methods.

The integration of optimization-techniques has already been realized in various software packages, but there is a substantial difference between using a spreadsheet only as a comfortable interface to linear programming, or enhancing its functionality with such mathematical models by explicitly taking into account the context and the scope of variability provided by a spreadsheet [Ang 87] .

5. Final remarks

In this paper we addressed the question, how to design a DSS-generator, such that the effort for building a specific DSS is small but at the same time the user-interface reflects the individual semantic structuring of the scope of actions.

A conceptual answer to the question raised above has been proposed here.

Through the a priori specification of a context underlying a DSS-generator a mental frame is defined for

1. confining the problem-domain,

2. integrating the various components of a DSS-generator using the concept of a semantic structuring of its scope of variability,

3. defining, representing and manipulating objects, relations, models and operations compatible to the user's mental processes and   hence

4. facilitating the design of specific DSS reflecting the individual scope of actions.

References

[AA 86]   ANGEHRN Albert, ARNOLDI Massimo
          A geographical DSS-Generator
          Working paper, Institut für Operations Research, ETH-Zürich.
[Ack 87] ACKERMANN David
          Handlungsspielraum, mentale Repräsentation und Handlungsregulation am Beispiel
          der Mensch-Computer-Interaktion.
          Inauguraldissertation Universität Bern.
[Ang 87] ANGEHRN Albert
          A New Approach for applying Linear Optimization in Spreadsheets.
          Working paper, Institut für Operations Research, ETH-Zürich.
[Bös 86] BÖSZE J. Z.
          EPILOG: Evaluationsplanung im Dialog.
          Unveröffentlichte Diplomarbeit im Fach Informatik, ETH-Zürich.
[Dre 83] DREYFUS H.
          Why current studies of human capacities can never be scientific.
          Berkley Cognitive Science Program Report No 11, Okt., Inst. of Cognitive Studies.
[Fis 87] FISCHER Gerhard
          Making Computers more useful and more usable.
          Cognitive Engineering in the Design of Human-Interaction and Expert Systems, pp. 97-104

[Hac 78]   HACKER W.
           Allgemeine Arbeits- und Ingenieurpsychologie.
           Bern: Huber.
[Hol 83]   HOLLNAGEL E.
           Cognitive systems engineering: New wine in new bottles.
           Int. J. Man-Machine Studies, 18.
[Hud 87]   HUDSON Scott
           UIMS Support for Direct Manipulation Interfaces
           Computer Graphics, Vol. 21, No. 2, pp. 120-124
[HHN 85]   HUTCHINS Edwin, HOLLAN James, NORMAN Donald
           Direct manipulation interfaces.
           Human-Computer Interaction, Volume 1, pp. 311-338
[Kee 87]   KEEN P.G.W.
           DSS The next decade.
           Decision Support Systems 3 .
[Nor 86]   NORMAN D.A., DRAPER St.W. (eds)
           User centered system design. New perspectives on human-computer interaction.
           Hillsdale N.J.: Lawrence Erlbaum.
[PL 87]   PFEIFER Rolf, LUETHI Hans-Jacob
           Decision Support Systems and Expert Systems: a complementary relationship
           Expert Systems and Artificial Intelligence in Decision Support Systems, Sol/Takkenberg/De Vries Robbé
[Sim 60]   SIMON H.A.
           The New Science of Management Decision
           Harper & Row, New York
[Sim 81]   SIMON H.A.
           The Sciences of the Artificial
           The MIT Press, Cambridge, MA
[SC 82]   SPRAGUE Ralph, CARLSON Eric
           Building Effective Decision Support Systems
           Prentice-Hall
[Uli 78]   ULICH E.
           Über das Prinzip der differentiellen Artbeitsgestaltung
           Industrielle Organisation, 47.
[Uli 84]   ULICH E.
           Psychologie der Arbeit.
           In: Management Enzyklopädie, Band 7. Landsberg: Moderne Industrie.
[Uli 85]   ULICH E.
           Arbeitspsychologische Konzepte für computerunterstützte Büroarbeit.
           SPECTRUM Nr. 14.
[WF 86]   WINOGRAD Terry, FLORES Fernando
           Understanding Computer and Cognition
           Ablex Publishing Company

BEYOND THE DESK TOP METAPHOR:
INFORMATION RETRIEVAL WITH AN ICON-BASED INTERFACE

Annelise Mark Pejtersen and L. P. Goodstein
Risø National Laboratory
Department of Information Technology
DK 4000 Roskilde, Denmark

INTRODUCTION

The advent of modern information technology has a significant effect on users' work situations. Functional requirements for the support of specific professional activities are being integrated in work stations which give the user access to all kinds of information from a host of sources, e.g., from local databanks, mail services, instruments, laboratory test results and external databases. One of the user's critical problems is to be able to navigate in a set of different distinctive databases, each with its own type of information, design intent and justification, etc. The requirement exists that this information be processed, coordinated and displayed in such a way that the contents and form directly can match the user's need and choice of strategy in the current task. This calls for a new approach to the design of the user interface, which will be described in this paper (Pejtersen, 1987).

Databases can be considered as multidimensional storehouses of items of information. In principle, a standardized and generally applicable iconic interface can be developed if a repertoire of icons can be designed to represent the topology of the storehouse as well as the related navigation rules. In addition, however, content-specific icons are needed for each given domain. Hence, this approach calls for a metaphor for each domain and its associated information retrieval and processing task spectrum. This use of icons stands in contrast to the widely used "desk top metaphor" which merely relates icons to an earlier generation of technology (folders, in and out baskets, etc.). Thus the metaphor consists of a set of computerized graphic representations of these desk top tools without any effort to relate them to the user's present work situation.

It is the aim of the project to investigate how such an interface with icons can support the user's navigation in databases by a graphical representation of the function of the system as well as its information contents in relation to the user's task. The particular context chosen is the retrieval of fiction in public libraries.

A DATABASE FOR FICTION RETRIEVAL

As argued in the preceding section, a multidimensional, relational database in which items can be identified rapidly and with good resolution in response to users' queries is a primary requirement. The structure used for the database design in the present experiments was developed from empirical investigations of user behaviour in libraries. Field studies by Pejtersen (1979, 1980, 1984, 1987, 1988) have led to the formulation of a search space. Analyses of end user-intermediary searches in libraries have shown that users express their reading needs in a way which can best be represented in this type of multifacetted or multidimensional classification system.

The contents of the various facets are related to: 1. Author's intention with the document such as to give the user an emotional experience, information, education, etc. or to promote ideas, e.g., social criticism, philosophical attitudes, etc. 2. Frame or setting of the subject matter content in terms of time and place, i.e., the geographical, historical, social, or professional surroundings, etc. 3. Subject matter of a document in terms of action and course of events ('plot'), psychological development/description, social relationships. 4. Accessibility, the physical characteristics of a document, readability, printing, physical format, publisher, etc.

In order to support user access to literature in a database system, it should be possible to identify and locate items by employing search terms in any of these facets of the user demand or in combinations of them. Thus, design of computer-supported retrieval systems has to build on a suitable classification system as well as a database sensitive to queries in terms compatible with the various facets reflecting user needs. This is not the situation for fiction retrieval alone but is also relevant in other applications such as engineering design and emergency management.

As a result, the information retrieval task in libraries will involve a mapping between two separate multilevel problem spaces, the user need and the contents of available bibliographical references. Fig. 1 illustrates this in the form of a document description in terms of the multidimensional classification system mentioned above (the left column) with the contents of the document to the right. The latter can be matched against the original user requirements structured with respect to the classification system. Two decision makers are typically involved in this task; the user who may only be able to formulate his/her reading needs in implicit terms, and an intermediary who may know only part of the contents of the individual databases and of their knowledge domain. The joint decision task during a search then will be to analyse/determine a user's need in terms compatible with the database structure, select documents and compare their match with the need. In order to make it feasible for the end user to access the databases directly, interfaces which guide the user's navigation in these complex structures are necessary.

By analysis of actual user behaviour in libraries, several different strategies for identification of documents to match user needs have been identified (Pejtersen, 1979). Some of these are:

- Analytical search. The intermediary is in control, explores systematically the dimensions of the user's needs, retrieves documents, compares aspects of needs with aspects of documents, suggests titles for the user's consideration and approval. This strategy is the rational, problem solving strategy.

- Search by analogy. The intermediary is in control and explores the user's needs by asking for information about the user's previous reading in order to be able to find 'something similar'. Prototypes thus identified are then analysed to identify search terms for new documents.

- <u>Browsing strategy.</u> An information seeker in a library may have a need which is so ambiguous that specification of a search template is avoided and, instead, the contents of a bookshelf or a database is scanned in order to explore possible matches between the intuitive current need and the available items.

It will be seen that these strategies are formulated at the same level of generality and can be used to specify the mental model and the categories of information which should be considered for the design of support systems and their interfaces.

These search strategies are discussed in a subsequent section with reference to experiments with computer-supported user interaction with bibliographic databases.

<u>NAVIGATION IN DATABASES</u>

It is important for the design of information systems for the casual users (of, for example, library systems) as well as for general users who can be confronted with unpredictable situations that the navigation in databases can be based on task-independent rules. The hypothesis of the experiments discussed in the following sections is that efficient navigation in a database will be possible only if the database structure can be embedded in a context which can be represented on the display interface in a way making it possible for the user to develop efficient sensory-motor manipulation skills. Since manual skills are typically a function of the spatial-temporal aspects of the environment, this will thus be enhanced if the abstract attributes of the items of the database are consistently recoded to positions in a spatial representation.

The direct manipulation paradigm is relevant in connection with navigating in databases. The sensory-motor control patterns at the automated level of behaviour are related only to the interface manipulation task itself; i.e., manipulation of items on the visible surface. The advantage of a mouse-based system is that the communication of spatial-temporal aspects in the perception-action loop remains intact. The commands to send to the computer are selected from a repertoire presented on the screen. They can be identified by means of their physical position, and are pointed at with the mouse before the selection order is transmitted by a 'click' action. This implies a direct relationship between the movement pattern and the perceptual control (see fig. 2). Consequently, very efficient navigation in a database would be possible if the abstract attributes of the items of the database could be consistently recoded to positions in a spatial representation and these locations identified perceptually, while navigation in the space is analogically controlled by patterns of movement.

THE BOOK HOUSE METAPHOR

For library systems, as for most professional databases, there are a number of serious problems:

- the number of abstract dimensions of the databse is rather high,

- the number of items in the database is large,

- and, in particular, the attributes for search are not typically formulated ecplicitly by the userts.

In general, therefore, an intermediary (computer and librarian) is necessary to translate book characteristics to user terms and/or to conduct the search on behalf of the user.

The library system of this project is designed for novice or casual end users who can be adults or children. It was therefore important to adopt a metaphor for the system, which gave a symbolic representation of the system and was easy to remenber and understand. The metaphor had to be compatible with the user's daily experiences and, at the same time, be easily associated with the structure of the database system. The metaphor also had to be familiar, arouse positive feelings in the users and seem natural for the domain it represented. The Book House was chosen as a metaphor of a library as well as a metaphor of a house built with books just like the well known pancake house. The book is the reason for, the object of and the target of the acts of the users during a search. The house is the symbol of the database system in which the user has to navigate.

When the user has entered the Book House, he/she walks through rooms with different arrangements and forms of books with several illustrations of users performing different search strategies. The user can thus perceive the links through which he/she can select user category (children, adult) or search strategy in the respective rooms. See figs. 3-6. The room for choice of search strategy includes representation of the strategies which were identified in the earlier studies. They are represented as users looking at the shelf for books similar to their previous reading, as users sitting at a desk and combining information items shown as objects representing the dimensions of the their needs, as users browsing through books picked up randomly from the bookshelf or as users interested in browsing through icons reflecting book contents.

The Book House has a number of working rooms having a metaphoric link to different, selectable strategies or routes for information retrieval in the database. The user can enter the working room that matches the way he/she wants to perform the search task. In each working room, a number of icons are available. These icons represent a symbolic reference to the particular search strategy that is available in this room together with a number of icons to choose for actions to control the search (see later). At the same time, each working room has books on shelves or tables, which increases the user's spatial impression. The storehouse and work room metaphor were inspired by the ancient Greek Simonedes' (500 BC) mnemotechnical trick: To imagine the objects to be remembered placed along a familiar street or in a familiar room. See also Fuller (1898) and Miller (1957).

In the Book House four different rooms make the same database information available for user perasal, but permit the search to be tailored to the current user need. The user can shift strategy by choosing a different work room and thus can navigate freely in the database.

Analytical search

Referring to fig. 5, if the user selects the person who is sitting at the desk and working, the user enters the room that supports the carrying out of an analytical specification of needs in terms corresponding to the multidimensional classification scheme which has been implemented in the database. The information content of the database which is relevant to this particular strategy is displayed in the figure as icons. There are thirteen of them. For example, the world globe icon represents geographical book subjects, the clock icon represents the time period of books. The theatre masks refer to the emotional experience provided by the books. The view out of the window to a village, a big city or the sea makes it possible to choose the setting for the books. With the mouse, the user can select one of these icons and thus get access to the particular set of subject terms to be displayed from the database. The analytical work room enables the user to combine terms from one or more of these dimensions by choosing new icons - one at a time. When a classification icon is chosen, relevant subject terms are displayed on the screen as an open book. See fig. 7 and 8.

Search by analogy

When the user selects the person looking for similar books at the lefthand bookrack, another room is entered. The user can open a book with an author and title index and identify "a good book", and the system will automatically attempt to find other books which include as many indexed attributes of the model book as possible. The description of these books will then be presented in an open book format in decreasing order of relevance. The multifacetted classification scheme is used to generate weights for all the books in the database in relation to the model book.

Browsing through books

The choice of the browsing strategy is well suited for the user who has no specific need, but wishes to skim through descriptions of the books in the database. From the room for choice of this strategy, the system immediately shifts to an open book with a book description. The user can step through descriptions which are randomly chosen and desplayed on the open book format.

Browsing through icons

The browsing strategy also includes an iconic version where the icons can be used for intuitive searches. Instead of browsing directly in book descriptions as above, an intermediate process of selecting among icons containing book content information is employed.

When a user does not have a well formulated information need, but accesses the information system with an intuitive retrieval approach, there is a need for a quick bird's eye view of the contents of the database. Skimming through several pages of subject terms selected within one or more of the dimensions of the classification scheme is a feasible way, but it can be a rather slow and tedious job due to the high number of terms. It is our hypothesis that icons can be a more information economic way of performing intuitive searches. If icons are used to represent the contents of books in the database, the user will eb able to replace the skimming of therms with the skimming of a much smaller number of pictures. A single picture can communicate many different dimensions of meanings and thus includes subject terms from several different dimensions of the classification scheme. An icon with soldiers in a war can at the same time tell the user something about the time period and the country involved in the war by means of a flag, a uniform, the weapons, etc. A conventional verbal search in a database would require access to the subject matter dimension, the time dimension and the place dimension in order to achieve the same. In addition to being more effective, the skimming of icons has the possibility of providing an aesthetic and emotional experience to the user and, at the same time, gives the user potentially new perspectives on a topic.

When the user chooses to skim and select icons, this means that a multidimensional search takes place on the basis of only one system entry or route in the system. Whenever an icon is chosen by the user, a Boolean search is performed on all the subject terms that are allocated to that particular icon. Icons can have a number of parallel themes (e.g., fig. 9 with travel. OR imagination) and thus a Boolean OR combination will be performed.

The user will eventually be able to choose one or more icons during the intuitive search. When more than one icon is chosen, a Boolean AND search is initiated between the icons. In this way a complicated formal Boolean search including many ANDs and ORs can easily be conducted by the user. In large databases with thousands of search terms, the advantage of this method is its great potential. The number of ducuments as a result of an iconic search will rapidly be reduced and, by choosing a small number of icons on an intuitive basis, the user rapidly reaches a relevant subset of the database to skim through.

MEMORY SUPPORT AND THE BOOK HOUSE METAPHOR

In the system under discussion, an attempt has been made to exploit the capabilities of computers for flexible display presentations by relating the information items to their locations in a virtual space, a storehouse, in which four dimensions of the multidimensional attribute space are represented by their location in a room, while the reamining, relevant dimensions are taken care of y arranging for several rooms and departments in the storehouse. In this way, it will be possible to transfer Simonedes' mnemotechnic trick to a multidimensional representation or, in other words, to use the idea of George Miller (1968): information i a question of 'where'.

This representation will make it possible for a user to search the spatial analogy of the database through the use of mental strategies similar to those mentioned earlier in the discussion of library systems. Compared with a physical collection of items computers have the advantage that the same information item can be located in several different places and, therefore, a data space with more than three dimensions can be represented by a number of rooms. In this way, a user can 'browse' according to location, if the rooms representing the most relevant dimensions are entered.

Other strategies mentioned depend on specification of the search
attributes, either directly via an analytical search or in terms of
a model example, a search by analogy. Since the needs are only
implicitly formulated by the user, it is generally necessary to show
the possible dimensions for user's choice (recognition is easier
than recall).

In this spatial or topographic metaphor, an analytical search is a
kind of selectively 'addressed' search in a domain chosen from a
display of a 'workroom' showing the landscape of topical items which
can be selected. Using the analogy of a city map, one has an
indication at least of the street one wants to visit together with a
helicpter which will bring one there directly. Being there, one will
look at the houses. In the 'browsing strategy', one doesn't know the
address but will recognize what is sought when it is seen. This
means pass through the streets of the city until an item is
recognized. In a library, this implies scanning the physical books
on the shelf. In a computerized system, however, a subspace of, or a
'channel' through the multidimensional space, can be chosen by
specifying some aspects of the target which are known (either what
is wanted or what is not wanted). In this way, the difference
between analytical search and browsing in a computerized system is a
question of degree, not of categories.

DESCRIPTION OF THE USER-BOOKHOUSE DIALOGUE

It can be useful to see how some of the above concepts are realized
in terms of a description of the user-system dialogue. The dialogue
flow is shown in fig. 10 which attempts to compress the many options
provided by the system onto a single illustrative representation.
There are four main interaction phases:

A)   Select one of two dialogue forms.

B)   Select one of three book data bases.

C)   Select one of four search strategies.

D)   Examine resulting book descriptions; revise search criteria and reexamine the search results; process eventual candidates.

A) The Book House system allows the user to choose between conducting book searches through use of the traditional keyboard-based command dialogue which all Danish public libraries have access to and experience with OR by means of the mouse-based Book House system. This section covers the latter approach only.

B) After choosing the mouse-based dialogue, the user is asked to select the appropriate database. There are three possibilities - the children's bookbase covering literature for children up to about sixteen years of age, the adults' bookbase or the total bookbase covering both children's and adults' books. A single mouse selection is required.

C) At this point in the dialogue, the user must decide how the search for books will be carried out. The Book House provides four alternatives:

1.   an analytical search,
2.   a search by analogy,
3.   browsing in pictures,
4.   browsing in book descriptions.

1. If the user selects to carry out an analytical search, the next step in the dialogue is to identify with the mouse the specific search terms which reflect the current need. First the user must select a relevant dimension from the set of thirteen icons shown in fig. 7 (e.g., plot, setting, accessability, etc.). This leads to the display on the screen in an open book format of the first page og the corresponding index of terms for the selected dimension. As indicated in firgure 8, the user can narrow his/her attention to a specific part of the index via a "look up" with an optianal alphabet where the first two letters of the desired index term have to be chosen. The user can also browse through the various pages of the index. The longest index has about fifty pages, the shortest just one page. With the mouse, the user selects the desired index term. This word appears in a dedicated "current search profile" area near the bottom of the screen.

The Book House immediately performs a search and responds shortly thereafter by displaying the number of books found. Each selection results in a new automatic search using the current total profile of search terms.

As stated, the user can continue the process by selecting another dimension, seeing a new index of terms and selecting new index terms with the mouse. The user can also undo the selection of index terms - in the reverse order of their selection.

The Book House carries out an automatic Boolean search after the user has chosen his/her index terms. An AND is used between dimensions of the classification scheme. An OR is used for terms within the dimension, depending on which dimension it is.

At some point in this iterative process of selection, automatic search and display of results, the search will undoubtedly produce zero books. The Book House provides the user with the possibility of asking for "more books". This prompts the system to perform a new search with ORs between terms instead of ANDs. The reverse is also possible in case more than 100 books are found; i.e., the user can ask for "fewer books. In a normal dialogue, the user exits from the analytical search by asking to see the books which the Book House has found. See D) below.

2. If the user wants to find a book which resembles one he/she is already familiar with, the find similar books input should be selected with the mouse. The user must then specify the title of the known (reference) book - either directly from an index of titles which is displayed, or indirectly by first browsing through an author index and then selecting the desired title. Again an alphabetical look up is possible and/or the user can browse through the indices. Selection of the desired title produces a display of a description of the reference book on the screen. See D) for continuation of the dialogue.

3. If the user has no specific (or specifiable) need, there are two possibilities of browsing in the selected book base. By selecting browsing in descriptions of books, the user can decide to go to a direct perusal of randomly selected book descriptions from the book base. See D) for the next phase.

4. The user can also select browse through pictures. This option gives the user the possibility of adding a new dimension to the process of finding suitable books by asking him/her to utilize the associations triggered by one or more of 108 icons (in sets of eighteen) to select books for viewing. The selection and editing process is the same as for analytical searching except that pictures are the medium instead of single index terms. A textual description of each selected icon appears in the text area. In addition, the Book House performs a search after each icon selection - as described previously for the analytical approach - so that the user gets direct feedback as to the number of books found. After each search, the user can decide to see the books which were found.

D) In a normal dialogue, this phase of the dialogue is entered from each of the above four searches: after either the analytical specification or the browse in pictures selections have been made and see books has been chosen with the mouse, after a reference book title has been specified in a find similar books dialogue or after the user has desired to browse in book descriptions.

A host of options now become available independent of the search strategy selected. Firstly, a description of the first book of the current set is displayed on the screen organized in accordance with the classification system. The user can browse through the set and can initialize his/her browsing with the first, the last or the middle book in the set. The number of the book in the current set is displayed in the corner of the screen. (If "find similar books" was chosen, the reference book will of course be book 1 of 1.). The user can now repetitively:

-   Save interesting candidates in the Book House for later browsing and/or request that hard copies of interesting descriptions be printed - e.g., for use in finding the books on the shelves. One can also see previously saved book descriptions.

-   Find similar books which, if the analogical input was selected, will as a start use the reference book as the basis for finding (at least) ten other similar books in the selected book base. However, the option can be used at this point in the dialogue in connection with any current book description on the screen.

- Modify the current need which gives the user the option of adding (one or more) or removing (only one) search terms from the current search profile (which incidentally can become a combination of index terms and icons). Each change generates an automatic search, the number of books found is displayed. At the present time, only the current book set is retained by the system.

This description has only dealt with a "normal" dialogue trace. Several possibilities of looping and restarting are possible which could no bte depicted in the figure so that, for example, users can shift strategies, abandon current searches, choose a new data base, etc.

ICON-BASED INTERFACE DESIGN

When icons are designed to improve the user's interaction with and comprehension of a database system, the most important design issue is the perception of content or message when reading an icon on the interface display surface. This will depend more on the retrieval context in which anicon is displayed than on its representation or form. In general, both the user's task and whether the user is a novice or an expert will greatly influence his/her perceptive interpretation. Icons can be perceived in three different ways (Rasmussen, 1986, Panofsky, 1962):

- Identification of objects and the relations between objects in the form of an icon. Based on previous experience with these objects and their relations, the icon's behaviour in reflecting acts or events is intuitively perceived as a space-time related signal by the user.

- The meaning of objects, acts or events in an icon is determined by convention. The user's perception based on experience is extended with a knowledge of professional, social, historical conventions of meaning. Icons are perceived as signs related to rules for actions. The user acts on these signs and uses them for a choice of action and further control of the system.

- The meaning of an icon is interpreted by the user in relation to the user's knowledge about symbolic values of objects, acts or events. The symbolic meaning can be subjective or match professional, social or historical knowledge or interpretations. Icons are perceived as symbols; the user understands the symbols and uses his/her understanding to predict or explain the function of the system.

This distinction between the perception of iconic information as signals, signs or symbols is dependent on the user's context-dependent intentions during his/her task (e.g., searching for literature). Therefore, for the designer the challenge is to provide a match between the context of the search and the icons which ensures that the user perceives the icons in a way that matches current intentions.

In the current project, we have primarily focussed on the design of (a) icons as signs for rules of action during a search and (b) icons to provide a symbolic representation of the semantic information content of the database - i.e., the substance of the books in the database. An expert may perceive both these signs and symbols as signals, which will be efficient if the task is familiar and predictable. However, in this experiment we have designed an interface for novice users, and have tried to create a context for the proper match between the function of icons as signs and symbols and the user's perception of these icons. In terms of fig. 2, this implies that display icons should be chosen which simultaneously present a close mapping onto effective cues at the levels of movement and action control (their sign function) and onto the semantic content of the database which is compatible with the user's planning level (their symbolic meaning).

The form of icons

The various technical means available for generating screen icons lend themselves actually to an enhanced communication of appropriate functional purpose to the user.

For example, icons drawn with available computer drawing programs have a clean and sharp appearance on the screen. These icons con support the designer's desire to provide the user with a clear graphic object as a distinctive cue and action link. An example is the UNDO icon shown in fig. 11.

The other method is to scan hand drawn icons into the system using TV techniques. These icons can have a completely different impact. They are more fuzzy and soft in appearance and have an impressionistic flavor. There is not the same efficient and direct message transfer as with computer-drawn icons. They have more of a narrative function and form and can hopefully set the user's facilities for interpretation and comprehension in focus. Each icon has its individual and artistic form to support the communication of the intended subject matter. There is no standardized production: every icon requires the generation of an individual drawing followed by scanning, retouching and coloring. This technique can support the generation of icons for the creation of the illusion of a metaphor as well as for pictures for browsing in the form of symbols for the subjects and contents of books. Fig. 12 illustrates a typical icon of this type where the "muddiness" of the icon gave during an evaluation experiment described in a later section associations to: estate, politics, power, authorities.

In some cases, iconic representations have to serve both purposes; i.e., as a sign indicating the "act here" link and as a symbol referring to the context of the action. This can also simplify the dialogue. In information retrieval, symbolic references to the meaning of information items without reference to the direct search activity may be very helpful for an experienced user. In the Book House, these types of icons are used for describing the various dimensions of the classification scheme and for identifying the various search strategies. If feasible, it might be desirable to extend the production techniques described above to be able to combine the clear sign drawing with the more fuzzy symbols. However, in the latest version of the Book House all icons have been produced with a combination of computer drawing techniques and TV techniques. This was the result of some pilot studies which demonstrated problems with the understandability of "fuzzy" (scanned) icons on a small screen.

Icons as signs for action

Icons that are intended to function as cues for action often have graphic objects that have some similarity to the content of action. In general, this similarity refers to the physical appearance of an object related to the action in question. In the present context, however, similarity to representation in the interface of higher level structures also justifies the term 'icon'. By definition, signs and icons in their action queuing function refer to the action by mere convention. The connection may be formally instructed or discovered by the user empirically.

Different principles can be used for selection of icons to serve as signs. The choice of significance for signs can be based on criteria as, for instance, easy remembering, easy guessing by the novice, relation to population stereotypes. Given the many degrees of freedom underlying the design of iconic signs, a general principle should probably be adopted as design aid in order to have an intuitive context for guiding users. Therefore, a taxonomy of signs from a cue-agent-action scenario may be useful for design. See fig. 13. The examples in the taxonomy are taken from well known icons encountered daily. The form of signs may be related to any of the items in the sequence of the action scenario, and a taxonomy will be related to the different sign references given in the figure. Different mnemotechnical principles can be used, relating signs to all of the different elements of the cue-agent-action scenario.

A few examples from some of the Book House displays can be relevant. Fig. 11 gives an overview of most of the "sign" icons. Fig. 8 illustrates the stage in the dialogue where a choice of index terms in one of the dimensions of the classification systems can be made. Figure 14 shows the description of a retrieved book. The following describes some of the icons in more detail.

Item from taxonomy	Description of icon
State to reach	Book House icon in upper left hand corner. The doors are closed. The user can at any time end his/her search by pointing at this icon and

can thus "get out of the Book House".

State of affairs

Number of retrieved documents: shown in the lower right hand corner. One of three icons informs the user about the state of affairs after a choice of index term; a bookcase is shown either full, half-full or with only a few books. In addition the number of books found is given.

Object to use

See books: the previously mentioned icon can also be activated in order to get a display describing the books which the Book House has found.

Delete search term. The last choice can be deleted by selecting the eraser icon on the top line.

State to reach

Room for choice of database: the user can interrupt his/her search and start over again by choosing the same or a new database. The icon is a miniature representation of the full scale display of database selection.

Object to use

Print book: The icon with a printer is used to request a printout of the current book description.

Open book with marked corners: All information on books (and index contents) is displayed in an open book format with marked leaves so that the user can work his/her way through the material forwards or backwards. The lower right and left marks turn one page at a time. The upper marks jump larger intervals.

Action to perform

Find similar books. The user can ask the Book House to find books similar to the one currently on the screen. The icon shows the act of comparison between two books.

Change search: If the user wants to revise the current set of search terms, selecting this icon on the top line will call a new display of the book description which colors in red the indexed terms and allows a revised selection to be made. The icon reflects the new display by itself being a small segment of text with red and non-red letters.

Save book: Any book description currently on the screen can be saved for later perusal. The icon shows a hand which will take the book and put it away.

All the displays have a help icon in the upper right hand corner in the form of a lifebelt (i.e., an "object to use" icon). Activating this icon gives the user a set of help texts on the screen. At present, this separate help facility is more of a supplementary static type since the user also is always presented with a short text description of every icon when the mouse is moved over the icon.

EXPERIMENTAL EVALUATION OF THE PROTOTYPE

Evaluation of icon-index term match

In connection with supporting the search strategy based on browsing in pictures, an experiment was conducted to determine whether it was feasible to draw icons on the basis of content terms chosen from the different dimensions of the classification scheme. Secondly, there was an interest in determining whether there would be a sufficient consensus between the designers' perception of match between icons and index terms and that of different groups of potential users of the system.

Based on the most frequently used terms in the database, 108 icons were drawn by the designers. The subjects had five choices for each icon. Three of these were the terms from the index which the designers had used as the basis for drawing the icon. The fourth was a check term not at all related to the intended message of the icon. The fifth gave the subject the opportunity to answer that none of the terms matched the icon.

Three experiments were conducted. One with 13 trained librarians, the second with 10 adult users of the public library with different professions, and the third involved 18 children (nine boys and nine girls) from 8 to 13 years of age. Among the adult subjects there were 13 women from the mid-twenties to the mid-fifties and 10 men from the mid-twenties to the mid-sixties.

Each of the 108 icons with its four associated subject terms was displayed on an overhead projector to the subjects, who then on a paper with the terms for the appropiate icon marked one or more of the terms which they found relevant. Each icon was displayed on the screen for 25 seconds in order to get the subjects' intuitive impression of the meaning of each icon. The icon was displayed first, and then the related terms. Thus, the same order was followed as the order in which a user would meet icons and terms in the interface. After the experiments, subjects were encouraged to comment on the icons regarding which they found easy or difficult to comprehend.

The analysis of the data from this study resulted in good indications of the users' criteria for interpreting the meaning of an icon. Most of the icons were associated with one or more of the terms used as a design basis for the icon. Four of the 108 icons caused problems. The adult subjects were not able to identify a relationship between terms and icons in two cases. The children had the same problem with two other icons. Difficulties arose when icons were too detailed to communicate a clear message (see e.g., fig. 15 for the icon and a distribution of answers from the subjects). Icons that attempted to represent an abstract notion such as "feelings" or "togetherness" by referring to concrete objects failed. Subjects did not agree when the symbol chosen to illustrate a concept was not a generally known prototype or expressive enough in provoking the associated meaning.

Some icons resulted in a clear choice of one term out of the four possibilities. See fig. 16. Other icons gave a more distributed response to the terms. Distributed responses seem to relate to different factors. One factor is the nature of terms chosen for each icon. Some icons had terms that had a strong semantic relation. This led to highly distributed responses. For example, one icon had crime, criminality, showdown, judiciary system. Another factor is that some icons were simply not "strong" enough, i.e., one example gave almost equal weights to homosexuality, famous people and music.

Of course, other icons had terms which semantically had little in common. These icons gave more peaked distributions of responses. Similar peaked responses were received with icons possessing a clear prototypical symbol chosen to illustrate a concept (e.g. Figure 17, where the heart, cross, and anchor are symbols of love, belief and fidelity and is at the same time a concrete picture of a heart, anchor and cross). Another example is when the icons show children and signify children. When the icon directly represents the object that the icon signifies, no problems arise.

A significant feature was that the childrens' responses were much more distributed than the adults' responses and, in many cases, the women's responses were more distributed than the male subjects. Thus age and sex seems to influence subjects' interpretation of icons.

The experience gained from this experiment was used in the further design of icons as well as in the implementation of terms with icons in the interface. Only icons that had terms with 50 percent of consensus or more were implemented in the system. When less than 50 percent of the subjects agreed on the meaning of an icon, the icon was redrawn. When more terms were selected as being meaningful for a given icon, only those terms with 50 percent or more of the votes were assigned to the icon. As a result of this policy, there is a difference between the meanings of icons in the database with adult books and in the database with childrens' books. When the user chooses an icon in the childrens' database, a Boolean search is initiated using more and sometimes different subject terms than with the same icon in the adults' database.

Further evaluation of the Book House prototype

The prototype Book House will be evaluated in a public library for six months. Experiences with this prototype will be generalized in order to make the results useful as guidelines for the design of information retrieval in databases using integrated work stations in other contexts. The evaluation will be carried out through a combination of on-line logging of user interactions with the system, interviews and questionnaires. The last-named item covers a complete set of paper questionnaires to be filled out at various phases in the user/Book House interaction as well as an on-line session where the user is asked for his/her detailed opinion about the icons.

AKNOWLEDGEMENTS

The project is supported by Denmark's Technological Council. The project partners are Jutland Telephone, Regnecentralen A/S, The Royal Art Academy and Risø National Laboratory (Department of Information Technology).

REFERENCES

1. Pejtersen, A.M., Olsen, Sv. E. and Zunde, P.: A retrieval aid for browsing strategies in bibliografic databases based on users' associative Semantics: A term association Thesaurus. In: Knowledge Engineering Expert systems and information retrieval. Ed: Wormell, I.. Taylor Graham, 1988.

2. Pejtersen, Annelise Mark: Search Strategies and Database Design. In: Tasks, Errors and Mental Models. Eds. L.P.Goodstein, H.B.Andersen and S.E.Olsen, Taylor and Francis, 1988.

3. Pejtersen, Annelise Mark and Rasmussen, Jens: Information Retrieval in Integrated Work Stations. Paper presented at the Second ICAK Conference, Japan, November 1987. To be published in the proceedings: Information and Knowledge, Tokyo 1988.

4. Pejtersen, A.M. and Rasmussen, J.: Design and evaluation of user-system interfaces or of user-task interaction? A discussion of interface design approaches in different domains for application of modern information Technology. In: Empirical Foundations of Information and Soft Ware Science. Eds: Zunde, P. et. al. 1987. published by Plenum Press.)

5. Rasmussen, Jens: Information Processing and Human-Machine Interaction: An Approach to Cognitive Engineering. North Holland 1986.

6. Bewley, W.L. et al: Human factors testing in the design of Xerox's 8010 "Star" office workstation. In: Human factors in computing systems. ACM. North Holland 1984.

7. Pejtersen, A.M.: Design of a computer-aided usersystem dialogue based on an analysis of users'search Behaviour. In: Social Science Information Studies, no. 4, 1984 p. 167-183.

8. Pejtersen, A.M.: Design of a classification scheme for fiction based on an analysis of actual user-bibrarian communication, and use of the scheme for control of librarians' search Strategies. In: Theory and Application of Information Research. Ed: Harbo, O. and Kajberg, L.. London, Mansell, 1980, p 167-183.

9. Pejtersen, A.M.: Investigation of search strategies in fiction based on an analysis of 134 user-librarian Conversations. In: IRFIS 3. Ed.; Henriksen, T.. Oslo, 1979, p. 107-132.

10 Miller, G.A.: Information is a question of where. In: Psychology and Information. Am. Docum. 19. (19

11. Fuller, H.H. (1898): The Art of Memory. St. Paul, Minnesota: National Publishing Company.

LISA ALTHER: KINFLICKS 1977

Front Page Colours: White, red and black

Front Page Pictures: Faces

Subject Matter: A woman's visit to her mother's sick-bed
                           and her revival of her youth, student
                           days and marriage. Her experience of her
                           mother's death.

Place: USA. Tennessee.

Setting: Southern states. Middle-class. High
                           school, Feminism.

Time: 1960'ties.

Cognition/Information: Realistic description of the American
                           society and of a woman's love affairs,
                           her development and identity problems.
                           The relationship between mothers and
                           daughters.

Emotional Experience: Humoristic.

Literary Form: Novel. Related in first and third
                           person. Feminist novel. Developmental
                           novel.

Readability: Average.

Typography: Normal

                           A record from a Fiction Database. It
                           illustrates the multi-dimensional input
                           to an online retrieval system. All
                           information in a record can be retrieved
                           by a boolean search of keywords. The
                           record can also be retrieved by the
                           selection of an icon that shows arguing
                           females.

Figure 1 Multidimensional structure of the database with example
         of book content to be matched to user need.

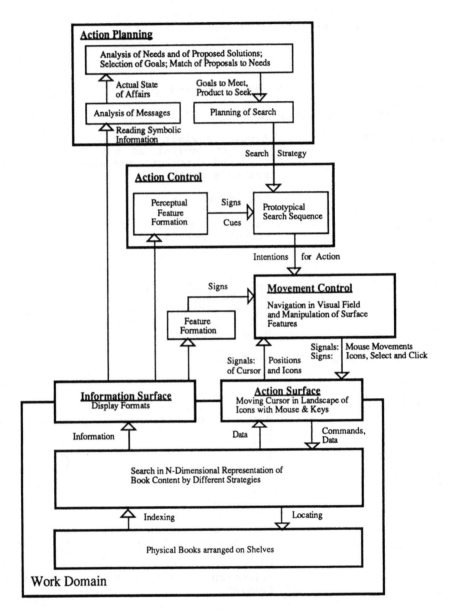

Figure 2 Structure of the different levels of cognitive control of the interaction through an interface to a library system. The distinction should be seen between the control of physical manipulations, intentional actions and planning of the activity.

Figure 3   Display of the Book House which is the first iconic
           "room" seen by the user

Figure 4   Display of the hall to the Book House where the user
           selects the database to be used

Figure 5 Display of the strategy selection room for adults

Figure 6 Display of the strategy selection room for children

Figure 7   Display of the analytical workroom

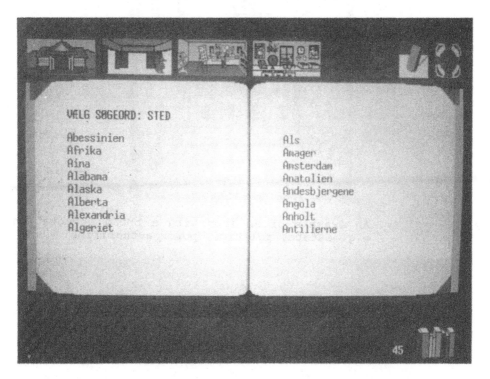

Figure 8 Display of an open book with the display of the
contents of a typical index of search terms

Figure 9 A typical contents icon based on the topics of travel
or imagination

Figure 12   An example of an icon with a broad connotation -
e.g. estate, politics, power, authorities.

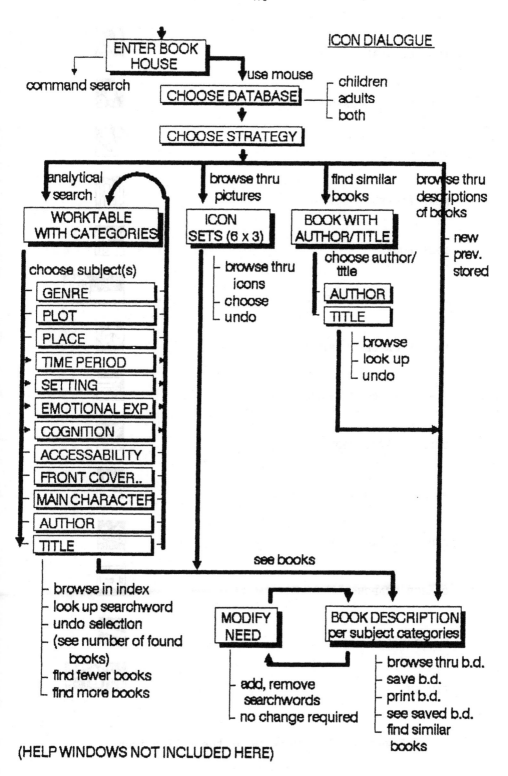

Figure 10 A map of the dialogue flow using the Book House.

LOOK-UP YEAR

ALPHABETIC LOOK-UP

UNDO

MORE BOOKS

LESS BOOKS

SEE BOOK DESCRIPTIONS

SAVE BOOK DESCRIPTIONS

SEE SAVED BOOK DESCRIPTIONS

DELETE SAVED BOOKS

PRINT OUT BOOK DESCRIPTION

FIND SIMILAR BOOKS

CHANGE SEARCH

NOT WANTED

FINISH

Figure 11   An overview of the action icons.

SCENARIO FOR DEFINITION OF SIGN REFERENCE.

```
        1. )              2. )              3. )              4. )
IF <STATE> --> THEN <ACTOR> --> DO <ACT> --> WITH <OBJECT> -->

                5. )
IN-ORDER-TO <GOAL, TARGET>
```

Design of signs icons can be based on reference to any item in
the action scenario:

1. *The state of affairs* needing attention.
    Traffic signs: A 'steam engine' signals crossing trains; be
    careful;

2. *The actors* who should care.
    Lady's and gents on restroom doors;

3. *Action* to perform.
    Sign with man walking on stairs;

4. *Object* to use.
    Garbage can icon;

    Object not to use.
    'Deleted' cigarette;

5. *State to reach*.
    'Light-on' icon;

    State to avoid.
    'Flame' signalling no-open-fire;

6. *Symbolic reference*
    Reference to the meaning of information items;

*. *Nothing*. Pure convention.
    'Red light' at street crossing;

Figure 13   The action scenario taxonomy for icon sign design.

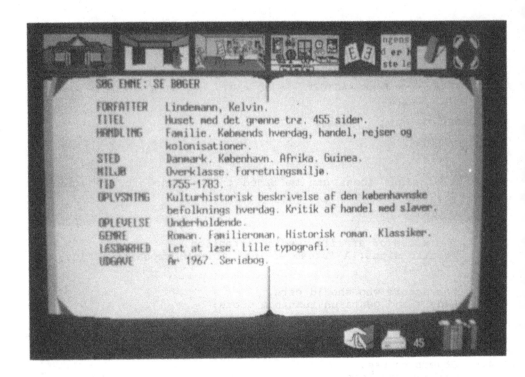

Figure 14   Display of a typical book description in the Book
             House

Figure 17   The heart, cross and anchor are symbols of love,
             belief and fidelity.

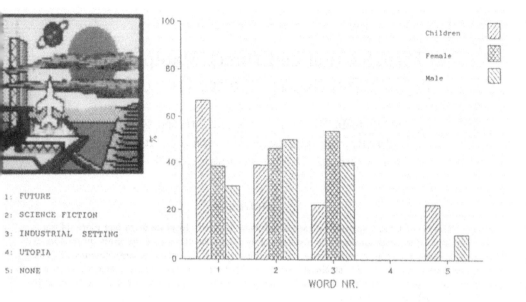

Figure 15 A contents icon that received a broad interpretation.

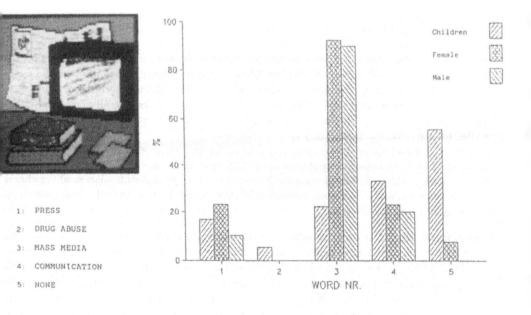

Figure 16 A contents icon that received a narrow interpretation.

Visualization and Direct Manipulation in User Interfaces: Are we Overdoing it?

Klaus Kunkel   Thomas Strothotte

Institut für Informatik, Universität Stuttgart

Azenbergstr. 12, D-7000 Stuttgart 1, F. R. Germany

Abstract

The current tendency on the part of software designers to place more and more information onto the computer screen is resulting in an increased burden on end-users' physiological capabilities and cognitive resources. Users must constantly survey a large amount of data, resulting in a considerable strain on their eyes. Furthermore, the work on their primary task is often seriously disrupted when direct manipulation techniques are used to issue commands to the application program.

In this paper we propose the use of bimodal input – speech coupled with direct manipulation – as a means of allowing users to take fuller advantage of the visualization of information. We describe an empirical study with 72 senior high school students and manufacturing apprentices working with two prototypical interfaces for a program to produce technical diagrams. One interface had the usual unimodal interaction (i.e., direct manipulation only), while the second allowed bimodal interaction. An improvement of over 15% in the subjects' working-speed was attained with the bimodal interface. Further, no significant increase in their cognitive workload was observed. Our results suggest that speech may be a viable complement to direct manipulation techniques in user interfaces as a way of supporting complex visualizations.

1   Introduction

User interfaces with direct manipulation are characterized by their high degree of visualization [Shn83]. The user manipulates on the screen different representations of the objects of the application in a relatively syntax-free manner. At the same time, the commands which are available to him for selecting the current mode of operation of the application are typically presented in the form of menus. Since both the objects of the application and the menus are available to him in parallel, his attention can move freely between the two.

An often cited advantage of such user interfaces is the uniformity with which the user operates [HHN86]. Virtually all operations are carried out by moving the mouse and clicking its buttons while feedback is always obtained visually. We consider there to be two fundamental drawbacks of the visualization and direct manipulation of objects of the application and simultaneously of the menus for command selection:

Physiological stress. In order to activate a command in a menu, the user must first direct his line of vision to the menu field and monitor the movement of the mouse cursor to that field. After activating the command, he must scan the screen for the place where work on the application is to continue and again monitor the movement of the mouse cursor. These steps cause considerable strain on his eyes, and take a non-trivial amount of time to carry out. The problem is aggravated by the current tendency to pack more and more information onto the screen.

Cognitive stress. The user's work on his primary task, working with the objects of the application, is interrupted. He is forced to shift his attention away from the application to the menu for command selection and finally back again. The constant shifting between the user's primary task and the operation of the program results in significant load on his cognitive capabilities.

We conjecture that these drawbacks are a consequence of the overuse of visualizations and direct manipulation in present user interfaces. While selecting and activating commands is necessary, this should not interfere with the user's cognitive processing capabilites available for his primary task.

We conjecture also that the negative effects on the user can be reduced by introducing multiple modes of I/O. Under such circumstances, the user can work with each aspect of the program in a different way. While bi- or even multimodal user interfaces may increase the overall cognitive workload, in the bimodal case, the user employs cognitive resources which are left unused in the unimodal case. Further, we conjecture that for bimodal interaction, the cognitive capacity remaining for the primary task is larger than for the unimodal interaction.

In this paper we introduce an empirial study to test our conjectures. Subjects work with a prototypical application in which speech input can be combined with direct manipulation. Related work is discussed in Section 2. Section 3 describes the experiment of which the results are surveyed in Section 4. The results are discussed in Section 5.

2 Related Work

In the past, speech recognition devices have been used in man-machine interfaces primarily to augment or replace the keyboard. Several studies have been carried out in which speech was used in text- and program editors, primarily to enter commands. The results of these studies have not been overwhelming. For example, Leggett and Williams [LW84] found that speech took about 25% longer than keyboard entry of programs, although the error rate was lower with the speech. In a similar study, Morrison et al. [MGSP84] found no significant difference in the amount of time nor error rates for entering the commands of a text editor with speech compared to the keyboard.

One of the problems with these approaches is that while the hands are offloaded by the use of the speech, the cognitive capacity which is freed is not used in any useful way. We thus began to look for ways of combing speech input with direct manipulation techniques. Our initial experience with a Pascal program editor [Pfl87] indicated that this combination is most useful when both modes are used most of the time and when there is a certain balance between the amount of time the user works with the speech and the amount of time he works with the mouse. These observations form the background for the present study.

3 An Experiment

3.1 Goals

The purpose of the present empirical study is to compare the quality of two prototypical user interfaces for the same application. When working with the first interface, the user enters information unimodally (strictly via direct manipulation) he works bimodally (with direct manipulation and speech input) with the second interface. To assess the quality of the interfaces, we studied such parameters as the amount of time taken by subjects to successfully complete given tasks, their cognitive workload and their preferences when given a degree of freedom. To gain further insight into the user's mental workload, we also study how these parameters differ under time pressure.

3.2   The Application

As a prototypical application for the study, we chose a simple graphics editor. We were unable to use a commercial product (such as MacDraw on the MacIntosh) because they are implemented as "black boxes" into which speech input cannot readily be integrated, and because they offer a too rich repertoire of commands to be controlled in an experiment. Thus we designed and implemented a "stripped down" version of a drawing program. The user can draw rectangles, circles and lines and enter text. Further, he can move around or erase existing objects. The commands for drawing an object such as a rectangle can either be specified by "clicking" the appropriate field with the mouse or by speaking aloud the name of the command. In either case, the portion of the menu corresponding to the activated command is converted to reverse-video, thus giving the user visual feedback. The object itself is then drawn by moving the mouse cursor to one corner, pressing a button while moving the cursor to the opposite corner. This method of drawing objects is familiar from the MacIntosh interface.

3.3   Hypotheses

We postulate the following:

H_1: The cognitive workload is higher when working with the bimodal user interface than when working with the unimodal interface.

H_2: The time a user needs to complete a drawing with the bimodal user interface is less than with the unimodal interface.

3.4   Method

The graphics editor was implemented in C on an IBM PC-AT with a Grundig BGB36 monitor, used in its monochrome mode with a resolution of 640x350 pixels. For speech input, the Votan VPC 2000, a commercially available speech recognition device, was used.

3.5   Subjects

The sample consists of 23 senior high school students (10 females, 13 males) and 49 metal-manufacturing apprentices (3 females, 46 males). The average age of the subjects was 18.5 years (s=2.3). Forty-two subjects (58.3%) had some experience with computers (essentially some knowledge in programming in BASIC); eight of the subjects (11.1%) were already familiar with the mouse. Thirty persons (41.7%) were totally inexperienced.

3.6   Design

To compare the two different interfaces we made use of a repeated measure design. The subjects were trained in the use of both interfaces in highly standardized single sessions by drawing several diagrams from a prepared set (see Figure 3.6 for an example). In order to minimize experimenter influences, the training instructions were given in writing. The experimenter intervened solely when occasional hardware or software problems occured. To avoid carry-over and order-of-learning effects, the interface to be learned first – whether the uni- or the bimodal one – was attached randomly. After the training, subjects were randomly assigned to the three test conditions:

(A) direct manipulation only,

(B) direct manipulation with speech input,

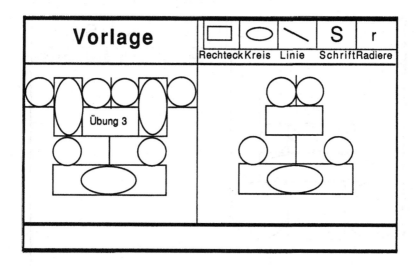

Figure 1: Sample diagrams used in the study. Subjects were presented with a diagram on the left half of the screen ("Vorlage") and were to reproduce it on the right half.

(C) free choice of input mode (command selection).

The subsequent inspection of the data showed that subjects' occupation, age, sex and computer experience were evenly distributed over these test conditions.

During the test, subjects drew three pictures twice each, once under time pressure and once without time pressure.

To measure the cognitive workload, users were occupied with secondary tasks at irregular intervals (every 10 to 20 seconds). The purpose of the dual task method is to produce measurable performance, where users are performing tasks with a relatively high cognitive component which require few overt responses and produce low error rates. The rationale underlying this method is that human processing resources are limited, therefore if an additional task can be made to compete for those limited resources, there will be a measurable deterioration in performance [Bro78]. The tasks consisted of simple shape-recognition and arithmetic exercises (see Figure 3.6). The user had to press a button of the mouse (not used for drawing) once if the answer was correct and twice if it was incorrect. Upon pressing the button once, an equals-sign ("=") appeared on the bottom of the screen; upon pressing the button a second time, this sign was negated (i.e., changed to "≠"). The exercise disappeared 1 second after the users' response, or 5 seconds after being posed, whichever happened first.

Finally, subjects completed a short questionnaire at the end of the session. They were asked about the learnability and ease of use of the interfaces, which interface they would prefer if they had to decide on one of them, their knowledge of programming languages and about some sociodemograhic items.

Figure 3.7 illustrates the run of events in the experiment.

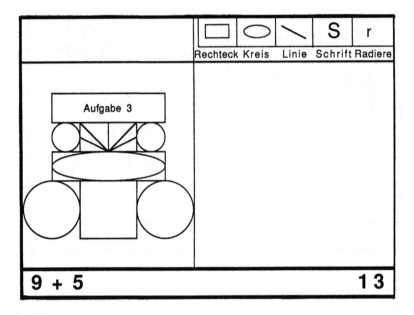

Figure 2: Secondary tasks. The secondary task is either a simple shape-recognition or arithmetic exercise at the bottom of the screen.

3.7 Dependant Variables of the Experiment

All actions of the subjects – while working with the interfaces – were registrated in background, i.e., unnoticed by the subjects[1]. The data collected represent variables such as the total amount of time needed to complete the drawings, number of drawing operations, number of command specifications by mouse clicks and speech input, number of deletions and shift operations, the positions of the objects drawn (x- and y-coordinates of the mouse position at the beginning and at the end of the drawing operation), the time elapsed between a command specification and the beginning of the corresponding drawing operation, the time elapsed between the end of drawing and the beginning of the next action, the time elapsed during which the mouse remained stationary longer than one second, the number of correct and incorrect responses to the secondary tasks, and the number of secondary tasks which were left unanswered.

4 Results

In the statistical analysis[2] for testing the hypotheses H_1 and H_2 we included only the samples of the test conditions A and B. For detecting possible significant differences between the samples, we compared their baseline data, obtained by subjects' performance while drawing under time pressure with both interfaces at the end of the training period. T-tests for independant samples showed no differences between the two samples in the average amount of time needed to complete the drawings, neither for the unimodal nor for the bimodal interface. T-tests for paired samples showed no difference between the two interfaces with regard to the total amount of time needed for Sample A. Subjects of Sample B worked significantly faster with the bimodal interface. F-values

---

[1]Subjects were informed in advance that the data would be collected.
[2]The statistical analysis was carried out with SPSS/PC+ on an IBM PC-AT.

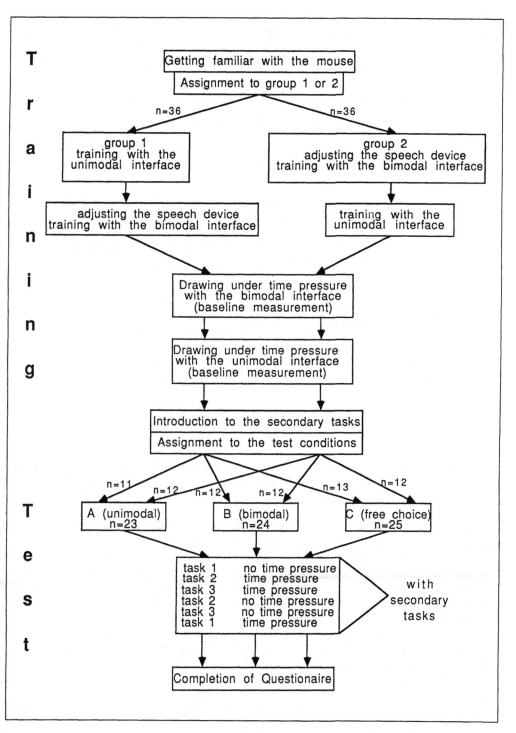

Figure 3: Run of events of the experiment.

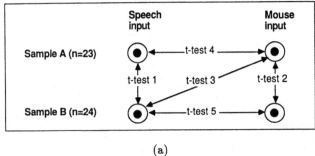

(a)

t-Test	Mean$_B^A$	S.dev.	F-Val.	Prob.	t-Val.	df	Prob.
1	10.77	2.21					
	10.35	1.43	2.38	.046	.75	35.5	.458
2	10.73	3.50					
	11.28	2.29	2.33	.049	-.64	37.7	.523
3	10.73	3.50					
	10.35	1.43	5.97	.000	.48	28.9	.637
	Diff.mean		Corr.				
4	-.447	1.69	.775	.000	-1.24	21	.228
5	-.932	1.70	.672	.000	-2.69	23	.013

(b)

Table 1: Testing the baseline data. Part (a) shows the t-tests numbered 1 to 5, while part (b) shows the numerical results.

indicate that the variance of the tested variables are significantly inhomogeneous in the samples ($p < .05$). The results of a two-factor repeated measure analysis of variance of the baseline data are in accordance with the findings reported above. The results of testing the baseline data are summed up in Table 4.

The two-factor repeated measure ANOVA run with the data of the test period led to the following results. Hypothesis H_1 could not be validated. The cognitive workload, as measured in responses to secondary tasks, did not differ neither between the samples nor within the samples between the conditions of working under time pressure or not. Only if the variable 'time needed to complete the drawings' is included in the analysis as a constant covariate, there is a slight tendency ($p = .079$) of a higher cognitive workload working with the bimodal interface under both conditions (see Table 2 and Figure 4).

The analysis supplied evidence for hypothesis H_2. Subjects who were working with the bimodal interface needed significantly less time to complete the drawings (and Figure 4). Whereas subjects of Sample A were not able to enhance the speed with which they worked in the test conditions, related to the baseline measurement, subjects of Sample B could increase the speed from baseline measurement to the condition 'no time pressure', and again from the one test condition to the other. The F-value of the between-subjects effect (the interface factor) amounts to $F = 5.84$ ($p = .020$). The 'time' within-subjects effect is documented by a value of $F = 7.75$ ($p = .001$) (see Table 3).

Repeated Measure Analysis of Variance					
Between-Subjects Effect Source of Variation	SS	df	MS	F	Sig. of F
within cells	4647.51	42	110.65		
regression	340.18	1	340.18	3.07	.087
constant	21284.31	1	21284.31	192.35	.000
sample(A,B)	358.20	1	358.20	3.24	.079
'Secondary Tasks' Within-Subjects Effect Source of Variation	SS	df	MS	F	Sig. of F
within cells	1585.73	42	37.76		
regression	8.24	1	8.24	.22	.643
secondary task	52.34	1	52.34	1.39	.246
sample by secondary task	.02	1	.02	.00	.981

Table 2: Testing hypothesis H_1.

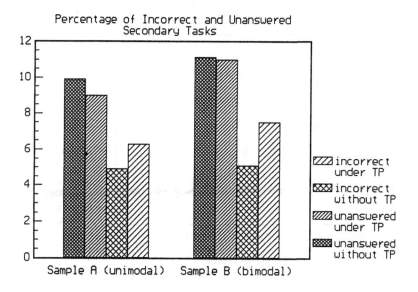

Figure 4: Summary of data for testing hypothesis H_1, comparing subjects' performance on secondary tasks under time pressure (TP) and without time pressure.

Repeated Measure Analysis of Variance					
Between-Subjects Effect Source of Variation	SS	df	MS	F	Sig. of F
within cells	390.84	45	8.69		
constant	14014.33	1	14014.33	1613.54	.000
sample(A,B)	50.70	1	˙50.70	5.84	.020
'Time' Within-Subjects Effect Source of Variation	SS	df	MS	F	Sig. of F
within cells	221.63	90	2.46		
time	37.19	2	18.59	7.55	.001
sample(A,B) by time	12.00	2	6.00	2.44	.093

Table 3: Testing hypothesis H_2.

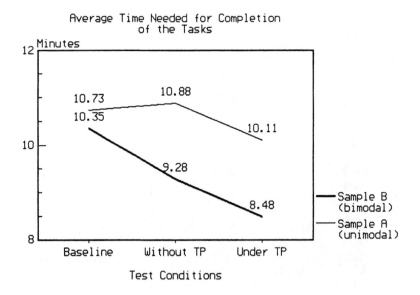

Figure 5: Summary of data for testing hypothesis H_2, comparing subjects' performance under time pressure (TP) and without time pressure.

Subjects' responses on the questionnaire indicate a pronounced but not significant preference for one of the two interfaces. Sixty-two percent of the entire sample (n = 72) would prefer the unimodal interface. No significant deviations between the samples A, B and C occured.

5 Discussion

Although empirical support for hypothesis H_2 was found and further investigations seem to be neccesary before rejecting hypothesis H_1 definitely, some results of the experiment are hard to explain. It was expected that the subjects would need more or at least the same time as measured as baseline for completing the drawings when they are additionally occupied with secondary tasks. While Sample A followed this expectation, Sample B could enhance the speed significantly in both conditions.

A possible explanation is that using the bimodal interface needs more training before it reveals its power. We believe that this is not the whole truth, because the sequence of the drawings to be done in the two test conditions is fixed in a manner which should, if this is the only source of effect, prevent significant differences between the conditions. We tend to the interpretation that the types of secondary tasks used here interfere less with the method of working with the bimodal interface and therefore subjects are able to develop a more economical strategy to master the primary tasks. The cognitive strain of visualization are smaller when commands are specified by speech than when selected with the mouse. This would suggest the existence of additional free cognitive capacity, which could be exploited to perform the tasks.

Another surprising result is that the subjects behaved in a reserved manner to the bimodal interface. Some reasons may be related to those about speaking to a telephone answering system. A more important reason might be the at times unsatisfactory reliability of the speech input device. Though the device was adjusted to every person's individual voice, the rate of incorrectly recognized commands varied enormously: In the training period the device produced an average of 18.6 misunderstandings. The standard deviation was s = 9.4, the range of faulty recognitions extended from 0 to 43. There exists a significant correlation of error rate with preference of interface of $r_{pbis} = .30$ (p = .01).

A further source of discomfort with the bimodal interface might be that correcting a failed drawing operation is only possible by verbalizing the command 'delete' explicitly and thus the mistake becomes public.

6 Acknowledgements

We would like to thank Prof.Dr.R. Gunzenhäuser for his support of our work. We are also indebt to Th. Fehrle for several fruitful discussions, particularly in the early phases of this work, as well as Dr.K. Klöpfer for help in preparing the raw data for its statistical analysis.

References

[Bro78]   D. I. Brown. Dual task methods of assessing workload. *Ergonomics*, 21(3):221–224, 1978.

[HHN86]   E. L. Hutchins, J. D. Hollan, and D. A. Norman. Direct manipulation interfaces. In D. A. Norman and S. W. Draper, editors, *User Centered System Design*, Lawrence Erlbaum Associates, Hillsdale, N.J., 1986.

[LW84]   J. Leggett and G. Williams. An empirical investigation of voice as an input modality for computer programming. *International Journal of Man-Machine Studies*, 21(6):493–520, 1984.

[MGSP84] D. L. Morrison, T. R. G. Green, A. C. Shaw, and S. J. Payne. Speech-controlled text-editing: effects of input modality and of command structure. *International Journal of Man-Machine Studies*, 21(1):49–63, 1984.

[Pfl87]   H. Pflieger. *Entwurf und Implementierung eines Diktatsystems für Pascal*. Diplomarbeit, Institut für Informatik, Universität Stuttgart, January, 1987.

[Shn83]   B. Shneiderman. Direct manipulation: a step beyond programming languages. *IEEE Computer*, 16(8):57–69, 1983.

TEACHING A SPREADSHEET APPLICATION -
visual-spatial metaphors
in relation to spatial ability,
and the effect on mental models

Gerrit C. van der Veer and Robert Wijk
Free University, Amsterdam

Teaching a computer application for non-computer specialist requires a general strategy, starting with the analysis of the user's virtual machine, along with the definition of the conceptual model of the user interface. From this definition to a useful set of metaphors, knowledge of relevant user variables and analysis of the task domain is required. Well chosen metaphors will help novices to grasp the principles of the functionality and interaction with the system, although the metaphors presented need not be part of the resulting mental models after the initial learning process.

For a well known spreadsheet system, a field study was performed on 54 office workers who attended a two day course on this application for a PC. Visual-spatial metaphors (including animation) were developed, as the structure and dynamics of the system were too complicated for a two dimensional visual description (as was in fact provided by the user interface of the system).

In general, the metaphors were sufficient to guide most participants to understanding of the functionality and skill in interacting with the system. The resulting mental models showed striking individual differences in mode of representation, including descriptions on the different levels of Moran (1981). It turned out that for this user group knowledge of the external functionality was not related to knowledge of the system. Spatial ability was strongly related to knowledge of the system at the end of the course, and only in a restricted way to knowledge of the external functionality.

1. INTRODUCTION

1.1. Teaching for the mental model

Users of a computer application need a clear and consistent knowledge structure of the system they interact with. This knowledge (the mental model, in the terminology of Norman, 1983) only concerns that part of the system, that is directly relevant to the task delegation by the user to the system, the user interface. This model is the source of the expectation the user has about the reaction of the system to his behaviour. It will guide his planning of the interaction, and will help the interpretation of the system's reactions (Norman, 1983, 1986). A perceived deviation of the system's behaviour from the expectations will lead to an adaptation of the mental model.

The conceptual model of the user interface has to be developed with the explicit aim to be parallelled by mental models, individually different representations of the system by different users, all of which will start by being a novice to this system. In designing the user interface, the knowledge of human learning will have to be applied to make adequate use of the possibilities of adaptation and flexibility that are available.

Moran (1981) proposed a representational framework, enabling the description of the conceptual model of the user interface on the one hand and the intended mental model of the user on the other hand. An important aspect of his analysis is the description of knowledge about the human-computer interaction in levels. When discussing the compatibility between users' mental models and system's conceptual models we distinguish the following levels:

a. The task level corresponds to the tasks which can be performed in the system. (A "task" is intuitively defined as something which a user wants to achieve, and which is complex enough to require more than one simple action, cf. Card, Moran and Newell, 1983).
b. The semantic level concerns the conceptual operations and conceptual objects with their relevant attributes as defined for the task by the system.
c. At syntax level the commands available for accomplishing the operations defined at the semantic level and the wording of the system's feedback are described.
d. The key-stroke level represents handling of the physical devices which is required to issue the commands, and the physical implementation of the feedback, as far as it is relevant to the human-computer interaction.

Users will differ in their mental models, dependent on their a priori knowledge of the external task domain and of related systems, and dependent on their prefered style of representation of information, e.g. verbalising or visualising.

The conceptual model of the user interface should be presented to the user, taking into account relevant characteristics of human learning and user variables. The learning process that leads to the mental model will be based on analogies to known situations and systems. The learning process may be facilitated by providing adequate metaphors. (van der Veer, Felt, van Muylwijk and van Biene, 1987, van der Veer and Felt, 1988).

1.2. Designing metaphors

The learning process that leads to a mental model, evidently has to start somewhere. Most of the time the system to be learned will be used for a kind of application, of which the user has already some prior knowledge, even if that may be of a non-computerised variant of the task domain. Building a new mental model for the computerised situation will be based on available knowledge of situations and systems. New models are built analogous to existing models.

For the choice and construction of an adequate metaphor, both the level of the description of human-computer communication it represents and the mode of representation are important. Pictorial schemas and graphs are useful to represent structures and semantic relations, animations may illustrated processes, verbal descriptions are helpful to explain task analysis and task delegation. This choice of representation mode cannot be made without considering the levels of communication we derived from Moran's analysis. For task level and semantic level metaphors may refer to known situations, systems and structures, or may be constructed by combining known concepts and schemes. For the syntax level one will often need to construct a clear description that represents sequences, conditions, parameters. It may be better not to call these constructs a metaphor, but just a "description" in the form of a BNF syntax, state transition diagrams, a set of production rules, or natural language.

Van der Veer et al. (1988) propose a general strategy for the dealing with the problem of helping the users to adequately represent in their mental model the system they are using. The approach starts from the analysis of the system the user has to learn, focusing on the conceptual model of the system. If the system concerned is an existing one, this is no trivial task, since often the available documentation does not cover all levels of description, or presupposes knowledge of the underlying system covered by the user interface (van der Veer and Felt, 1988). Once the conceptual model is described and the user interface identified by this description, the next step is the definition of the user's virtual machine (UVM, see Tauber, 1985), which is a specification of the conceptual model as far as it is relevant for a certain user group and a specified task domain. The third step is the choice and construction of appropriate metaphors intended to induce adequate mental models for the users. Different aspects will contribute to this choice: the expected knowledge of the users at the task domain, relevant user characteristics and individual differences, and the structure of the user interface as analysed in levels of human-computer interaction (Carroll, 1983; Carroll and Thomas, 1982; Houston, 1983). Several distinct metaphors might be referred to for the same conceptual model, each illustrating a few aspects of the new system to be learned (Rumelhart and Norman, 1977).

Clanton (1983) refers to metaphors specially in relation to the design of systems. His distinction in different kinds of metaphors is also relevant in teaching existing systems:

a. Functional metaphors are chosen in order to reveal the relation between the system's functionality and the user's task perception. A spreadsheet is a traditional example of this kind of metaphor, enabling the user to structure his task delegation and the objects and actions referred to analogous to tools and methods in a traditional office environment.

b. Operational metaphors aim at referring to actions in such a way that the user's "natural" expectation of the meaning and results are confirmed. Like functional metaphors, they may be incorporated in the user interface. Object manipulation is a well known example. They may also be constructed especially for teaching purposed, as will be shown in this study where we will apply them for process dynamics.

c. Organisational metaphors show how notions on location and structure of information in the system may be used for planning and application. Clanton did not identify existing systems that employed this type of metaphor in the user interface. In the current study we will illustrate this type for the representation of semantics.

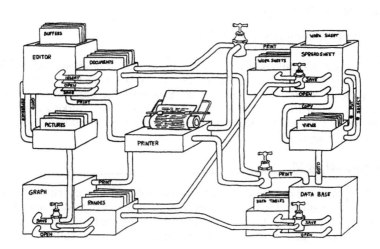

Figure 1. Example of an integrating metaphor (van der Veer and Felt, 1988)

d. Integrating metaphors represent the integration of system components and subsystems, in relation to the accomplishment of complex tasks. Van der Veer and Felt (1988) applied this type of metaphor for an integrated office system, comprising database, spreadsheet, editor, graphics, and information management. For the structure of the semantics of the system (the tools, objects and actions and their structural relations) a visual-spatial metaphor was developed as illustrated in figure 1. The tools are represented by boxes, the objects by documents, the relations by tubes and taps, and the actions are denoted by their keywords, indication the information flow that is produced by the command.

1.3. Teaching and evaluation

Application of metaphors for the introduction of a system to a novice asks for a strategy of teaching and evaluation. One important point in this strategy is the identification of relevant user characteristics (van der Veer, Tauber, Waern and van Muylwijk, 1985). A well chosen set of metaphors should appeal to knowledge, strategies and abilities of the intended user group. The teaching should, moreover, cope with individual differences between users that are relevant for the ability of grasping the relevant aspects of the system with the help of the metaphors and exercises offered.

Evaluation of the metaphors and the related teaching might be approached via an experimental situation. Especially the characteristics of the intended user group, however, are in some cases not easily simulated in an experimental sample. A field study may be preferred for the validity of this aspect, although this is payd for by a loss of control and of the possibility of manipulation of variables. This contribution reports on a field study, as the opportunity was offered to us. We got the possibility to measure relevant user characteristics, to analyse the system and design the teaching and the metaphors, to observe the actual course and to measure and record relevant effects.

Evaluation asks for the planning and design of various kinds of indications of effects. The mental model that results from the teaching can only be investigated in an indirect way. Actual performance during and after the course provides an indication of the adequacy of the mental model and related skills and knowledge. A teach-back method (see van der Veer, in press) gives an impression of the user's mental representation including completeness and correctness. An inventory at the end of the course may also ask for users' preferences for metacommunication (asking help form an expert, reading the course material, exploring the system), as an indication of how they would find the knowledge their mental model does not provide.

2. AN EXAMPLE: A SPREADSHEET SYSTEM

An example of recent applications of computers is the domain of office automation. Novices in this kind of applications often start in a position of being an expert on the task domain, at the same time having no experience whatsoever on the use of computers. The introduction of new applications will make them occasional users, who will spend only part of their working time in direct interaction with systems. As we had the opportunity to study this type of application, we will use this as an illustration of our approach.

2.1. The conceptual model

Analysis of the system and definition of the conceptual model form the first step to design adequate metaphors. Formal methods for the representation of conceptual models and the user's virtual machine are developed, e.g. by Tauber (1988). These are especially needed for the construction of user interfaces. For our goal, however, an less formal description will suffice.

In this case we started with the analysis of the available documentation and tried to build a complete and correct conceptual model of the system by comparing the impression the documents offered with our own experience in exploring the system. A diary was kept of this efforts, showing a kind of step by step evolution of the conceptual model. Every notion derived from the text was first recorded, than evaluated at the actual system, and revised if necessary. The revision was again recorded and argumented. Sometimes a notion needed several revisions before it could finally stand further testing.

Contrary to our intentions, we observed that this method, guided by the available documentation led to the formation of a conceptual model at syntax and interaction level firstly. Especially for the semantic level of description a lot of revisions were needed. In fact the documentation hardly contained any relevant details regarding the system's functionality. Indications were often implicit in the choice of command names and in the structure of the command hierarchy, but in these "sources of knowledge" a lot of inconsistencies were incorporated that in fact misguided the usage as we found in a pilot study on users who had learned the system from available documentation (Wijk, 1987).

2.2. The UVM

Definition of the user's virtual machine means tailoring the conceptual model of the system to the intended user group and their task domain. The user group in the case of this study consisted of employees of a large insurance company, whose daily jobs included a lot of calculations in relation to databases of a relatively simple nature. The relevant functionality of the system for this group may be characterised as the use of the basic spreadsheet functions without too much application of advanced database functions. Van Wijk (1987) reports on the frequency of use of the different facilities of this system by 11 employees of the same company, who learned the system from available documentation and applied it regularly in their jobs. For these users, a multi-layered model of the spreadsheet seemed to be relevant, showing layers representing (from inside to outside) the formal definition of the content of cells, the actual value of the content, and the formatted appearance of the cell on the screen (see figure 2).

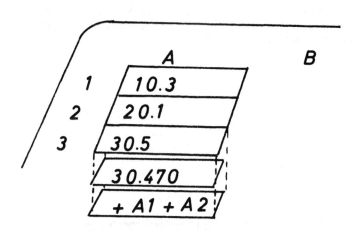

Figure 2. Multi-layered model of spreadsheet

Another aspect of the system that is relevant for this group of occasional users is the way in which the issueing of commands is enabled by the user interface. The system in this study offers the users a choice between menu selection of (hierarchically structured) commands, or the typing of the first characters of the consecutive menu choices. This leads for many experienced users to a skill in typing character strings that each represent one complete action, in the sense of a basic task as defined by Tauber (1988). A fragment of the conceptual model of the hierarchically structured basic tasks (part of the syntax level) is illustrated in figure 3.

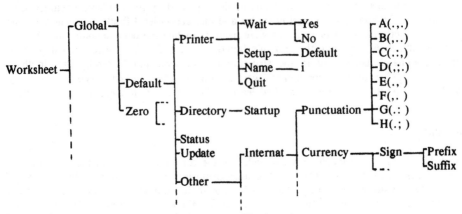

Figure 3. Fragment of the syntax of basic tasks

2.3. Construction of metaphors

The overall structure of the semantics of the system was illustrated with the help of an organisational metaphor (see 1.2.), illustrated in figure 4. In analogy to the tree structure of the syntax, the main tools in the system are represented by trees with a common root structure. The different facilities within the spreadsheet proper (the largest tree) are represented by main branches, grouped together on the base of their semantic relation. Information transfer between the facilities and between a facility of the spreadsheet and another tool are denoted by falling apples, indicating the direction of the information flow. The actions are labeled with their keywords, indicating the path in the tree structure they will activate.

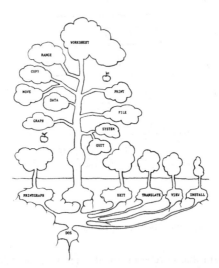

Figure 4. organisational metaphor of semantics (main tools and facilities)

Figures 5-7 show organisational metaphors illustrating some detailed semantic features. In Figure 5, illustrating the graphic facilities, the attributes that are requested in the action of defining the graph are written alongside the icon we choose to represent the actual information object (the apple). The possibilities to either ask for a preview at the screen, or for the storage and subsequent output on the printer, are represented with images indicating the actual orientation of the result.

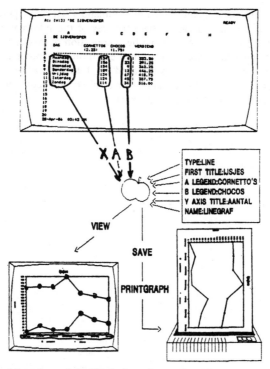

Figure 5. Metaphor of manipulation of graphic objects

The semantics of the command pair SAVE and RETRIEVE ask for the notion of the storage of an unknown number of different information objects, that may be retrieved in a random access mode. The typical fruit case illustrated in figure 6 represents this type of storage location.

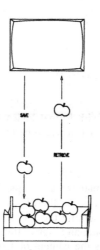

Figure 6. Semantic metaphor for storing and retrieving files

Special attention was given to the semantics of the command PRINT. Apart from the "natural" interpretation, illustrated with a denotation of the attributes of the information package written at the side of the icon for the information object, another application of this command is in fact a special kind of storage action, on which occasion again the printing attributes are requested from the system. This connoted information is thereupon saved for future occasions, at which the Dutch proverb APPELTJE VOOR DE DORST ("an apple for a thirsty moment") hints, which, alas, has to be translated with the proverb "a nest egg" (figure 7).

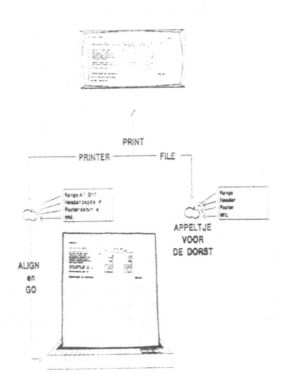

Figure 7. Metaphor for printing actions

The application of logical operations in a database is a problem for most users in the intended user group (who will not have any experience with formal logics and notation). Definition by example will be an adequate metaphor, which is in fact provided by the user interface of the system, like the spreadsheet idea itself.

For the process that results from the execution of a macro in the spreadsheet system an operational metaphor (see 1.2) in the form of an animation was designed, from which figure 8 gives a single view. In the actual animation, to be displayed on the PC, the caterpillar climbs the three, crosses the different elements of the macro (representing the series of command-codes on the first line of the macro), until it reaches the end-of-command sign ("tilde"). The animal then drops from the end of the branch onto the worksheet, eats the content of a cell of the worksheet (as the last command of the series invokes the ERASE action), goes down one cell (illustrating the semantic meaning of the second line of the macro), and subsequently repeats the macro, since the last line in this example indicates the call of the same macro.

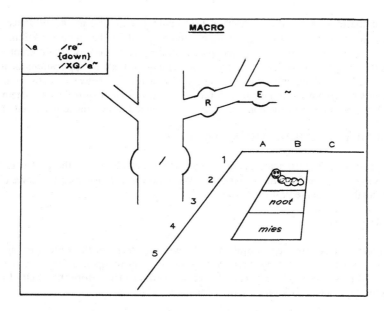

Figure 8. operational metaphor for the dynamics of macro facilities

Representation at syntax level is closely related with the actual appearance and physical characteristics of the interface, e.g. the lay out of the screen. For systems with alternative ways of interaction this may lead to contradicting descriptions. In the actual system the beginning user will be happy to let his interaction be guided by a menu, displayed on top of the screen. The line immediately below the line of menu options most of the time shows the sub-menu that will be offered if the option is chosen that is momentary blinking (an action of attention of the menu cursor). For novices this leads very often "naturally" to a syntactic model of a top-down tree of menu choices. After considerable training (e.g. 25 hours) most users turn to the possibility of manual input of the first characters of these choices. This results in the behaviour of defining a command string consisting of sequence-dependent single characters, keyed in as if typing from left to right. This is (at least sometimes) accompanied with an internal model of the syntax consisting of the commands (or their first character) structured in a horizontal tree, top-left. Offering novices one of these representations on paper will either support the original "natural" mental representation or the one that may be found after some experience with the system. In view of the fact that the novices in our study might be expected to become experienced users, we choose to offer them the representation of which figure 2 is a fragment as an organisational metaphor of syntax.

2.4. Relevant user characteristics

The way in which users develop a mental model, and the applicability of the mental model, may be an effect of individual differences (van der Veer et al., 1985). In this respect the current system has as an important characteristic a structured domain that is always only very fragmentarily visible, and thus difficult to survey for the user at the terminal. This is a characteristic of both the spreadsheet as a place for objects, and of the command structure.

Spatial ability is therefore a potentially relevant user characteristic that might influence the results of the course. Some empirical findings of other studies point in the same direction. Egan and Gomez (sited by Rothkopf, 1986) found that spatial ability was related users' different amounts of success for both storage and retrieval of patterns for changing texts in applications of text processors. Van der Veer, van Beek and Cruts (1987) mention a relation between spatial ability and the use of a graphical programming language. In the case of the current spreadsheet system, in a pilot study a correct representation of the command structure seemed to be related to spatial ability.

3. A FIELD STUDY: TEACHING THE METAPHORS

We had the opportunity to participate in the design of the metaphors and the first course that was given on the subject in the insurance company. We followed the teaching for several groups of employees. In total we observed 54 cases.

3.1. The students

All students might be characterised as professionals, who had to learn the system for application in their current job. Some were sent by their chef, others voluntarily applied for the course. The age varied between 18 and 63 years, there were 13 women and 41 men. More than half of all students had at least some experience with other applications at a PC.

In order to measure relevant user characteristics, we applied the DAT Space Relations test (Bennet, Seashore and Wesman, 1959), and we asked the students to fill in a questionnaire on experience with other systems.

3.2. Organisation of the course

The course itself took two full days. In cooperation with the teacher (an employee of the company) a detailed script was prepared, including all metaphors and points marked for explanation. The order of treatment was organised in a list of topics that were related to meaningful unit tasks a user could delegate to the system. The teaching on each unit task was structured in such a way that first the task level was covered, followed by semantics, syntax, and key-stroke level.

For the sake of hands on experience, one general exercise was designed, covering most types of objects and actions, in a logical way referring to students' prior experience in their jobs. Only for the explanation of the macro facilities a specific exercise had to be designed. For details on the organisation, see Wijk (1987).

3.3. Evaluation measurements

Students' preference for metacommunication after the course (additional information on aspects of the system not completely known by the user) was measured via systematic self reports on preference for different sources (on-line, documentation, experts, colleagues, course material and representation of the metaphors).

The resulting knowledge on the system was measured by separate questions on task level, semantic level, syntax level, and key-stroke level of the system. For details, see Wijk (1987).

The mental representation can only indirectly be investigated. We applied a teach back procedure (van der Veer, in press), of which figure 9 gives an example.

> explain to a colleague who does not know ****
> but who has some experience with PCs how to
> construct a graph from a table
>
> use the rest of this page, write in short sentences
> and / or draw sketches and / or graphs etc.

Figure 9. Example of teach back task

4. RESULTS

4.1. Knowledge of the system

As we measured the users' knowledge of the system with separate questions aiming at the different levels of description we derived from Moran, we were able to calculate the relation between the correctness at these levels. Table 1 shows only the Spearman correlations that were significant ($p \leqslant .05$).

	semantic level	syntax level	key-stroke level
task level	n.s.	n.s.	n.s.
semantic level		.68	.52
syntax level			.68

Table 1. Correlations between the different levels of knowledge, $n = 54$

The results indicate a clustering of knowledge at semantic, syntax, and key-stroke level, apparently unrelated to knowledge at task level. We interpret this as two different dimensions, (a) knowledge of the actual system and (b) knowledge of external functionality, the first one indicating the insight of users in the system itself, the other indicating their general ideas of the benefit of any spreadsheet system.

4.2. Representations of the system

The users' mental models were investigated with the help of a teach-back method, that provided us with an insight in the different representations users built of the system. The representations we collected were mainly correct, indicating effective mental models. A major source of difference was the level of representation. More than half of them could be identified as semantic level descriptions, although we found individual representations at all different levels and at several combinations of levels. Figures 10-14 show several examples. The metaphors as presented in the course were not often found. Figure 15 illustrates a rare occasion.

> **** has the possibility to select from a database
> (is a group of data regarding similar information,
> e.g. members of your aerobic dance group. For
> each person data are recorded like name,
> address, city, telephone number, age etc)
>
> If you want to find members from a certain age
> group, then you write down which class (e.g.
> between 40-250 years) and **** will check all
> persons. if it finds such a person falling in the
> age group, it copies all data concerning this per-
> son to a different place, presenting you with the
> requested overview. In case of a group of 10
> members, you may do this on the face of it, but
> with a large society the computer is much
> quicker.

Figure 10. A user's representation at task level

> -   make a graph with command "Graph"
>   / Graph
>   X Range ...
>   Y Range ...
>   Titles First
>   Titles   X-axis
>   Y-axis
>   Name
>   View

Figure 11. A user's representation at syntax level

> put the data for the figure in columns, ordered in
> horizontal and vertical data, take care for the gra-
> duation of the axes. Choose the relevant columns
> via Graph, choose titles and descriptions, and
> view in between as often as possible the results
> via View.

Figure 12. A user's representation at semantic level

- go to Graph in the menu
  - indicate the kind of graph (Type);
  - indicate Range of X;
  - indicate Range of A (if necessary up to F);
  - if necessary indicate Legend;
  - mark on Graph menu level View
- if to be kept, "save" for later print
  with PrintGraph.
- Quit

Figure 13. A combination of semantics and syntax representation

G(raph)
T(ype)
L(ine)
X C8..F8

Figure 14. Key-stroke sequence with syntax indication

database kind of card desk
important to know how and where
1) how notated
3) input data
2) where it should go

database
how where
e.g.:

field name	NAME		ADDRESS	record

field

actions: / = backslash
F = file
r = retrieve, put in database (external)?

Figure 15. Teach back protocol representing course metaphor

4.3. Preference for metacommunication

As part of the questionnaire the students answered after the course, we collected their preference for sources of help in situations where there knowledge of the system would fail. The answers showed a variety in prefered sources, but documentation and exploration of the system were both mentioned by the majority of the students. Only a minority mentions colleagues or experts (who are in fact available in the company). "Active" help by the system is a potential source for about 10 per cent, and the course metaphors score only 20 per cent. Obviously most students think they are able to solve problems without any active help.

The sources of help may be classified as internal to the system and external to the system. In our student group, there was no correlation between preference for internal metacommunication and preference for metacommunication outside the system.

Our data show significant correlations (p $\leqslant$ .05, n=54) between knowledge of external functionality (see 4.1.) and both preference for metacommunication outside the system (.27), and preference for internal metacommunication (.35). There is a significant correlation between knowledge of the actual system (see 4.1.) and preference for internal metacommunication only (.44).

4.4. Spatial ability

Spatial ability was investigated in relation with the scores on the knowledge questions. It was significantly correlated to both knowledge of external functionality (.29), and knowledge of the system (.56).

5. CONCLUSIONS

The general approach of analysing the user interface of an existing system, describing the conceptual model and defining the user's virtual machine, and designing metaphors for teaching, has proven to be successful in case of a spreadsheet system. Users knew most of the relevant aspects of the system (the UVM) after 2 days of teaching. Although we are unable to apply statistical tests, we get the impression that the problems the users of the pilot study mentioned did not occur in the group that attended our course.

The users' knowledge at the end of the course can be differentiated in knowledge of the system and knowledge of the general functionality of spreadsheet systems. Knowledge of the system at semantic, syntax, and key-stroke level are strongly related.

Mental representations differ between users. The semantic level is most often represented, but descriptions at all levels may be found, and various combinations are also present. The metaphors used in teaching are seldom reflected in the users' representations after the course.

Preference for sources of metacommunication after the completion of the course indicate that users generally estimate themselves competent enough to find out for themselves, using documentation or actively exploring the system. The more a user knows the actual system, the more he relies on the system as a source of metacommunication. The more a user understands the general functionality of spreadsheet systems, the more he prefers metacommunication sources both inside and outside the system.

Spatial ability is a significant and strong predictor for knowledge of the actual system (semantics, syntax and key-stroke level) after the course, and, to a much lesser extend, of knowledge of the general functionality of spreadsheet systems.

6. REFERENCES

Bennet G.K., Seashore H.G., and Wesman A.G. (1959). A manual for the Differential Aptitude Test, 3rd edition. The Psychological Corporation, New York.

Card S.K., Moran T.P., and Newell A. (1983) The psychology of human-computer interaction. Erlbaum, Hillsdale, N.J.

Carroll J.M. (1983) Presentation and form in user-interface architecture. Byte, 12, 113-122.

Carroll J.M. and Thomas J.C. (1982) Metaphor and the cognitive representation of computer systems. IEEE Transactions on Systems, Man, and Cybernetics, 12, 107-116.

Clanton C. (1983) the future of metaphor in man-computer systems. Byte, 12, 263-270.

Houston T. (1983) The allegory of software. Byte, 12, 210-214.

Moran T.P. (1981) the Command Language Grammar: a representation for the user interface of interactive computer systems. International Journal of Man-Machine Studies, 15, 3-50.

Norman D.A. (1983) Some observations on mental models. In: A.L. Stevens and D. Gentner (Eds.), Mental Models. Erlbaum, Hillsdale, N.J.

Norman D.A. (1986) Cognitive Engineering. In: D.A. Norman and S.W. Draper (Eds.), User centered design. Erlbaum, Hillsdale, N.J.

Rothkopf differences among users in instructive information exchanges with computers. In: F. Klix and H. Wandke (Eds.), Man-Computer Interaction Research MACINTER-I. North-Holland, Amsterdam.

Rumelhart D.E. and Norman D.A. (1977) Analogical Processes in Learning. In: J.R. Anderson (Ed.), Cognitive Skills and their Acquisition. Erlbaum, Hillsdale, N.J.

Tauber M.J. (1985) Top down design of human-computer systems from the demands of human cognition to the virtual machine. Proceedings 1985 IEEE workshop on languages for automation - cognitive aspects in information processing. IEEE computer Society, Los Angeles, CA.

Tauber M.J. (1988) On Mental Models and the User Interface. In: G.C. van der Veer, T.R.G. Green, J.-M. Hoc and D. Murray (Eds.), Working with Computers - Theory vs Outcome. Academic Press, London.

Veer G.C. van der (in press) Users' representations of systems. In: F. Klix and H. Wandke (Eds.), Man-Computer Interaction Research MACINTER-II. North-Holland, Amsterdam.

Veer G.C. van der, Beek J. van, and Cruts A.A.N. (1987) Learning structured diagrams - effect of mathematical background, instruction, and problem semantics. In: P. Gorny and M.C. Tauber (Eds.), Visualization in Programming. Springer Verlag, Heidelberg.

Veer G.C. van der and Felt M.A.M. (1988) Development of mental models of an office system. In: G.C. van der Veer and B. Mulder (Eds.), Human computer interaction - Psychonomic Aspects. Springer Verlag, Heidelberg.

Veer G.C. van der, Felt M.A.M., Muylwijk B. van, and Biene, R.J. van (1987) Learning an office system - a field study on the development of mental models. Zeitschrift für Psychologie, Suppl. 9, 46-58.

Veer G.C. van der, Guest S.P., Haselager W.F.G., Innocent P.R., McDaid E.G., Oestreicher L., Tauber M.J., Vos U., and Waern Y. (1988) An interdisciplinary approach to human factors in telematic systems. Computer Networks and ISDN Systems, 15, 73-80.

Veer G.C. van der, Tauber M.J., Waern Y., Muylwijk B. van (1985) On the interaction between system and user characteristics. Behaviour and information technology, 4 (4), 289-308.

Wijk R. (1987) Opzet en evaluatie van een cursus voor gebruikers van een spreadsheet systeem. Masters thesis. Free University, Department of Psychology, Amsterdam.

SOME HCI ISSUES CONCERNED WITH DISPLAYING QUANTITATIVE INFORMATION GRAPHICALLY

Jenny Preece

People and Computer Interaction Systems

Mathematics Faculty, The Open University

Milton Keynes, MK7 6AA

England

1   Introduction

Cartesian graphs are one of the most frequently used methods for displaying the quantitative relationships between two variables. These graphs may have precisely labelled scales which show the ranges of values of the variables. Alternatively, the scales may not be precise or they may even be absent. When this is the case the intention of the person who constructed the graph is generally that it should be used for examining trends in the data. Showing trends in data in this way is common practice in political and economic articles in newspapers. In fact, the distortion or absence of scales is a well known ploy for encouraging the reader to draw the conclusions desired by the journalist. However, the more positive reason for only labelling the axes of graphs and omitting precise scales is to help readers to interpret trends in data rather than to focus on individual points and possibly miss the general meaning shown in the graph. Poor graph interpreters generally give point interpretations at the expense of describing the trends in the data. [1,2,7]

In this paper I shall briefly describe how graphs are used for showing trends in data before going on to describe some common interpretation metaphors and how the use of such metaphors is stimulated by the visual appearance of the graph display and the domain to which the graph relates. I shall then discuss a study in which subjects were asked to interpret the trends in two syntactically identical graph displays, which related to different domains. The results of this study will be discussed from the point of view of how the subjects' interpretations were influenced by the two domains. I shall also propose a classification of graph interpretation types and show typical examples of some types through the use of visual chronological models of individual pupils' interpretations. These models show clearly when the interpreter was relating the graph to its domain and when either the syntax of the graph or its domain dominated the interpretation. Finally, I shall propose some morals for HCI concerning the display of data in graphs and draw some conclusions.

2   Showing trends in data with cartesian graphs

When graphs are designed for showing the trends in two or more pairs of variables they can provide a very rich form of visual information.   This is well recognised by the designers of scientific simulations and of specialist statistical and graphical software packages.   Now that "visualising" concepts has been assisted by improved computer graphics even on small and comparatively inexpensive machines and by the trend to research visualising, there will be an even greater use of this kind of graph.   Already it is quite common to see graphs like those in figures 1, and 2.

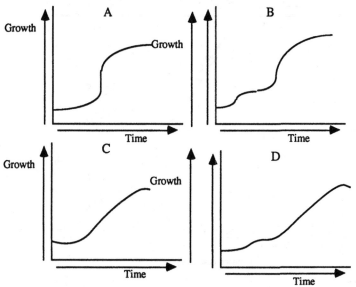

The graphs above represent generalised growth patterns in different types of organisms. Match the growth pattern curve with one of the statements below.

The change in numbers of cells in a closed bactrial culture.

The volume changes during the growth of an arthroped.

The length changes during development of *Xenopus*.

Dry mass changes in development of a seed plant.

Figure 1. A question from a Joint Matriculation Board advanced level biology examination paper. (June 1978)

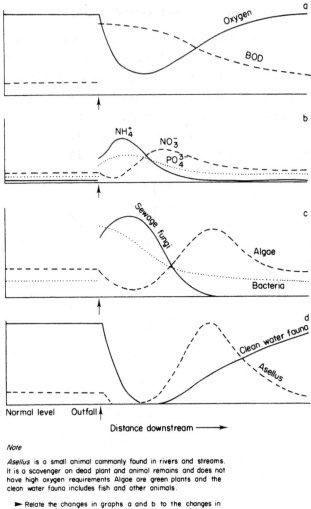

Figure 2. Exercise from a S.C.I.S.P. Ordinary Biology Text. (Mowl et al., 1974)

Figure 1 is taken from an exam for English senior school pupils. It shows the growth patterns for four different organisms and the question requires the pupils to interpret the trends and to match their interpretation with their domain knowledge and to select the correct answer from the four possible organisms listed. The second question is from a school textbook and it requires pupils to interpret the trends in a number of inter-related graphs each showing two or more pairs of variables. The graphs in this second figure are unusually complicated and represent a complex biological situation in which ecological stability is temporarily disturbed. A part from the complexity of the curves, notice also that there is no indication at all of the scales for each curve. Although this encourages pupils to focus on trends there is also a disadvantage; some subjects assume that a higher curve indicates a larger absolute quantity than a lower curve and this notion then predominates their interpretations.[1,3]. Notice also the small arrow, which can be mis-leading for some subjects, who interpret it as indicating that substances are going up rather than the point at which sewage is introduced into the stream. The graphs do, however, provide a valuable way of 'visualising' the changes that occur in the stream as a result of sewage pollution.

3 Some common mis-interpretations and incorrect metaphors

There are a number of reasons why graph displays can be difficult to interpret or mis-leading.[1,4] There may be too much information (e.g. too many curves or too much textual information), poor screen resolution, inappropriate use of colour, and inappropriate scales. In certain circumstances, however, these are not the main reasons why a particular graph is or is not difficult to interpret. The domain and specific context to which the graph relates may influence how well it is interpreted. What is more, the physical form of the graph in relation to its domain may influence how the graph is interpreted.[1,3,4,7] In order to facilitate this description it is helpful to describe the graph in terms of its semantics, general domain, syntax and presentation characteristics. The semantics of the graph is the meaning that the graph contains (e.g. information about distance travelled and speed in the graph in figure 3; the general domain is world knowledge about cars and the way they behave and the meaning of distance and speed; the syntax of the graph is the axes and the curves; and the presentation characteristics are aspects such as whether the whole graph was displayed at once or drawn from left to right, the resolution, the colour etc. The syntax and the presentation characteristics of a graph may be viewed differently for graphs with different semantics and different domains.

This paper aims to present the following three theses concerning the way trends are interpreted from graphs:

(1)   Syntactic and presentation characteristics can provide powerful cues when related to general domain knowledge and these cues can encourage visualising and the development of visual metaphors.

(2)   Subjects' visualisations and metaphoric interpretations can be so powerful that they over-ride semantic correctness.

(3)   The reason why these semantically incorrect metaphors and visualisations can be powerful and pervasive is that they 'make sense' within the general domain to which the graph relates.

There were many examples of mis-leading visualisations and metaphors from the subjects (over 300 14 and 15 year olds [1,2,3,4])who took part in the tests and experiments. Graphs showing variables from domains involving roads, hills, streams and trajectories were frequently interpreted as though they showed a different representation of those objects. For example, when asked to interpret the graph showing the distance travelled and speeds of three cars in figure 3 by answering the question "Does black overtake blue, or does blue overtake black? How can you tell?" several pupils gave answers similar to the following:

(S.R.)   "Because the curve for the black car goes further up."
(R.L.)   "The line goes further up to show a faster speed."
(G.H.)   "The end of the line is higher at the end."
(R.D.)   "Because the black car goes further up the page than the blue."

For the question "What happens to the red car? (Does it speed up, slow down or what?)", The answers given include the following:

(J.S.)   "It turns off to the right."
(C.H.)   "It crashes."
(K.B.)   "It turns around the corner and then disappears out of sight."

There were also other examples. Questions involving the interpretation of gradient frequently caused problems for subjects who were not well trained to use graphs. Figure 4 contains a graph which was produced by a computer simulation. The simulation shows pictorially the changes in the number of organisms in a population. Subjects were then asked to sketch a graph to represent the changes that they had just seen using a digitising tablet.[3] After being asked to describe what their own graph showed the computer produced a graph for comparison. The subjects were then asked a number of carefully structured questions which involved explaining changes in gradient or comparing the gradients of their own sketch with the computer generated graph. There were many occasions when 'rising fastest' was interpreted as 'the highest curve' or 'the furthest curve' or 'the curve which appeared to be produced quickest' and

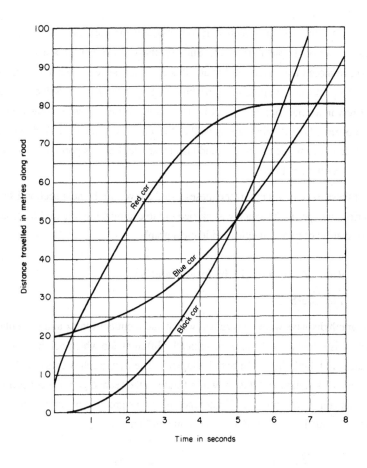

Figure 3

even 'the curve which had the most "little notches"'(i.e. small breaks due to the poor graphics resolution!)

Figure 4

Another example which is interesting to consider is the use of additional symbols such as the arrows on graphs in figure 1. Such symbols can be very mis-leading because they have more than one use in life and this encourages the subject to consider another kind of representation rather than concentrating upon the graph. Subjects interpreted the arrow in a simplified version of figure 1 in the following ways: direction - it went up; movement - is moving up; as well as the way it was intended - it happened here. In a different example an arrow could also mean: look at this point or indicate a process- x changes to y.

All of these examples support the theses listed above. In the next section I shall describe an experiment which was carried out to examine the role of the domain on the interpretation of two syntactically identical graphs.

4   Role of the domain in interpretation

4.1   The method

Two graph displays were constructed which had identical syntax and presentation characteristics but which were semantically different and which belonged to different domains, although they were both biological. The first graph is concerned with the pollution of a stream and it is shown in figure 5; the second graph is concerned with what happens to the amount of light reaching plants growing under a large tree when the tree is drastically pruned and it is shown in figure 6.

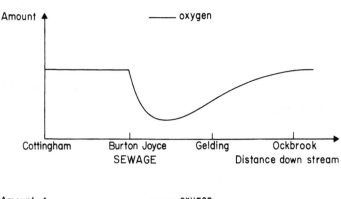

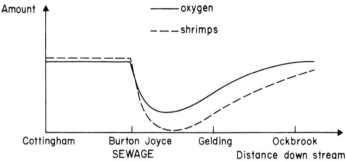

Figure 5

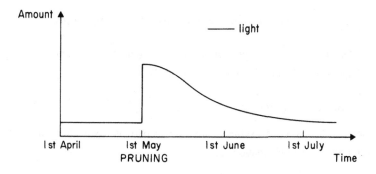

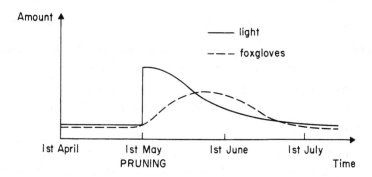

Figure 6

Twenty subjects aged 14 and 15 years took part in the experiment. Ten subjects did the task involving the graph in figure 5 first before proceeding immediately to the graph in figure 6. The other half of the subjects did the tasks in the reverse order. The subjects were carefully selected based on their general graph interpreting ability on standard tests and half of the subjects were boys and half were girls. (For a more detailed explanation of the experimental procedure and selection of candidates see references [1,2]) Each pupil was interviewed individually using the same questions for approximately half an hour by the author. The pupils were shown the first curve of each display on paper and asked to explain it and then prompted for more information. Then they were shown the second curve which was presented as a transparent over-lay and they were asked the same questions. So for each task domain shown in figure 5 and 6 for example, the following sequence of events was followed:

(1)   Present first curve (i.e. oxygen or light)

(2)   Ask Q1: "Can you tell me in as much detail as possible what happens ..(..to the oxygen in the stream when there is pollution? / ..to the light under the tree when the tree is pruned?)"

(3)   Prompt: " Thankyou, anything else?"

(4)   Present over-lay containing second curve (i.e. shrimps or plants)

(5)   Ask: Q2: "Now, can you tell me in as much detail as possible what happens to the ..(..the shrimps? / ..the small plants?)"

(6)   Prompt: "Anything else?"

On some occasions when a subject's answer was particularly unclear the interviewer asked for additional information.

The interview was recorded on audiocassette tape and later transcribed for analysis.

4.2   The results and the construction of visual chronological models

The protocols were analaysed in two ways; one method was quantitative and the other was qualitative. In this paper I shall first mention the quantitative method briefly and then focus on the qualitative analysis. The experimental design employed and the method of data collection was selected primarily so that the richness of the data could be examined qualitatively.

Although there were only 20 subjects a method of scoring the responses was devised and a quantitative comparison of the subjects' performance on each of the tasks was made. These results indicated that performance on the 'orchard task' was slightly better than on the sewage task. This result was anticipated since the 'sewage task' provided greater scope for pupils to construct incorrect visualisations. However, the number of subjects did not warrant statistical treatment, so the results must be regarded tentatively. A full report of the scoring method and the results is provided in [1,2]

The qualitative analysis involved examining and classifying subjects' responses in such a way that whatever cued or subsequently drove the response could be identified. This classification was devised through a number of pilot studies in which the following five categories were identified as the cueing and driving agencies for the interpretations:

- syntactic - a graphical description driven by the syntax of the graph

- pictorial - the subject is viewing the graph as a picture

- domain - the domain drives the interpretation

- domain drifting - the domain drives the interpretation to such an extent that the interpretation bears little relation to the real semantics of the graph display. Such interpretations generally include guessing.

- balanced - well balanced description in which syntax and domain are inter-related. This type of interpretation generally results in a correct semantic interpretation.

With prompting there may be recovery from any of the first three types of interpretation but recovery from domain drifting is rare.

The aim in constructing models of individual subject's interpretations was to see where particular types of interpretation were used and whether the types were transitory or relatively fixed. Figure 7a shows a generalised model of these types of interpretations. It is itself an example of a representation which requires a fair amount of explanation! In figure 7a there are two parts to the figure; a small graph and a diagram of the interpretion. Both of these representations can be thought of as being divided into three parts as shown by the dotted vertical explanation lines in figure 7b. These three divisions represent the three parts of the graph: the part before the event of pollution or pruning took place (the ecological disturbance); the area of ecological disturbance itself; and the area of recovery after the disturbance. The small graph contains numbers and these numbers indicate the order in which a subject attempted to interpret the display so figure 7a shows that the subject interpreted the area of ecological disturbance first, followed by the area of recovery and did not pay attention to the first part of the graph at all.

The diagram of the interpretation in figure 7a is also divided horizontally. The middle portion represents the actual interpretation and the top portion shows when information about the domain was brought into the interpretation and the bottom portion shows when syntactic descriptions were given. The unshaded area in the domain and syntax areas is also divided to represent the potential for using these sources of information to describe the three areas of the curve. Figure 8 shows typical models for each of the five interpretation types. The shaded areas in the middle show which parts were actually used in the interpretation.

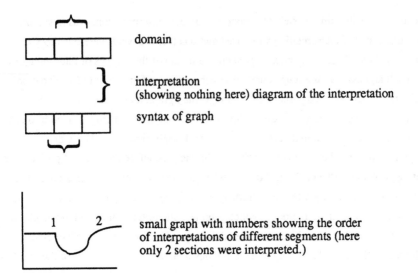

domain

interpretation
(showing nothing here) diagram of the interpretation

syntax of graph

small graph with numbers showing the order
of interpretations of different segments (here
only 2 sections were interpreted.)

Figure 7a

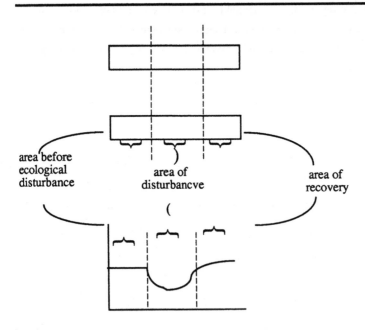

area before
ecological
disturbance

area of
disturbancve

area of
recovery

Figure 7b

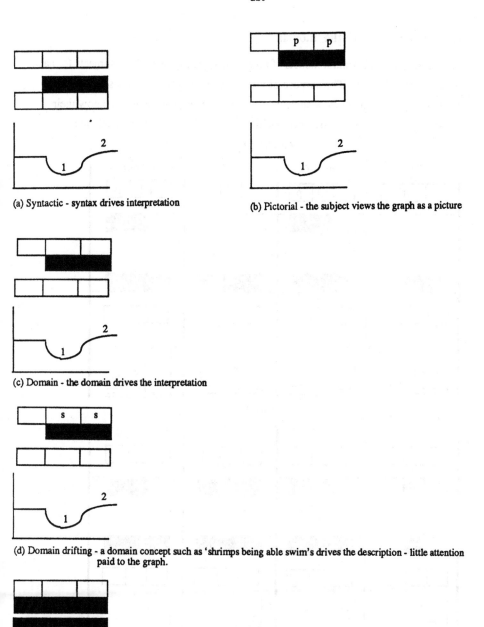

(a) Syntactic - syntax drives interpretation

(b) Pictorial - the subject views the graph as a picture

(c) Domain - the domain drives the interpretation

(d) Domain drifting - a domain concept such as 'shrimps being able swim's drives the description - little attention paid to the graph.

(e) Balances - domain and syntactic information are correctly inter-related. All sections considered in order.

Figure 8 Typical models for each of the five interpretation styles

4.3   Discussion of the models

Figures 9, 10 and 11 contain models of the real interpretations of three subjects for each of the two graph tasks. The purpose of including these examples is to show, through this modelling technique, how subjects used their domain knowledge and how their pictorial visualisations and their personally constructed metaphors mislead them.

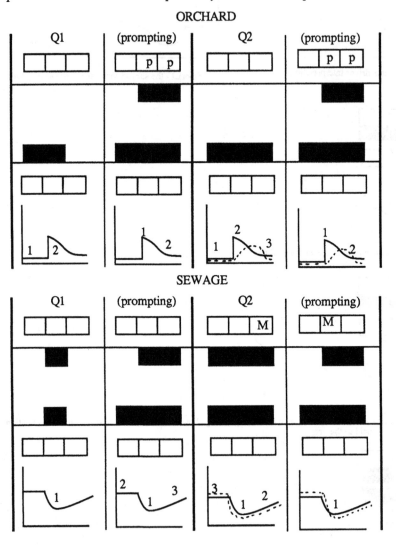

Figure 9 A pictorial account of K.A.'s protocol.

(p = pictorial interpretation; m = movement)

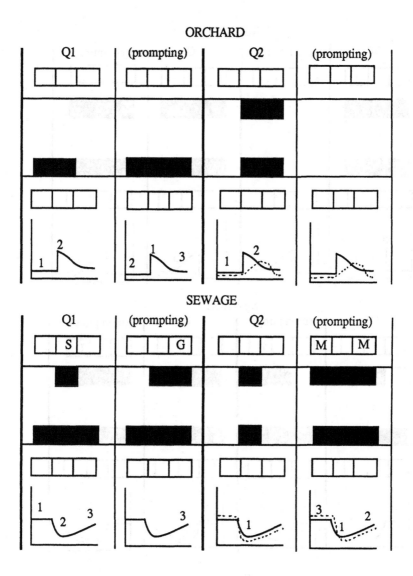

Figure 10 A pictorial account of L.K.'s protocol.
(S = space; G = guess; M = movement)

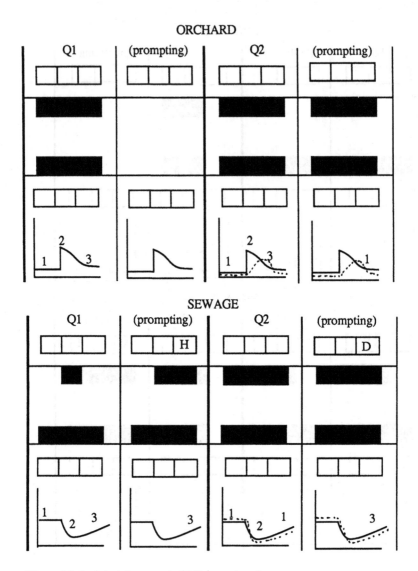

Figure 11 A pictorial account of I.R.'s protocol.
(D = domain drifting)

The models in figures 9, 10 and 11 are constructed in the same way as the examples shown in figure 8 except that they represent the whole of the interview described in section 4.1. The heavy vertical lines at the beginning and before Q2 (i.e. question 2) indicate that the first curve was presented and then the over-lay for the second curve respectively.

KA (see figure 9) interpreted the two graphs in the following way. For both curves in the 'orchard test' she gave syntactic descriptions and when prompted she added even more syntactic description and also gave pictorial descriptions. In the pictorial description she described the curves as though they represent the physical position of the light source. Her interpretation of the 'sewage test' is similar in that the interpretation starts off syntactic and then becomes pictorial after prompting in the second question. In her description she interpreted the graph as though the shrimps were moving in the water. This interpretation was fairly common and was recorded for several pupils. It seems that the notion of shrimps being able to move either up and down in the water or further along the stream away from the source of the pollution is powerful. Pictorial interpretations were common for the 'sewage test' but not for the 'orchard test'. This can also be seen in LK's interpretation.(figure 10) where prompting on the second question of the 'sewage test' led to a pictorial interpretation in which the shrimps were again said to move. The explanation given to explain the fall in the curve for oxygen was that 'the sewage took up the space and forced the oxygen down', so again we see how the domain knowledge along with visualising can misguide. This kind of explanation was common, for example another pupil said: "There are a lot of shrimps before the sewage gets into the stream and as it gets in they dive down very low ..." IR's protocols in figure 11 are included for comparison. They show well balanced correct interpretations in which the syntax of the graph is correctly explained in terms of the domain to give good semantic descriptions. Nothing could be added to his answer to the first 'orchard test' question and very little to the second question. His answers for the 'sewage task' were not quite as complete and prompting on the second question led to the inclusion of some irrelevant domain knowledge - i.e. domain drifting. (In the original models [1] any increase or decrease in the amount of information given by the subjects was also included but for clarity this extra detail has been omitted from this account.) It is also interesting to note that, with the exception of the last subject, IR, the subjects tend to focus on the central area of the curves. This behaviour was common amongst the less good interpreters and it led them to over-look vital information. You will also have noticed that the 'sewage task' is adapted from the graph shown in figure 2 but the arrow has been omitted. It was included in early pilot studies but it encouraged some pupils to think that the shrimps and the oxygen moved up!

The results of the analyses strongly support the theses mentioned in section 2. The 'sewage task' particularly encourages pupils to visualise the syntax of the graph in ways which make sense to them in terms of their already existing knowledge of the domain. In this way they temporarily view the graph as though it is a different kind of representation. The addition of the arrow in the tests used in early pilot studies encouraged this incorrect visualisation.[1] In general the conclusion that can be tentatively drawn is that the subjects interpreted the 'orchard task' better than the 'sewage task' because they were less likely to be encouraged to adopt incorrect visualisations by the domain.[1, 2] However, the qualitative nature of the data and the small number of subjects do not permit a more concrete statement to be made. Further experiments are needed to support this evidence.

5   General conclusions and morals for HCI

In the earlier discussion I have tried to select examples from a number of tests in which subjects were required to interpret the trends shown between one or more pairs of variables represented in a cartesian graph. Through these examples I have shown that there is evidence to support my theses that:

(1)   Syntactic and presentation characteristics can provide powerful cues when related to general domain knowledge and these cues can encourage visualising and the development of visual metaphors.

(2)   Subjects' visualisations and metaphoric interpretations can be so powerful that they over-ride semantic correctness.

(3)   The reason why these semantically incorrect metaphors and visualisations can be powerful and pervasive is that they 'make sense' within the general domain to which the graph relates.

In order to show statistically that these theses are correct many more experiments would be necessary and with more subjects. Similarly, the work should also be related directly to HCI by using computer generated displays for all the tests. It is unlikely that the same kinds of findings would be made if the subjects were scientifically trained in the use of graphs. However, there are a number of morals which can be drawn, at least tentatively, concerning the use of graphs with programs designed to be used by the general public and in education. Even though it is now very popular to try to capitalise on the potential of better and better graphics becoming available at lower and lower prices we should proceed with care. There is much development work involving visualisation which masquerades as research. Research into the use of cartesian graphs and other graphical representations in text have pointed out that assumptions about the how easy it is to understand these representations can be misguided.[8,9,10] HCI specialists should learn from this research with text. The potential for mistakes with computer generated displays is even greater than with text because of the flexibility and sophisticated displays which are possible with this medium. Two general morals which should be accepted are that 'not all visual representations are helpful' and that 'the usefulness of some visualisations may be strongly affected by the domain that is being represented' For these reasons technical and aesthetic artefacts should be avoided and when information from another visual system is used it should be included with care.

Having said this, the potential of using computer graphics for researching the use of visualisations and developing visualisations to facilitate understanding is an exciting prospect and one which should be explored fully.

Acknowledgements

The author particularly wishes to thank Claude Janvier who contributed many key ideas during this research. She also wishes to acknowledge and thank the following people who commented on various stages of the work: Margaret Brown, Thomas Green, Celia Hoyles, Ann Jones, Diana Laurillard, Tim O'Shea and David Pimm.

References

[1]   Preece, J. Interpreting trends in cartesian graphs. PhD. Thesis. The Open University. Milton Keynes. 1985

[2]   Janvier, C. and Preece, J. Interpreting trends in multiple curve cartesian graphs. Accepted for publication by The Journal of Instructional Science.

[3]   Preece, J. A Study of pupils' graph concepts with a qualitative interactive graph sketching program. Computer Education, 8, 1, pp 159-163. 1984

[4]   Preece, J. Graphs are not straightforward in T.Green, S. Payne and G. Van der Veer.Eds. Proceedings of the Conference of Cognitive Ergonomics. Academic Press. 1982

[5]   Joint matriculation Board. Advanced level Biology Examination Paper. June 1978.

[6]   Mowl, B., Hall, W., and Bausor, J., Patterns 4: Interactions and change. Longman. London 1974.

[7]   Janvier, C. Uses of situations in Mathematics Education. Educational Studies in Mathematics. 11, 1980.

[8]   Funkhouser OSIRIS 3. Historical development of the graphical representation of statistical data. 1937

[9]   Ehrenberg A.S.C. ABA Statistical Meetings. Detriot, 1981.

[10]   MacDonald-Ross, M. 'How numbers are shown: A review of research on the presentation of quantitive data in texts'. IET Monographs. The Open University, Milton Keynes 1977.

Implementing Direct Manipulation Query Languages Using an Adequate Data Model

Rainer Gimnich
IBM Scientific Center Heidelberg
Tiergartenstr. 15, D-6900 Heidelberg, F.R.G.

Abstract

Human factors work in the areas of database use addresses the design of the user interface of interactive database applications as well as the design of the on-line interface of the database system itself. Some conceptual prerequisites of using direct manipulation in an on-line database interface are discussed. It will be shown that choosing an adequate data model is vital in investigating the application of this style of interaction in complex database environments requiring a high level of abstraction. As an example, an advanced data model is introduced. In this model, the semantics of operating directly on a graphical database interface is specified, possible ambiguities are revealed, and a way of implementing the interface in an existing (e.g. normalized relational) database environment is shown.

1. Formal Specification and Prototyping of User Interfaces

The term *specification* in software development is not used in a uniform sense: there are specifications of requirements (also called "definitions") and of designs, of processes and of their results (also called "documents"). But these meanings of the term *specification* have in common that a precise description of the external behavior of a system is intended without describing its concrete internal realization. Specifications emphasize *what* the system does, contrasted to *how* it is (or will be) implemented.

By a formal specification we understand a word of a formal specification language, and *formal* here refers to a clear and unambiguous semantics definition. Among the benefits of formal specifications in the early stages of software development (requirements engineering, design) we find that these descriptions enable to reason and prove properties about an intended software system (e.g. perform consistency checks) before the first line of code is written.

The concept of formal specification is well complemented by *rapid prototyping*. A prototype of a software system shows its external behavior before the system is fully implemented. Thus, some of the quality aspects, such as efficiency and robustness, may be neglected. An increasing number of research activities aim at automatically transforming design specifications into corresponding operational forms, for prototyping, for testing purposes, or even for final implementations.

Those parts of a software system that handle the user's interaction with it are usually separated in a *user interface management system (UIMS)*. This supports an efficient implementation, reuse, and adaptation of user interfaces.

In a logical model, a UIMS consists of three components [Edmo82, Green85]:
- Presentation
- Dialogue Control
- Application Interface

The user interacts directly with the Presentation component, which generates the screen display and reads data input by the user. The Dialogue Control mediates between the user and the application program. This component processes the data transferred by the Presentation component and sends data to the Application Interface to be processed by appropriate application modules. In turn, the Dialogue Control component manages requests from the application program which require a user's reaction. The Application Interface model is a representation of the application from the point of view of the user interface and defines the semantics of the application.

The specification of a direct-manipulation database UIMS, which will be presented here, concentrates on aspects of the Application Interface, while syntactic (Dialogue Control) and lexical (Presentation) aspects of interaction are tackled briefly.

2. User Interfaces to Database Systems

Database systems are viewed in the context of integrated information systems, and it is obvious that their interfaces to end-users should require least personal effort in learning and handling the relevant system functions. Furthermore, it is necessary that the interaction principles can easily be remembered over time and that, to a certain extent, the interface is tailorable to individual needs.

By a *database user interface* we understand an on-line interface or shell to a *database management system (DBMS)* rather than the user interface of an interactive database application program which was built using the application program interface (API) of the DBMS. In the following, the term *application* is used to denote the underlying software system that the UIMS is to access. In our case the application is a DBMS.

User interfaces are generated on the basis of defined *interaction languages*. Typically, an interaction language consists of (linear) formal language, natural language, and graphical language elements. The decision for a particular interaction language to be used for (particular parts of) the interface is application-dependent and requires a careful task analysis (cf. [GerRoh87]).

In the case of DBMSs, interaction languages are necessary for introducing and handling data: a *data definition language (DDL)* and a *data manipulation language (DML)*. To enable the user to retrieve information from the database, the *query language (QL)* portion of the DML is most important to be elaborated on the user interface.

Particular effort is required in the design of interaction languages which are predominantly graphical and where the user interface shall allow for a direct manipulation of the graphical objects. Despite the relative ease of learning and using such interfaces, they are difficult to specify and implement properly.

One outstanding example of a direct-manipulation database user interface is the work by Herot [Herot80, Herot84] on a "spatial data management" prototype for geographical applications.

McDonald [McDo86] provides a multi-media data management system combining computer graphics and video techniques. A prototype has been implemented for a hospital supply database system.

A recent example by Kim, Korth, and Silberschatz [KiKoSi88] introduces a graphical query language based on the universal relation model.

Wong and Kuo have presented their Graphical User Interface for Database Exploration (GUIDE) [WonKuo82]. They have explicitly addressed the following problems they experienced with traditional database interfaces based on linear-formal interaction languages:

- *memory load:* e.g. to remember the data structures; names, types, and units of attributes; meanings of acronyms;
- *inappropriate external data models:* e.g. implicit referential integrity;
- *no feedback in query process:* no stepwise formulation of queries built up on intermediary results;
- *no levels of abstraction for schemes:* e.g. only relation and attribute levels;
- *no mechanisms to overview large databases:* no "meta-data browsing".

The central idea is that the so-called *conceptual data model* on which the DBMS is built (e.g. normalized relational data model [Codd70]) will not always be appropriate if used on the user interface level (so-called *external level*). Why not use "higher", more user-oriented data models here and define transformations of each external model to the conceptual model? Wong and Kuo decided to use an entity-relationship model (cf. [Chen76], also [Sowa84]). The approach presented in the following sections will rely on a *non first normal form (NF^2)* relational data model [SchPis82, DKABE86, PisAnd86, PisTra86] for the external level.

3. An Approach to Direct-Manipulation Database User Interfaces

Database querying can be viewed as an iterative process on three operation levels:

1. Selection of relevant information domain ("universe of discourse")

2. Stepwise formulation of information request (query)

3. Processing of query result

A user interface accounting for flexible interactive work must provide appropriate transitions between these levels. These transitions may be implicit, e.g. if the information domain is extended or reduced during query formulation.

The database interaction language and the user interface based on it mainly hold for requirements on operation level 2. Although some of the development principles can be extended and adapted to level 1, some additional concepts, such as super-icons, need to be applied there [Rohr88].

The UIMS under development refers to hierarchical views on data structures. Hierarchical views can be built automatically from normalized relational database schemes by analyzing the referential integrity constraints [Gimn88]. In cases where this analysis results in a graph which is not tree-structured, a spanning tree of this graph may be selected. An example of a simple DEPARTMENTs database presentation is shown in Fig. 1.

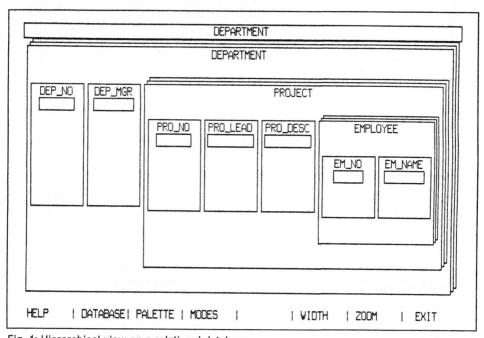

Fig. 1: Hierarchical view on a relational database

In its central part, this screen shows the structure of a data object named DEPARTMENT and indicates that there is a set of instances of this sort by presenting, in this lexical form, a special frame indicating several spatially arranged sheets. Each element of the set of departments consists of a department number (DEP_NO), a department manager (DEP_MGR), and a set of projects (PROJECT) each of which is, in turn, structured as a tree-like hierarchy. There is a clear indication that the information in each department instance consists of *one* department number, *one* department manager, and a set of projects that belong to (or run in) this department. These *x:one* and *x:many* relationships are naturally read from top to bottom. The structures can be shifted and displayed from several points of view. In fact, each complex object's name may be placed in the top position, and the dependencies are then shown from the view of this root element. This view transformation operation provides for a flexible comprehension of object dependencies while keeping the hierarchical representation style (Fig. 2, Fig. 3). View transformations may be applied deliberately before or during query formulation. As to querying, the most significant operations are selecting (complex or atomic) objects for their values to be output, and entering restrictions on data values into the text fields (special windows) of atomic objects.

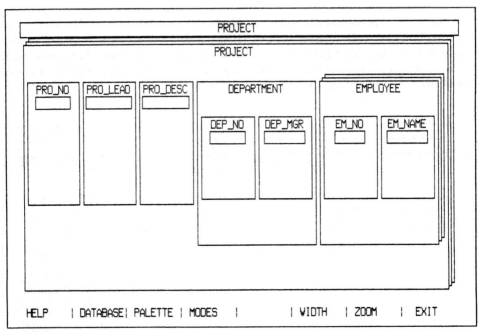

Fig. 2: PROJECT view

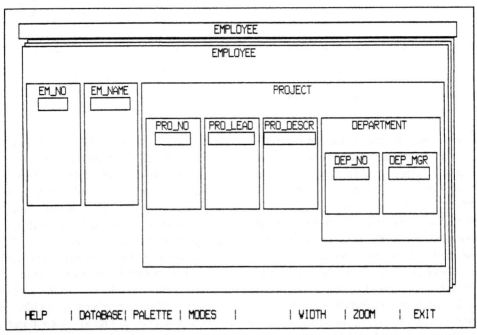

Fig. 3: EMPLOYEE view

Besides the central presentation part, there is a scroll bar at the top of the screen repeating the name of the root element. Horizontal scrolling is useful in large trees.

In the bottom line of the screen there is a pop-up menu list. The menus provide functions for detailed help information, database selection, color palette selection and definition, mode display and change, adaptation of presentation width, and zooming.

The Dialogue Control component defines the structure of the interaction and retains state information. Only part of the information received from the Presentation is handed on to the Application Interface. User input that only affects presentational aspects is processed and information is directly sent back to the Presentation component. In contrast, user input interpreted as operations like database selection or querying, which also require a presentational response, are relevant to the application.

The Dialogue Control handles direct-manipulation interaction structures in an application-independent manner. It thus abstracts over lexical aspects, such as geometry and coloring, and manages strict hierarchies like trees and forests with labelled nodes and edges.

The Application Interface (here: interface to a DBMS) interprets these hierarchies as complex sets of data. Concerning the most significant application-relevant operations, the selection of objects will be interpreted as data projection, while the modification of an object (e.g. by text entry) is interpreted as data restriction.

4. Formal Semantics Specification

The Application Interface model is described following a constructive, model-oriented approach. A well-established method in this approach is the *Vienna Development Method (VDM)* [BjøJon78, Jones80, Jones81, Bjør81, BjøJon82, Jones86, BJMN87].

VDM is a method for the complete process of software development, not only for specification, and it is based on denotational semantics. As to specification, the central idea in VDM - in contrast to algebraic or axiomatic methods - is to construct directly a model of the object to be described. This is done using mathematical concepts and notation: arithmetics, first-order logic, basic data structures such as lists, sets, and mappings. In a layered top-down development, the most abstract descriptions of objects and operations built in terms of these concepts are systematically developed into more and more concrete forms ("reification"), down to a programming language representation. On each stage, the adequacy of the refined data structures and the correct modelling of the more abstract operations by their decomposed counterparts have to be shown.

On a VDM basis, a specification language similar to the language used in [GimEbe87] is used for the specification of the Application Interface component. The application-relevant aspects of the user interface are modelled by means of an *abstract data type (ADT)*, here called **DM_query** ("direct-manipulation query"). Those parts of the specification which are sometimes called "semantic domains" and "syntactic domains" in the VDM literature are presented in Fig. 4 in a simplified manner.

```
module   DM_query

definitions
            compl              := { tuple-set }
            tuple-set          := { tuple }
            tuple              := [ component-list ]
            component-list     := component
                                  | component , component-list
            component          := identifier : type
            type               := compl | atomic
            atomic             := integer | string | ...
            obj_id             := identifier


operations

            transform   :   compl × obj_id  →  compl

            project     :   compl × 2 obj_id  →  compl

            select      :   compl × 2 (obj_id × string)  →  compl
```

Fig. 4: ADT definitions and operations syntax (simplified)

Types are treated as sets. The type compl ("complex object") is modelled here as a set of tuple-sets. A tuple-set is defined as a set of tuples, and a tuple consists of components which, in turn, may be complex or else atomic (e.g. integers, strings). This object model corresponds to the *non first normal form (NF²)* relational data model.

In Fig. 4 the syntax of the abstract query operations is given in a mathematical function notation. The semantics of these operations has to be included in the specification. As an example, the view transformation operation is depicted:

$$
\begin{aligned}
&\text{transform} \quad : \quad \text{compl} \times \text{obj\_id} \rightarrow \text{compl} \\[1em]
&\textbf{pre-}\text{transform (co, new)} = = \\
&\qquad\qquad \text{is\_complex (object (new))} \wedge \text{is\_in (co, new)} \\[1em]
&\textbf{post-}\text{transform (co, new; co}') = = \\
&\qquad\qquad (\text{name (co)} = \text{new} \Rightarrow \text{co}' = \text{co}) \\
&\qquad\qquad \wedge \ \text{name (co}') = \text{new} \\
&\qquad\qquad \wedge \ \text{co}' = \{ \text{depdt (new)} \ \# \ \text{restruct (co, new)} \}
\end{aligned}
$$

Fig. 5: Semantics of transform operation

The semantics of an operation of the ADT is specified by means of two predicates: a pre- and a post-condition. The pre-condition is a relation on the input parameters, stating the applicability of the operation. In practice, error or exception handling will be initiated if the input parameters do not meet the pre-condition. The post-condition describes the non-exceptional effect of the operation by relating input to output parameter values. For distinction, output values are marked with a prime. Especially, the effect of the operation on the internal "state" of an instance of the ADT needs to be recorded.

In the example, the pre-condition states that a view transformation on some complex object co can only be applied to a "sub-object" of co which, in turn, is a complex (and not atomic) object. The post-condition says that the state of an object co remains unchanged, if it is transformed to itself. Further, the name of the transformed complex object will be that of the second input parameter (new), and co' (i.e. co *after* the application of this operation) is the set of those tuples which are dependents of new, concatenated with components gained from rearranging (nesting or unnesting) the structure according to the dependencies. The auxiliary functions (is_complex, is_in, etc.) as well as the basic types (string, identifier, etc.) are assumed to be imported by the module.

Applying the transform operation to, say, a DEPARTMENT view to change it into a PROJECT view (cf. section 3), will yield:

```
    transform (DEPARTMENT, PROJECT)
  = {  depdt (PROJECT) # restruct (DEPARTMENT, PROJECT) }
  = {  depdt (PROJECT) # unnest (DEPARTMENT, PROJECT) }
  = {  [  y.PRO_NO, y.PRO_LEAD, y.PRO_DESCR, y.EMPLOYEE ,
          DEPARTMENT:  [ x.DEP_NO, x.DEP_MGR ] ]
        |  y In x.PROJECT,
           x In DEPARTMENT
      }
```

Fig. 6a: Semantics of transforming DEPARTMENT to PROJECT view

The last expression in Fig. 6a may be rewritten, with more "syntactic sugar":

```
  select   [ y.PRO_NO,
             y.PRO_LEAD,
             y.PRO_DESCR,
             y.EMPLOYEE,
             DEPARTMENT :   [ x.DEP_NO,
                              x.DEP_MGR
                            ]

           ]
  from     y In x.PROJECT,
           x In DEPARTMENT
```

Fig. 6b: Semantics of transforming DEPARTMENT to PROJECT view (continued)

This notation is borrowed from HDBL (Heidelberg DataBase Language) [PisTra86]. In fact, to improve readability, the specification language constructs applied in the examples below rely on a (slightly extended) version of HDBL.

To illustrate the other major operations of the ADT, namely **project** and **select**, let us assume first that the user chooses the objects department manager (**DEP_MGR**) and project description (**PRO_DESCR**) for data retrieval on the interface. This is handled by the **project** function which yields results in different structures according to the view (**DEPARTMENT, PROJECT,** or **EMPLOYEE**) the user has on the interface. The expressions representing the semantics of this projection in each view are shown in Fig. 7.

```
(in DEPARTMENT view:)

        select [ x.DEP_MGR,
                 PROJECT :  ( select [ y.PRO_DESCR ]
                                from   y In x.PROJECT   )
                 ]
        from   x In DEPARTMENT


(in PROJECT view:)

        select [ y.PRO_DESCR,
                 DEPARTMENT:  [ y.DEPARTMENT.DEP_MGR ]
                 ]
        from   y In PROJECT


(in EMPLOYEE view:)

        select [ PROJECT :  z.PROJECT.PRO_DESCR,
                            DEPARTMENT:
                               [ z.PROJECT.DEPARTMENT.DEP_MGR ]
                 ]
        from   z In EMPLOYEE
```

Fig. 7: Projection (example)

The semantics of projections on the same partial objects in each valid view are equivalent in the sense that, if the views are mapped to normalized ("flat") relational structures, then the correspondingly mapped projections will be identical.

When selections are used along with projections, the specification language helps in describing ambiguities. Assume, for example, that the user holds the **DEPARTMENT** view and merely chooses the top-level object (**DEPARTMENT**) and enters the restriction "= **SMITH**" into the project leader field. The semantics of this simple query can be specified in at least three ways:

```
(A)     select    x
        from      x in DEPARTMENT
        where     ( exists y in x.PROJECT:
                    y.PRO_LEAD = 'SMITH' )


(B)     select    [ x.DEP_NO,
                    x.DEP_MGR,
                    PROJECT :  ( select [ y.PRO_NO,
                                          y.PRO_LEAD,
                                          y.PRO_DESCR,
                                          y.EMPLOYEE
                                        ]
                                 from   y in x.PROJECT
                                 where  y.PRO_LEAD = 'SMITH' )
                    ]
        from      x in DEPARTMENT


(C)     select    atoms(x)
        from      x in DEPARTMENT
        where     ( exists y in x.PROJECT:
                    y.PRO_LEAD = 'SMITH' )
```

Fig. 8: Projection with selection (example)

Version (A) means that the values of all DEPARTMENT, PROJECT, and EMPLOYEE entries are to be displayed for those departments where there is at least one project whose leader's name is SMITH. In contrast, version (B) states that from all DEPARTMENT, PROJECT, and EMPLOYEE values only those projects led by a person named SMITH, along with their corresponding employees entries, will be output. Version (C) is yet another semantic variant of the graphically expressed query: the selection of a complex object is assumed as a shorthand expression for selecting its atomic dependents.

Strictly speaking, these different semantic interpretations lead to different graphical query languages. Experimental investigations will help in ultimately defining the semantics of the graphical operations, particularly in deciding which alternative will be most adequate to the user.

Besides its aid in clearly stating possible ambiguities in direct-manipulation queries, the formal specification also supports implementing a graphical query language as a kind of shell on an existing relational database system. The specified semantics serves as a reference in the translation process. An extended dependency graph is used for the internal representation of abstract objects, and graph algorithms are used to compose target language queries according to the specification.

As an example, the visually represented query of Fig. 9a will be targeted into an SQL (Structured Query Language) [IBM85] expression (Fig. 9b), which can directly be processed by any DBMS with an SQL language interface.

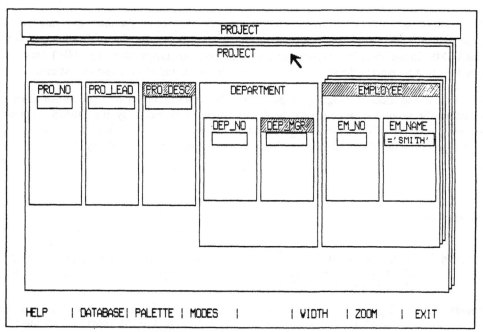

Fig. 9a: Sample query

```
SELECT    PROJECT.PRO_DESCR ,
          DEPARTMENT.DEP_MGR ,
          EMPLOYEE.EM_NO ,
          EMPLOYEE.EM_NAME

FROM      PROJECT ,
          DEPARTMENT ,
          EMPLOYEE

WHERE     PROJECT.DEP_NO = DEPARTMENT.DEP_NO  AND
          EMPLOYEE.PRO_NO = PROJECT.PRO_NO  AND
          EMPLOYEE.EM_NAME = 'SMITH'
```

Fig. 9b: Sample query translated into SQL

SQL is not to be confused with the specification language, particularly with those constructs based on HDBL.

5. Conclusion

A method of implementing a direct-manipulation user interface for database querying has been presented. A VDM based specification language is used to describe the application interface of this UIMS. In the specification language, we can define an appropriate (e.g. NF^2) data model which is used to express the semantics of graphically presented objects and operations.

The formal specification language supports concise descriptions of ambiguities and helps in mapping the graphical language to the target language provided by the DBMS. Different semantic readings of one graphical presentation can be taken as a defined basis for empirical investigations to decide which reading to prefer and to implement completely.

References

BJMN87   D. Bjørner, C. B. Jones, M. Mac an Airchinnigh, E. J. Neuhold (eds.), *VDM '87: VDM - a formal method at work,* Springer Verlag, LNCS 252, Berlin/Heidelberg/New York/Tokyo, 1987.

Bjør81   D. Bjørner, *The VDM principles of software specification and program design,* in: J. Diaz, I. Ramos (eds.), "Formalization of programming concepts", Springer Verlag, LNCS 107, Berlin/Heidelberg/New York, 1981.

BjøJon78   D. Bjørner, C. B. Jones (eds.), *The Vienna development method: the meta-language,* Springer Verlag, LNCS 61, Berlin/Heidelberg/New York, 1978.

BjøJon82   D. Bjørner, C. B. Jones (eds.), *Formal specification and software development,* Prentice-Hall International, Englewood Cliffs, NJ., 1982.

Chen76   P. P. S. Chen, *The entity-relationship model: toward a unified view of data,* ACM Trans. on Database Systems 1 (1976, 1), pp. 9 - 36.

Codd70   E. F. Codd, *A relational model of data for large shared data banks,* Comm. ACM 13 (1970, 6), pp. 377 - 387.

DKABE86   P. Dadam, K. Küspert, F. Andersen, H. Blanken, R. Erbe, J. Günauer, V. Lum, P. Pistor, G. Walch, *A DBMS prototype to support extended NF^2 relations: an integrated view on flat tables and hierarchies,* Proceedings of the 1986 ACM SIGMOD International Conference on Management of Data (Washington, D.C.; May 1986), pp. 356 - 367.

Edmo82   E. A. Edmonds, *The man-computer interface - a note on concepts and design,* Int. J. Man-Machine Studies 16 (1982), pp. 231ff.

GerRoh87   M. Gerstendörfer, G. Rohr, *Which task in which representation on what kind of interface,* in: H.-J. Bullinger, B. Shackel (eds.), "Human-Computer Interaction - INTERACT '87", North-Holland, 1987.

GimEbe87   R. Gimnich, J. Ebert, *Constructive formal specifications for rapid prototyping,* in: H.-J. Bullinger, B. Shackel (eds.), "Human-Computer Interaction - INTER-ACT '87", North-Holland, 1987.

Gimn88   R. Gimnich, *Transformation hierarchischer Sichten in einer graphischen Datenbankoberfläche* (Transforming hierarchical views in a graphical database user interface), Proceedings of 1st Workshop of the Gesellschaft für Informatik Working Group on Graphical User Interfaces (Bonn, March 23 - 25, 1988), GMD, Bonn (in German).

Green85   M. Green, *Report on dialogue specification tools,* in: G. E. Pfaff (ed.), "User interface management systems", Eurographic Seminars, Springer Verlag, New York, 1985, pp. 9 - 20.

Herot80   C. F. Herot, *Spatial management of data,* ACM Trans. on Database Systems 5 (1980, 4), pp. 493 - 513.

Herot84   C. F. Herot, *Graphical user interfaces,* in: Y. Vassiliou (ed.), "Human factors and interactive computer systems", Ablex Publishing Co., Norwood, NJ., 1984.

IBM85   International Business Machines Corporation, *SQL/Data System Concepts and Facilities for VM/System Product,* IBM Form No. SH24-5065, 2nd edition, November 1985.

Jones80   C. B. Jones, *Software development: a rigorous approach,* Prentice-Hall International, London, 1980.

Jones81   C. B. Jones, *Towards more formal specifications,* in: C. Floyd, H. Kopetz (eds.), "Software Engineering - Entwurf und Spezifikation", Teubner, Stuttgart, 1981.

Jones86   C. B. Jones, *Systematic software development using VDM,* Prentice-Hall International, London, 1986.

KiKoSi88   H.-J. Kim, H. F. Korth, A. Silberschatz, *PICASSO: a graphical query language,* Software - Practice and Experience 18 (1988, 3), pp. 169 - 203.

McDo86   N. H. McDonald, *Video-graphic query facility for database retrieval,* The Visual Computer 2 (1986, 2), pp. 72 - 77.

PisAnd86   P. Pistor, F. Andersen, *Designing a generalized NF^2 data model with a SQL-type language interface,* Proceedings of the 12th International Conference on Very Large Data Bases (Kyoto, Japan; August 1986), pp. 278 - 285.

PisTra86   P. Pistor, R. Traunmüller, *A data base language for sets, lists, and tables,* Information Systems 11 (1986, 4), pp. 323 - 336.

Rohr88   G. Rohr, *Graphical user languages for querying information: where to look for criteria?* Proceedings of the 1988 IEEE Workshop on Visual Languages (Pittsburgh, PA.; Oct. 10 - 12, 1988).

SchPis82   H.-J. Schek, P. Pistor, *Data structures for an integrated DB management and information retrieval system,* Proceedings of the 8th International Conference on Very Large Data Bases (Mexico City; September 8 - 10, 1982), VLDB Endowment, Saragota, CA., 1982, pp. 197 - 207.

Sowa84   J. F. Sowa, *Conceptual structures: information processing in mind and machine,* Addison-Wesley; Reading, MA., 1984.

WonKuo82   H. K. T. Wong, I. Kuo, *GUIDE: Graphical user interface for database exploration,* Proceedings of the 8th International Conference on Very Large Data Bases (Mexico City; September 8 - 10, 1982), VLDB Endowment, Saragota, CA., 1982, pp. 22 - 32.

MODELLING THE RELATIONSHIP BETWEEN
STATE AND DISPLAY IN INTERACTIVE SYSTEMS

M.D. Harrison & A.J. Dix
Human Computer Interaction Group
Department of Computer Science
University of York, Heslington, York, YO1 5DD, UK

ABSTRACT

For many interactive systems, and in particular designs influenced by the direct manipulation style of interaction, the user's ability to have immediate visual and manipulative access to all data is limited by the physical constraints of the display. A significant design concern therefore is the development of appropriate user models and complementary system models to support understanding of commands that are affected by these constraints. In this paper, the relationship between state and display is modelled mathematically to aid more precise understanding of the nature of direct manipulation as an interaction style, and the consequences of display boundary and other related limitations. Since it is unlikely that there is direct manipulative access to all data, we will distinguish between normal and exceptional models of interactive behaviour. Exception models describe the behaviour of the system when direct manipulation principles are transgressed.

Keywords: *interaction models, interactive system design, user-centred design, direct manipulation.*

1. INTRODUCTION

This paper is broadly concerned with issues of direct manipulation and visual interfaces in interactive systems.[1] We will define a class of interactive systems in which the state of the system is visualised within the display and there is a *consistent* relationship between what is manipulated (*state*) and what is perceived (*display*). More specifically, within the subset of such systems known as direct manipulation systems, we expect the display to "mirror" the part of the state that the user needs to know about.

Examples of such systems are:

(i)   a *display editor* in which the text is faithfully represented by a display; commands such as cursor movement and deletion modify underlying data and display equivalently.

(ii)   a *remote submersible* in which the attitude, position and velocity of the craft is reflected in dials and other iconic representations on a display. Changes in the state of the craft are reflected by changes in dial readings etc.

(iii) a *steam engine*[2] in which changes in water flow and temperature are represented schematically in a display.

The physical dimensions of the display often limit the user's ability to directly access data. A significant concern, therefore, is the way that these limits influence the design of interfaces. In this paper we model state and display and their relationship mathematically to enable understanding of direct manipulation as an interaction style more precisely, and to consider the effect of boundary limitation. Our purpose in developing a mathematical model is to make understanding more precise and to provide a design model, uncluttered by implementation detail, that may be used as a means of analysing features of interactive behaviour, and of producing implementations that are faithful constructions of these ideas.

In this paper, we are particularly concerned with the following two design issues and the development of associated design methods:

(i)   *consistency*: that the display gives an unambiguous view of aspects of the state that are important to the user; in practice ambiguities arise either because of inadequate data resolution or because the display format does not conform to the user's model of the structure of the manipulated data.

(ii) *completeness*: that physical characteristics of the display limit what is visible to part of the state only; few interactive systems provide a complete view of data, hence a strategy is required to make the state, as manipulated by the user, readily accessible through the display.

This work fits into a broader context of multidisciplinary research (computer science and cognitive psychology) in which principles of interactive behaviour[3] (generative user engineering principles) are being developed that can be used (in terms of a precise mathematical formulation) in the design of interactive systems and can be used (in terms of a colloquial or non-technical formulation) by users in understanding the operation of the commands of the interactive system.[4,5] These interaction principles tend to be expressed at different levels of detail and therefore may require contrasting but consistent models of an interactive system reflecting these levels. For example, some principles (actually algebraic properties of commands such as idempotence, commutativity and the existence of inverses i.e. recoverability) may be described in terms of an abstract model of system behaviour in which system state dominates; while others (for example the path of a mouse movement must be continuously visible) are expressed in terms of display only and therefore require a model of state that emphasises the display component. Yet other principles require models of style to support windows, menus or commands; and others (for example temporal principles) may require detailed understanding of the machine implementation. Finally, many interesting and useful properties relate state and display, and clarify physical constraints imposed by the display.

To illustrate the different levels of discussion of design principles, *state* and *display* models of interactive behaviour will be distinguished. Note that later we shall also investigate the distinction between exceptional and normal models of interactive behaviour. It is useful to consider exceptional and normal models separately, as often illustrated by work in cognitive psychology on modelling user error.[6,7] Although the separations described in the literature often deal with a rather different framework, we hypothesise that users of interactive systems develop an understanding of the regular behaviour of an interactive system separately from exceptional behaviour (such as occurs at display boundaries) and hence the two behaviours may be usefully presented separately. Here we consider system models of the regular behaviour of interactive systems, and use the models as a basis for the description of constraints that shape neighbourhoods in which this regular behaviour takes place. Our aim is to use these models as an aid to design to ease discussion of design alternatives. Clarifying the boundary between normal and exceptional will also aid explanation to users.

2. MODELLING STATE, DISPLAY AND VIEW

An important notion within the direct manipulation style is the idea of articulatory directness.[8] A crucial component of any support for this notion, is that the display gives a "mirror" representation of the manipulable state. As manipulations are performed on data, the effects of the manipulations are immediately visible in the display. As noted by Jacob,[9] visible representation may, in practice, be a very abstract picture of the state. Take for example:

* the remote submersible

    the *state* is the physical attitude, position, velocity and the environment of the submarine;

    the *display* consists of dials and other icons representing speed, direction and attitude, and a two dimensional view from a camera contained on board the craft.

- the ship's steam engine[2]

  the *state* is the simulation of the engine itself;

  the *display* schematic gives the status of flows and temperatures through the engine.

It may be appropriate to include the physical model being mirrored or monitored by the computer system. In the case of the submersible state is outside the computer system. As operations affecting the display are invoked, the physical state of the submarine or ship's engine is modified.

In order to model the distinction between state and display in a direct manipulation system, we require two models (we may model them as algebras since both models will include objects, operations and axiomatic constraints): a state algebra (S,C) consisting of state and *commands* on the state; and a display algebra (D,O) that consists of display and *operators* that manipulate display. For example, in the case of the remote submersible a change of velocity is either a modification of the attitude, speed and direction of the submarine or a change of illumination in the dials and icons of the display plus a renewed picture from the camera. We view them as algebras because we will be interested in the possibility of defining axioms on the commands and operations that govern their behaviour. Initially, at least, we treat the visual representation as entirely separate from the state representation. In practice, of course, the models are related since they represent two different views of the same artefact. At this stage we are not interested in the details of the implementation of state, display or the operations upon them or how the two models arise. As the design progresses, structure will be added to these basic models; the designer's task is to avoid early design decisions that commit to particular interface styles or implementations. All the detail necessary at this point is that C is a set of state transformations $(S \rightarrow S)$ and O is the set of display transformations $(D \rightarrow D)$. It is assumed in both models that parameters (that is what the command requires in order to produce its result) have been dealt with at some other level, somewhere in the mapping between physical inputs and commands.[10] The display may be considered to be a visual representation of some or all of the state (they are considered to be entirely independent) and might be, for example, an array of pixels (the details are not important).

The display is a view of some aspect of the state, so we construct a view mapping $(v:S \rightarrow D)$ that produces a visual representation of some or all of the state. The view mapping will also handle constant information to provide additional spatial information (template sugaring) to present to the user for example: a box outline of a data entry form, or menu, or information about mode. The two models may have a set of complementary commands in common, that is for $v:S \rightarrow D$, there exist two sets C' and O' of complementary functions. C' will consist of, for example, editing operations on text such as *insert*, *delete* and cursor movement, while O' consists of operations that change the state of pixels in the display, for example *cursor left* will move the illumination of the cursor one position to the left. These complementary sets may have the property that for any $c \in C'$ there corresponds an $o \in O'$, the *complement* of c, such that $\forall s \in S \; v(c(s)) = o(v(s))$, that is the commands are related by the view mapping, in a strong way (at least at this stage). It can be seen that an adequate description of mirroring is expressed in this coupling.

Two points emerge from the preceding discussion:

(1) The mapping from state to display, when complementary, affirms that the display is updated as the state is transformed by commands. Nothing is said about the user's understanding of the context in which commands are invoked. For example does the user perceive an operation on display or a command on state? Commands may be invoked within the state metaphor or the display metaphor. Dix [11] describes a model in which a reverse mapping from display to state is used to map the effect of operation invocations into the state.

(2) Typically, the data of interest to the user cannot be represented adequately within a limited display. The design of an interactive system involves the development of techniques for handling the whole, by showing an approximation of the data with enough detail for user purposes, and alternatively or additionally, by giving a partial view coupled with a strategy for revealing the whole.

It is the second of these points that will be pursued in future sections.

3. DISPLAY RESOLUTION

An important design problem is to develop an appropriate mechanism within an interactive system for presenting a partial picture of the state. We may think of the display as an approximation of the state in that it gives some detail of only part of the state. In this section we discuss and refine what we mean by approximation in the context of the state and display models. Clearly it is difficult to express the idea that a display is more approximate than a state, because displays and states are members of different domains (we are comparing state information with screen illuminations). One notion of resolution that may be adequate, but is too strong, is to say that, if one state is more approximate than another (we may abbreviate this by $s_1 \sqsubseteq s_2$ where $s_1, s_2 \in S$ are the two states) then the images of the two states: $v(s_1)$ must be more approximate than $v(s_2)$ as displays ($v(s_1) \sqsubseteq v(s_2)$). This definition of approximation is too strong if it demands that one state (or display) is *strictly* more approximate than the other state or display because it requires that any difference between the two states must be reflected in the two displays.

Part of the design process then, in such a framework, is to define an appropriate relation between states and between displays. The details of the relationship between states is not required in this account so we shall ignore it. In order to clarify approximation between displays, more information is required about the structure of the display. One example, a definition that will be used extensively throughout this paper, is that the display is a mapping between co-ordinates and pixels ($N \times N \rightarrow P$) where P is flat,[12] (in other words elements of P are incomparable with any other element than $\perp$ the least defined or undefined element). One display then will be more approximate than another ($d_1 \sqsubseteq d_2$) if co-ordinate positions in d_1 are the same as d_2 or they are undefined. One might imagine a least defined display as a display whose boundaries limit the display to nothing. A fully defined display, on the other hand, is a display with no boundaries, a display of everything displayable.

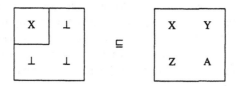

There are other more subtle approximation relations on displays that may be more appropriate in particular design cases. Systems often use icons or ellipses to abbreviate information on the display. Ellipses or icons are used to give brief visual references to information contained within state that would otherwise use substantially more display space. Such an arrangement requires a notion of approximation in which an icon is considered to be more approximate than the full display form of the information that it represents. A co-ordinate based relationship would not provide an appropriate description of this notion of approximation.

For present purposes, we take it that part of the design modelling role, carried out as part of the specification of an interactive system, is to formalise an appropriate partial ordering both on state and display. One significant property, that will be required of such an ordering, is that

if $s_1 \sqsubseteq s_2$ then $v(s_1) \sqsubseteq v(s_2)$

that is v is *faithful* with respect to these partial orderings (a property that is not too strong if the orderings are not strict orderings).

Since how and when commands behave in an irregular manner is of major significance to the user, an important modelling issue will be how properties of commands or operations are affected at the boundary. It will help us to analyse this behaviour if we define the least approximation of state that produces the same display under v as the whole state would, that is $s' \sqsubseteq s$ and $v(s') = v(s)$ and if n is strictly less defined than s' then $v(n) \neq v(s')$. As long as v is a monotonic function mapping S to D there will be a unique s', which is the minimal state under v to produce d. We shall define a function $f_v: S \to S$ that produces the minimal state. The choice of ordering will depend on the particular application. Our purpose is to consider general principles, not particular device issues.

4. PARTIALITY

An alternative tighter formulation of the connection between state and display models may be constructed by means of a panoramic[13] or "wide angle" view of the whole state. We require that what can be seen of the state through the view (v) is an accurate reflection, but this requirement is not sufficient to ensure that a complete picture may be constructed by the user. We need to ensure adequate views at boundaries and that no "holes" may occur where the view will not show the state.

A notion of observability is required that ensures that the entire state may be made visible consistently and faithfully. A wide-angle view of state is required, a mapping $v^+: S \to D$, that gives a "complete picture" of the underlying state; note we are not suggesting here that all interactive systems should be observable in this sense. The state of interest may be significantly smaller than the whole state. For example, in the case of the remote submersible example, a user is only interested in a partial picture of what is happening. He is only marginally interested in the internal workings of the submarine. However, on the other hand, an editor or spreadsheet system would require a more precise notion of predictability that incorporates a complete picture of the behaviour of the state.

In the following sections constructions will be described that ensure that the user can make up the whole display through a series of views. Hence v^+ should be constructible by means of passive commands that have no unwanted side effects.

4.1. Passivity

Passivity prescribes a set of commands that are harmless with respect to the part of state that contributes to the result of the system's execution. To produce a precise definition of passivity, more information is required about the state. The state may be structured by taking two mappings that extract some of the constituents of the state: $r : S \to R$ where R is the result and $f : S \to F$ where F is the set of frame information that defines, for example, what part of the state is displayed. A command, $c \in C$, is *passive* if for all $s \in S$, $r(c(s)) = r(s)$. In other words, the result part of the state remains unchanged.

Examples of passive commands may be found within a direct manipulation display editor such as: *cursor-left* and *page-forward*; and within an operating system, commands such as *list-files*. Notice that passivity is not completely harmless since for instance *delete*'s effect on state is not equivalent to *cursor-left* followed by *delete*.

4.2. Constructing v^+

The wide angle view (v^+) will generate a display that mirrors the whole manipulable state (probably the result component) whether visible or invisible under v. v^+ should satisfy certain obvious properties, both of consistency and completeness:

Consistency properties

- $\forall s \in S \quad v^+(f_v(s)) = v(s)$;

- $\forall s_1, s_2 \in S \quad s_1 \sqsubseteq s_2 \Rightarrow v^+(s_1) \sqsubseteq v^+(s_2)$;

A more reasonable assumption than v being complementary would be that v^+ be complementary, that is $\forall s \in S$, if $o \in O'$ is the complement of $c \in C'$ then $v^+(c(s)) = o(v^+(s))$. This requires that the whole viewable state mirrors the effect of complementary commands, not simply that which is viewed by v.

Completeness properties

v^+ is constructed "dynamically" by introducing a principle of *observability*. v^+ is generated by a sequence of states $\{s_i\}$ (produced by passive commands) being the least upper bound of a set of images of s_i under v. The least upper bound of two displays $d_1 \sqcup d_2$ (with approximation ordering as already defined) may be illustrated by means of the following picture:

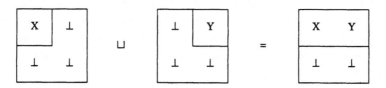

Hence, given a particular $s \in S$, we require a *strategy* $\{p_i\}$ (a set of command sequences $p_i = c^{i_1}; c^{i_2}; \cdots ; c^{i_k}$ where ";" composes commands and each c^{i_j} is passive). The strategy should generate a set of states with the following completeness properties: that the entire state should be visible through the panoramic view, and the panoramic view should contain an unambiguous representation of the result, or more precisely:

- $$r(\bigsqcup_{i=1}^{n} \{f_v(s_i)\}) = r(s)$$

  The result components of the least upper bound of the sequence of minimal states is equal to the result component of the original state.

- $$\bigsqcup_{i=1}^{n} \{v(s_i)\} = v^+(s).$$

  v^+ produces a display of the whole state s.

- $\forall s \in S : r(s)$ the result of the state s is contained within the display $v^+(s)$ in an unambiguous form.

Observability is stronger than required for many interactive systems, in particular for examples such as the submersible and steamer. For a general partial ordering, since a least upper bound is included, observability also highlights the possibility of display ambiguity that may arise when different parts of the state are capable of generating displays that are indistinguishable. These indistinguishable displays will not contribute properly to the panoramic display (since $d \sqcup d = d$). Systems may be designed that avoid the problem by using an iconic scroll bar to indicate where the display is in the context of the larger state. In practice, the definition that we have used here, because it is based on co-ordinates, ensures that a display is placed correctly within its co-ordinate background. A display produced by v is framed within a space of co-ordinates that all map to undefined ($\perp$).

5. NORMAL MODELS

So far in this paper we have explored the distinction between a state model and a display model without considering how these models may be used within a design methodology. In practice a designer's interest in the complementary effect of an operation is likely to be limited to subsets of states. For example when considering the behaviour of a command that uses a cursor to select parameter information from the state, one is interested in whether or not the required and resulting information is visible.

A more fruitful way of considering the complementary properties of state and display from a designer's point of view is to distinguish between an "unlimited" model of interactive behaviour, and a model that demonstrates the physical limitations of the display. For example, a designer might initially conceive of a text editor consisting of an arbitrarily long line with an associated cursor. At this level algebraic principles relating to state behaviour of the commands may be developed and applied, for example invertibility, commutativity etc. Physical constraints, imposed by dimensions of paper or display, will produce a requirement for new operations such as *cursor up* and *cursor down*. Also new behaviour of the existing commands will be required to deal with exceptional effects at boundaries, possibly conflicting with the originally required algebraic properties (for example commutativity and the existence of inverses may not be true at display boundaries). Neighbourhoods of the state, such as where manipulated information is visible, will provide context for investigating the complementary relationship between commands and operations. The display algebra operations characterise the boundary effects of commands.

There is therefore now a different emphasis in the use of these models. We are concerned about particular states, and whether properties true in the state model continue to hold in the display model. Constraints on commands and states are now required that will enable neighbourhoods for the two algebras to be complementary.

One example of a property that constrains the neighbourhood in which complementary properties should hold is *visibility*. A command is visible for a particular state if the command modifies visible data only, and produces a result in which all effects of the command are visible.

A relation is first defined between states: For any pair of states $s_1, s_2 \in S$ $vis(s_1, s_2)$ is true if $v^+(s_2) - v^+(f_v(s_2)) \sqsubseteq v^+(s_1)$ and $v^+(s_1) - v^+(f_v(s_1)) \sqsubseteq v^+(s_2)$.

This relation is complicated because of possible effects that might arise as state, that was visible in the display, becomes invisible, and previously invisible state becomes visible. The property requires that:

(i) the visible part of s_2 ($v^+(f_v(s_2))$) may change, but the invisible part of s_2 ($v^+(s_2) - v^+(f_v(s_2))$) where "-" defines all the co-ordinates of $v^+(s_2)$ that do not correspond to the visible part of s_2) is more approximate than what was initially visible under v^+.

(ii) a similar property relates the visible and invisible parts of s_1.

In short $vis(s_1, s_2)$ asserts that the only differences between s_1 and s_2 are visible in the display under v. Visibility is a particular form of this relation. A command c is *visible* in a particular state $s \in S$ if $vis(s, c(s))$, hence we are relating the initial state to the state after the command has been executed.

It is then possible to specify that regular properties of commands hold in states when a command is visible, for example given any $c \in C$ there corresponds an inverse $c' \in C$ such that $\forall s \in S$ for which $vis(s, c(s))$: $c'(c(s)) = s$. We may then demand that all displays must be visible for every state; this is equivalent to the technical property of *predictability* in interactive systems.[5]

6. EXCEPTION MODELS

Properties such as *visibility* establish neighbourhoods of validity for complementary property of algebras. However, as said in the introduction, it is likely that users distinguish between normal and exceptional properties of interactive systems with distinct mental models. Two models of an interactive system may be appropriate: the normal model which includes a number of algebras describing different normal properties of commands with more or less hindrance from the display or implementation; and the exception model that describes the effects of context and other factors generating discontinuities in the operation of user commands.

The *exception model* is concerned with the properties of commands as they are affected by display boundaries, cursor pointers and block boundaries (for example cut–and–paste boundaries). We will refer to these special points in the display or state as *pointers*. Given the example above, we may generalise the properties of commands that are expressed in the exception model. In the case of many interactive systems, for example display editors, these pointer effects are dominant in the user's perception of interactive behaviour and are therefore crucial to the user's understanding of the system.

For our purposes the exception model consists of an enumeration of cases that exhaust the possible effects on pointers. For example, taking a display editor [13] we notice that commands have exceptional effects (which may include complex interactions) in, among others, the following circumstances.

(1) *cursor pointers*: Certain commands change the state by modifying the cursor only. Cursor movement although *passive*, will affect active commands. For example:

$delete(uparrow(t)) \neq delete(t)$ some $t \in T$.

(2) *display boundaries*: Certain commands change the state by moving the display boundary, and have no other

effect on state. Other result transforming commands have exceptional effects at the boundaries, and it is appropriate to describe these effects separately. For example the effect when a command touches or crosses a boundary might be to have no effect on the result (contrary to normal principles such as invertibility) and sound the alarm.

(3) *cut–and–paste boundaries*: Special commands form and manipulate these boundaries. Commands will often have an ancillary effect to do the necessary work to accommodate these boundaries.

Types of exceptional case

The exception model should enumerate cases and prescribe generalised properties that occur at boundaries for example:

(A) *Commands whose only effect is to modify pointers.* It is necessary to express the interactions of these commands with other commands that use the state. We express these interactions as constraints: for any result transforming command $c : S \to S$ and a command $d : S \to S$ that modifies frame information only, $c(d(s)) \neq c(s)$.

(B) *Commands that have an exceptional effect as they cross boundary points.* Hence we express the behaviour of commands over a subset of the domain of the command. We require properties such as: if $c \in S \to S$ is a command that depends on the pointers generated by the *ptrs* function then for any $s' \in S$ such that $ptrs(s') \subseteq Bdry(s)$, c has the property that $c(s)=s$ and *bell* is sounded. Here $ptrs : S \to power(Ptr)$ generates cursors, Ptr is a set of pointers and $Bdry(s)$ is the set of boundary pointers for state s.

7. CONCLUSIONS

We have shown that it is useful to distinguish between state and display behaviour of interactive systems. In order to understand the physical limitations of the display we have further distinguished between the immediate display and the wider *panoramic* view available to the user by passive commands. By considering this, we have been able to describe the *consistency* between the immediate display and the wider view and between the effect of the users actions on the state and display. Further, we are able to define the *completeness* of this wider view with respect to the underlying state and the final result of the system.

It has also been useful to consider normal and exceptional models. Using a definition of *visibility* of commands, based on the immediate and wider views, we can define properties that fail at the display and other boundaries separately from the normal behaviour. The boundaries can be described in terms of pointers and this leads to a classification of commands based on their effect on these pointers.

We aim to produce a worked example of this layering technique in the context of a full specification of an interactive system. A design methodology using these models would clarify the level at which interaction principles apply, and the distinction between normal and abnormal behaviour.

8. ACKNOWLEDGEMENTS

We acknowledge with gratitude the stimulating environment provided by our colleagues in the interaction group at York. This research was part funded by the Alvey and Science and Engineering Research Council grant GR/D 02317.

9. REFERENCES

1. Shneiderman, B., "The future of interactive systems and the emergence of direct manipulation", *Behaviour and Information Technology* 1(3), pp. 237-256 (1982).

2. Hollan, J.D., Hutchins, E.L., and Weitzman, L.M., "STEAMER: An interactive inspectable simulation-based training system", *AI Magazine* 5(2), pp. 15-28 (1984).

3. Thimbleby, H.W., "Generative user-engineering principles for user interface design", pp. 661-666 in *Human-Computer Interaction — INTERACT'84*, ed. Shackel, B., North-Holland (1985).

4. Harrison, M.D. and Thimbleby, H.W., "Formalising guidelines for the design of interactive systems", pp.

161-171 in *People and Computers: Designing the Interface*, ed. Johnson, P. and Cook, S., Cambridge University Press (1985).

5. Dix, A.J., Harrison, M.D., Runciman, C., and Thimbleby, H.W., "Interaction models and the principled design of interactive systems", in *Proc. European Software Engineering Conference, Strasbourg*, ed. H. Nichols & D. Simpson, Springer Lecture Note 289 (1987).

6. Green, T.R.G., Payne, S.J., Gilmore. D.J., and Mepham, M, "Predicting expert slips", pp. 92-98 in *Human-Computer Interaction — INTERACT' 84*, ed. Shackel, B., North-Holland (1985).

7. Williams, M.D., Hollan, J.D., and Stevens, A.L., "Human reasoning about a simple physical system", pp. 131-153 in *Mental Models*, ed. Gentner & Stevens, Lawrence Erlbaum (1983).

8. Hutchins, D.L., Hollan, J.D., and Norman, D.A., "Direct manipulation interfaces", *Human-Computer Interaction* 1, pp. 331-338 (1985).

9. Jacob, R.J.K., *Direct manipulation*, Proceedings IEEE Conf. on Systems, Man & Cybernetics, Atlanta (1986).

10. Harrison, M.D. and Dix, A.J., "Towards models that clarify the manipulability of interactive systems", *University of York* (YCS 100) (1988).

11. Dix, A.J., *Formal Methods and Interactive Systems: Principles and Practice*, University of York (DPhil) (1988).

12. Schmidt, D.A., *Denotational semantics: A methodology for language development*, Allyn and Bacon (1986).

13. Dix, A.J. and Harrison, M.D., "Formalising models of interaction in the design of a display editor", in *Proc. Interact' 87 Stuttgart* , ed. Bullinger & Shackel, North Holland (1987).

A Software Engineering Environment for Developing Human-Computer Interfaces

Dr. A. Viereck
Universität Oldenburg, FB Informatik,
Postfach 2503, D-2900 Oldenburg

Abstract

Using the principles, methods, tools and processes of software-engineering, the development of software products becomes a standard technical procedure, with the aim of minimizing cost and time. From the view point of software-ergonomics the aids and resources of software-engineering are insufficient because there are neither methods nor tools relating the behaviour of the programs to that of the user. Since the expenses of creating a good interface for an interactive program can nowadays be higher than designing its functionality, we propose the following software-engineering environment model in which the psychological and ergonomic needs of the user are dominating.

1. Phased Interface Development

In software engineering there are many ways of splitting the development of software into a series of successive activities. Following Balzert [Balzert 82] we consider the software engineering environment to consist of six phases: planning, requirements definition, design, implementation, system testing and maintenance. For our purpose we regard the first four phases. Each of them has relations to and gives fixings for the user interface of the programs that are to develop.

At the end of the planning phase a product plan is defined which includes (among other things) global aspects for the human-computer interface to provide a vehicle of communication between user and developer. Within requirements definition there is built a product requirement specification that clearly and precisely defines each essential requirement for the software product, as well as the external interface to hardware and other software, and the user interface. A preliminary version of the user's manual is given. The next two phases deal with the way of working to realize the requirements and with the realization itself. Many aspects of functionality and of the user interface are detailed in these phases.

Each phase requires well-defined input information, utilizes well-defined methods and tools, and results in well defined products. But all these aids first of all concern the functionality and the way to realize it. The user interface - it's properties, different possibilities, and facilities - is not supported in a sufficient manner. We therefore propose to extract all the things connected with the user interface in the software development process from these phases and propose to provide an additional software engineering environment for developing human-computer-interfaces.

In addition to and integrated into the common software-engineering evironment models this proposal enables the software designer and programmer to take care of both the functionality and the user interface of the programs. The kernel of the software- engineering environment for developing human computer interfaces is a software ergonomic phase model consisting of four different phases:

-    The **conceptual phase**, where the basic approach of how to transpose preconditions and requirements for a given problem into an interactive program - the software ergonomic program concept - is given. The design of a program concept in regard to good dialog-behaviour implies - with the participation of the users - examining the organisation of work, the user-groups, their preliminary knowledge, technical preconditions etc.
-    The **structuring phase**, where an abstract dialog structure is built by decomposing the whole dialog into several parts (e.g. parts, where the user can handle specific aspects of the application, parts, where the user can manipulate the dialog behaviour, and parts, where the user can get help in specific situations) and fixings, how the user can work in these parts;
-    The **concretion phase**, where representing information is added to the abstract dialog structure to build a conrete dialog structure: which vocabulary is used for communi-cation, which syntactic or semantic properties and forms of expressions are employed;
-    The **realisation phase**, which consists of transferring a designed concrete dialog structure into specifications with all technical (system software and hardware) precon-ditions: What kind of input and output devices are used for which dialog-sequences? Where is which window-technique used and how? What about colors, fonts and other desk-top-publishing techniques and what about sound and speech? Which alternatives can users choose to individualize the interface?

In the process of developing interactive programs the designers analyse and discuss software-ergonomic aspects for each phase separately and transfer the results of an earlier phase to the subsequent phases by applying the resources of the respective phase until the program interface has been realised in all details.

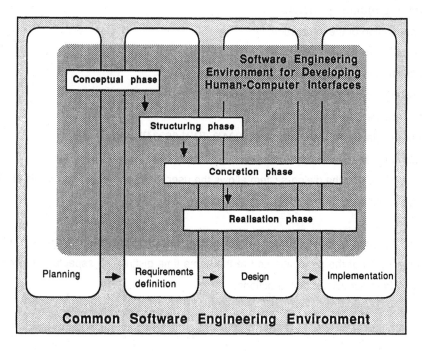

Fig. 1: Software Ergonomic Phase Model

2. The conceptual phase

The conceptual phase is the first phase, following the method of stepwise refinement for developing human-computer-interfaces. It is part of the common planning and requirements definition phases, and there is created the so called **software ergonomic program concept**, which builds a general framework for the human-computer-interface. The development of the concept is influenced by three partly contradictory aspects:
- by the desired behaviour and properties of the user interface,
- by the economic, technical, organisational and personal preconditions, and
- by the hardware- and software ergonomic perceptions for building user interfaces.

Since "hardware- ergonomics" is a relative old discipline with well known and generally accepted results we don't care about these aspects in this paper furthermore. Software ergonomics is a very young discipline with a lot of requirements, which often are neither generally known nor generally accepted.

For the development of the software ergonomic program concept we propose to follow the **software ergonomic principles**
- task-orientation of the interaction,
- self explaining dialog,
- user-controlled dialog,
- expectation conformity,
- fault-tolerance and transparence
as they are explained in the Din Norm 66234/8 ([DIN 66234]), and
- the individual responsibility of the user,
  which means, that the dialog-system allows the user to act corresponding to his abilities in a responsible way.

This could be done by using the following **conceptual-phase-methods**, that are a kind of operationalization of the principles and at the same time distinguish aspects of representing information from aspects of dialog-actions.

In human-computer-interfaces there are four basic dialog-action methods to build the dialog with:
- **Direct manipulation**, with methaphors, a separation of objects and functions, continuous feedback to incremental user input, window-technicque and pointing input devices.
- **Command orientation**, where the user chooses from the whole set of commands and specifies necessary parameters in a responsible way, when he is asked for input.
- **Multible choice**, where the user selects from some presented alternatives, when he is asked for input by the dialog system.
- **Data request**, where the user answers to a presented invitation to put data in.

The acting-oriented methods depend on information representing methods. The basic possibilities to represent information in human-computer-interaction are:
- The **Visual-pictorial** representation of information. Here the information is presented in form of pictures, figures, and/or pictograms. The user views them for instance on a screen, uses them for instance with a pointing device, or creates them with a graphic input device,

for instance a digitizer.

- The **Visual-textual** representation of information, where textual form for information representation is used. The user has to read or type those information to interact with the computer system.
- The **Audio-schematic** representation of information. Here the dialog system uses sound and melody to represent information.
- The **Audio-textual** representation of information, where interaction is held through speech input and output.

Depending on the economic, technical, organisational and personal preconditions the designer has to choose from the above methods and has to combine them to a software

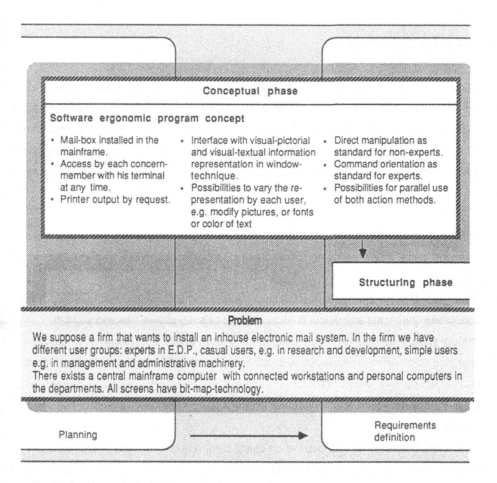

Fig. 2: Conceptual phase: Example for a software ergonomic program concept

ergonomic program concept, that fulfills the software ergonomic principles on the one hand and the behaviour and properties, the user interface is desired to have, on the other hand. Because of the uncountable number of variations for preconditions and possibilities for combining methods in relation to the preconditions there are usually given examples, that demonstrate, which software ergonomic methods should be used in a particular situation to have a good dialog behaviour (see e.g. [DIN 66234], [Lauter 87] or [Viereck 87]).

Because the decisions of the software ergonomic program concept are very general, the designer has now to structure the user-system-dialog through stepwise refinement with regard to both, the dialog-action methods and the information- representation methods.The structuring and concretion phase is dealing with these two refinements.

3. The structuring phase

In structuring phase there is given a description of the exact sequence of the intended dialog-action-methods without regard to representational aspects. The resulting structure therefore is called **abstract dialog structure**. To build the abstract dialog structure, requires knowledge about the functionality of the system that is to be developed. So the structuring phase starts in the common requirements definition phase, when the functionality of the program is given.

The first step in building the abstract dialog structure is a decomposition of the whole dialog into several parts. We propose to follow the application-independent partition first, which distinguishes:
- **Dialog-control-functions**, where the user starts, interrupts or finishes the dialog or an application, sets input and output devices, stores, deletes, copies files and so forth.
- **Dialog-styling-functions**, which enables the user to adapt the system to his habits, e.g. changing information representation, changing comprehensiveness and syntax of input and output, defining own functions.
- **Meta-functions**, which enable the user to interact about the dialog and give help in specific situations .
- **Application-functions**, that depend on specific applications, the user works with.
Secondly the application-functions have to be decomposed into parts. The way to do this is application-dependent.

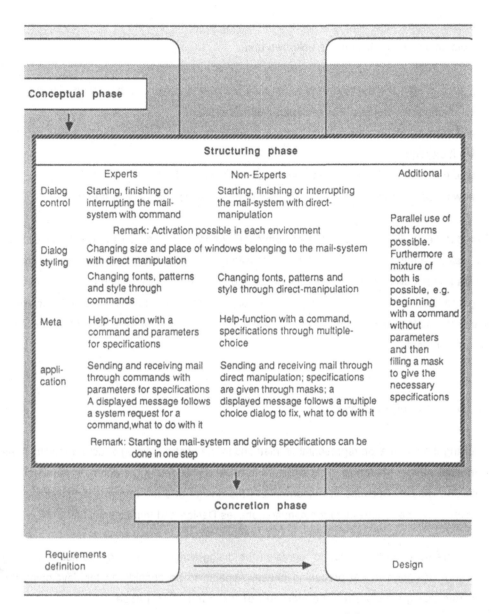

Fig. 3: Structuring phase: Example for fixings in an abstract dialog structure

Such decomposition makes sense in two ways. On the one hand there are formed clear units for the following studies, on the other hand there might be differences in how to employ the dialog action methods in the separate parts. For instance a user knows a little bit of managing control-functions, because of his work with the computer in his department with special applications. About the new application he knows little. So he feels good by using known functions, needs little help and uses commands, while he prefers direct manipulation or multiple choice for working in the unknown area.

In a second step the designer has to fix, how the user can work in the intended parts, i.e., which methods he can use. For each part one has to state:
- where to use direct manipulation, where commands, where multiple choice, where data input on request;
- where the user can choose between several of these methods;
- how these methods are mixed in one part or how they combine different parts.

One can generally say that in human-computer-interaction the initiative and responsibility of the dialog-system has to shrink, when the knowledge of the user grows. A casual user should be lead by the system in a moderate manner, e.g. with direct manipulation or multiple choice, to get to know the properties and operations of the system and to learn to use it. An expert wants to initiate dialog-actions, is able to take the responsibility for actions and to do his task with minor effort.

4. The concretion phase

Applying the information representation methods to the abstract dialog structure results in the **concrete dialog structure**. This structure is to be developed in the common requirements definition phase. Because of refinements in the design and the Implementation phase the concretion phase reaches into the common phases Design and Implementation.

There are several possibilities to represent the dialog-action-methods of the abstract dialog structure designed in the preceding phase. Aspects to be considered for developing the concrete dialog structure are the **methods of the concretion phase**:
- The vocabulary used in communication. This could be: natural-language words in visual-textual or audio-textual representation, alphanumerical codes in visual-textual representation, symbolic codes in audio-schematic or visual-pictorial representation, and pictures, drawings or diagrams in visual-pictorial representation.Usually you have a combination of several of these methods in the vocabulary of human-computer-interfaces
- The syntax of input and output. Here you have to distinguish: grammatical rules, limitations for the length of input and output or the dimension of drawings, restrictions for usable

characters, words or tones, and rules for the position (on a screen) to place input and output and for splitting in lines and columns.
- Semantic properties of input and output. This could be: formal redundancies in input and output, interpretation rules, and rules for managing inconsistencies and inconstancies in input and output.
- Form of expression in input and output. Human-computer-interaction can be polite and kind, short and stringent, precise and concrete.

We want to give a simple example in order to demonstrate different possibilities. Lets look at a dialog part in form of a data request to put in the time, consisting of seconds, minutes, and hours. It could appear in form of one word

> *"time?"*

or , more friendly, as a sentence

> *"Please put in the time"*.

In the second case the form of expression could be improved

> *"Would you please put in the time"*.

In all cases the user doesn't know the interpretation rules of the request: Which order and format is to be used? Is the input form optional? Often the rules of order and format are part of the request, wherby also syntactic limitations are given:

> *"Time? (SS,MM,HH)"*,
>
> *"Put in the time: HH:MM:SS"*.

A "correct" input to the first request would be

> *"15,13,10"*,

or to the second request

> *"10:13:15"*.

The syntax of this second input more closely correspond to German habits. If the system also accepts an input like

> *"10 hours, 13 minutes and 15 seconds"*,

or (better)

> *"13 minutes and 15 seconds past 10 o'clock"*,

further correspondance to German habits through formal redundancies and natural-language expressions in the input would be achieved. This is possible to realize in a dialog system. The following daily answer however, doesn't seem to be practical in relation to computer-systems:

> *"About quarter past 10"*.

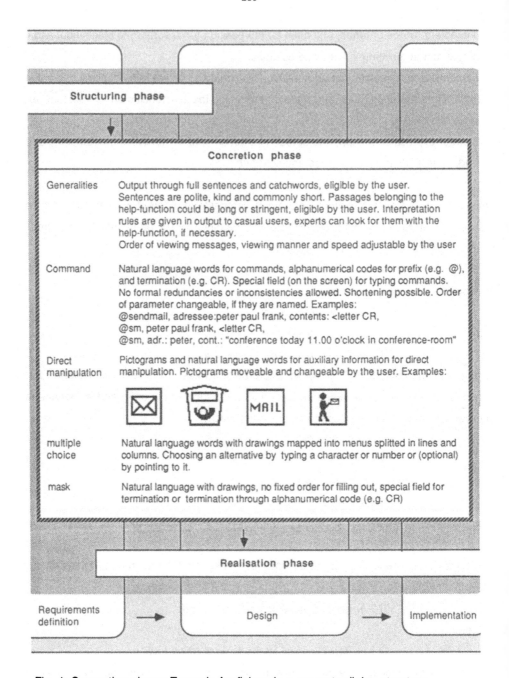

Fig. 4: Concretion phase: Example for fixings in a concrete dialog structure

Further syntactic restrictions for this dialog part are possible, e.g. limitations for the position and splitting of the input:

> *"Time?*   *Hours*   _ _
>   *Minutes* _ _
>   *Seconds* _ _"

or (more precisely)

> *"Time?*   *Hours*   _ _   *(00 .. 23)*
>   *Minutes* _ _   *(00 .. 59)*
>   *Seconds* _ _   *(00 .. 59)"*

In the second case the system shows the syntactic and semantic correct version for the input and takes the responsibility from the user.

In the concretion phase using the methods to build the concrete dialog structure out of the abstract structure the designer has to define - of course in regard to the software ergonomic principles -

- which pictures, pictograms, words, codes, grammatical rules and so forth are used in the dialog sequences,
- the user's possibilities of choosing between several methods to build his own conrete dialog structure.

5. The realisation phase

The last step in developing human-computer interfaces consists of transferring the designed concrete dialog structure into fixings, and finally into programs with all technical aspects. Here technical aspects do not only include the employed hardware but also the software-techniques and tools, usable to realize the concrete dialog structure are concerned. The following questions are to clearify:

- Which input and output devices are used for which dialog-sequences?
- Where is which window-technique used and how?
- What about colors, fonts and other desk-top-publishing techniques and what about sound and speech?
- Which alternatives can users choose to individualize the interface?

The designer has to start with these fixings within the phase of requirements definition. Here the determinations build the basis for the preliminary version of the user's manual and they can be used also for rapid prototyping, which enables the users of the system to work within the interface, to examine it and to provide for modifications in an early state of system

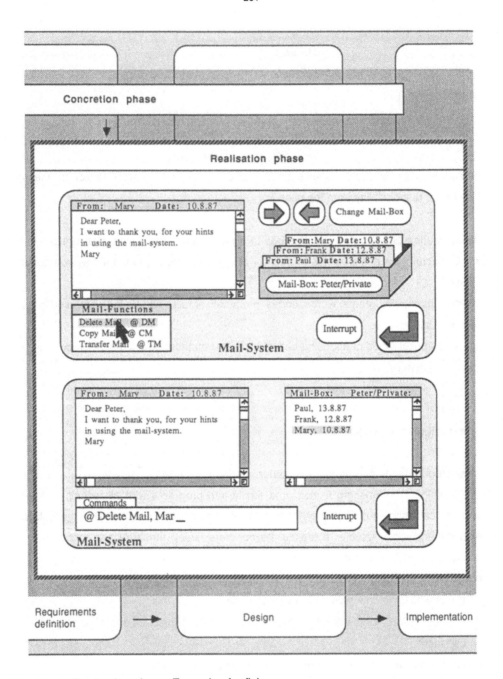

Fig. 5: Realisation phase: Examples for fixings

development. Such modifications are partly done in requirements definition and partly in Design or Implementation. So the realisation phase reaches into the design and into the implementation phase.

To determine the details of the human-computer interface in this realisation phase you have to respect the hardware-ergonomic results, just as the software-ergonomic principles and the results of psychological research of human behaviour and human learning in using computers.

For the design of pictograms, for instance, you have to notice the cognitive processing of pictograms, the abilities to remember pictograms in relation to an application, mental models of men by using pictograms, gestalt psychology criteria to form pictograms, e.g. contures, contrast, continuity, symmetry, orientation (see e.g. [Staufer 87]).

Screen-arrangement has to be done in regard to scientific findings about the number, layout and order of windows, about number, type and combination of colors or fonts, about methods to attract attention and so forth (see e.g. /Lauter 87/, [Nievergelt 83], [Benz 81], or [Benda 86]).

6. Conclusion

The presented phase model shows a way to systematically discuss, examine and realize the general criteria and aspects of software-ergonomics and to integrate the development of human-computer interfaces in the general software-engineering procedures. Using the phase model, the main activities for building the user interface of a programm occures in the requirements definition phase. Considering this and bringing the software engineering environment for developing human computer interfaces to an end, we propose to insert the results of the reflections to the user interface as an important part to the requirements specification document.

Literature

[Balzert 82]   H. Balzert: Die Entwicklung von Software-Systemen. Mannheim, Wien, Zürich: Bibliographisches Institut, 1982

[Benda 86]   H. v. Benda: Leitfaden zur benutzergerechten Gestaltung der Dialog-schnittstelle für Bildschirmarbeitsplätze von Sachbearbeitern in Büro und Verwaltung. Hamburg: Stollmann, 1986

[Benz 81]   G. Benz, R. Grob, P. Habner: Gestaltung von Bildschirmarbeitsplätzen.
                 Köln: TÜV Rheinland, 1981

[DIN 66234]   DIN 66234/8. Entwurf, Berlin: Beuth, 1986

[Lauter 87]   B. Lauter: Software-Ergonomie in der Praxis. München, Wien: Oldenbourg,
                 1987

[Nievergelt 83] J. Nievergelt, A. Ventura: Die Gestaltung interaktiver Programme.
                 Stuttgart: Teubner, 1983

[Staufer 87]   M. Staufer: Piktogramme für Computer. Berlin, New York: W. de Gruyter, 1987

[Viereck 87]   A. Viereck: Klassifikationen, Konzepte und Modelle für den Mensch-
                 Rechner-Dialog. Berichte aus dem Fachbereich Informatik, Nr. 1/87.
                 Oldenburg: Universität Oldenburg, Fachbereich Informatik, 1987

M.Lansky (University of Paderborn, FRG):

"Intrinsic Geometry in LOGO- Distance of Linear Segments"

1.Intrinsic Geometry in LOGO

Oriented curve in an oriented Euclidean plane -given a point of origin- may be described by a position vector function of a real parameter defined on some interval. We suppose, that this function has there continuous derivatives of sufficient high order with not zero derivative of first order. It is a well known fact, proven in differential geometry, that such curves are invariant with respect to a suitable group of parameter transformations. Various considerations become simpler, if we choose the length of arc "s" as the so called "natural" parameter. The curves are also invariant with respect to the group of Euclidean transformations; the choice of a coordinate system influences the form of functions used for description of curves and this circumstance can be sometimes tragical for the corresponding computer realization. According to Cesàro, we get a coordinate-free description of curves using their curvature "æ" (or the radius of curvature) as a function of "s" . This is the famous Cèsaro's approach to intrinsic ("natural") geometry ([1],[2]).

In the corresponding coordinate-free computer geometry, as e.g. in TURTLE geometry introduced by Papert in connection to LOGO, the curves are drawn as approximating polygons by means of commands FORWARD <DELTA s> and LEFT <DELTA Φ> (among others). The typical procedure is to divide equidistantly the natural parameter interval in n pieces of equal length <DELTA s> and evaluate stepwise the value of s, æ(s) and <DELTA Φ>=æ(s)*<DELTA s>, constructing thus some n-sided polygon. Alas, such an approximation is generally not the best one.

In [7] we proposed to parametrize s and Φ, preserving so the pleasant properties of intrinsic geometry of being coordinate-free, but opening on the other hand the possibility of a free choice of the parameter. It is obvious, that the goodness of such an approximation depends strongly on this choice, especially as the natural parameter s is generally not the best one. Related problems were already studied by Mehlum [3], Woodsford [4], Rogers [5]) and others.

In [9] we studied the problem of the best approximation of a curve by an n-sided polygon and the problem of the best parametrization. Such problems can be posed only if some suitable measure of "goodness" has been defined. For this purpose we proposed some measures for the distance of curves. Surprisingly enough, the concept of distance of curves is not quite usual. Many readers felt a need for a more elementary explanation of this approach. Therefore we present here for illustration of these fundamental concepts a complete theory of distance of linear segments, which are the elementary constituents of all aaproximating polygons.

2.Approximation of Curves by Polygons

Let c1, c2 be two curves defined in the above sense as vector-valued functions of their natural parameters s1, s2 on the intervals [s1α,s1Ω], [s2α,s2Ω] respectively. We adjust the common parameter tε[0,1] of these two curves linearly by means of the relations

(1)   s1(t) = s1α + t*(s1Ω − s1α) ; s2(t) = s2α + t*(s2Ω − s2α)

Then the distance of the curves c1, c2 may be defined invariantly by

(2) $\delta(c1,c2) = \int_0^1 |$ c2(s2(t)) − c1(s1(t)) | dt

or by

(3) $\delta(c1,c2) = \sqrt{\{\int_0^1}$ [c2(s2(t)) − c1(s1(t))]² dt }

or some other equivalent metric. These and other similar formulas can be taken for a measure of goodness of the approximation of the curve c1 by the curve c2 in the sense, that the approximation is closer (better) if δ(c1,c2) is smaller.
If for some fixed natural n

(4)   0 = t[0] < t[1] < t[2] <...< t[n] = 1

is a subdivision of the interval [0,1] and c2 is a polygon with corresponding edges

(5)   c2(s2α)=c2(s2(t[0])),c2(s2(t[1])),...,c2(s2(t[n]))=c2(s2Ω),

then for each k=1...n

(6)   c2(s2(t))=c2(s2(t[k−1]))+(c2(s2(t[k]))−c2(s2(t[k−1])))*

                 *(t−t[k−1])/(t[k]−t[k−1])   ; tε[t[k−1],t[k]]

is a straight line segment joining the edges c2(s2(t[k−1])) and c2(s2[k])).

The task of finding the best approximation polygon (with fixed n) to a given curve is solved by minimizing one of the integrals (2) or (3) with a substitution from (6), finding the edges (5) and the subdivision (4) preserving the properties (1) (see [9]!).

3.Distance of Linear Segments

Although the formulas (1) - (6) were originally used for planar curves, they do not lose their validity for curves in any oriented Euclidean space with a higher dimension. In order to get a formula for the distance of two linear segments AB and CD in such a space, we apply (2) to "curves" c1 and c2, constructed in agreement with (6) by linear equations

(7)   OX(t) = OA + t.AB   and OY(t) = OC + t.CD   for t from [0,1]

O being any point of origin and A, B, C, D being any not necessarily different points of the space. For sake of brevity, we use the notation like OA, AB,... not only for vectors, but also for segments; if we want to distinguish between vectors and segments, we stress for segments the notation "segment" OA, "segment" AB,.... This should lead here to no confusion. Substituting from (7) into (2) we get for distance the formula

$$(8) \quad \delta(AB,CD) = \int_0^1 |OY(t) - OX(t)|dt = \int_0^1 |AC + t.(CD - AB)|dt$$

(In this paper we do not investigate the application of (3) or similar formulas).

If we introduce a supplementary point E uniquely by

(9)   EA = DB   or   ED = AB

we get CD - AB = CD - ED = DE - DC = CE and then

$$\delta(AB,CD) = \int_0^1 |AC + t.CE|dt = \int_0^1 |CA - t.CE|dt =$$

(10)

$$= \int_0^1 \sqrt{(CA^2 - 2t.CA°CE + t^2.CE^2)}dt = \int_0^1 \sqrt{(e^2 - t.(e^2+a^2-c^2) + t^2.a^2)}dt$$

We see, that the solution depends only on the points A, C, E called "solving triangle", whose "sides" a, c, e are given by

(11) a = |CE| ≥ 0 ; c = |EA| ≥ 0 ; e = |AC| ≥ 0

and fulfill the inproper "triangle inequalities"

(12) a ≤ c + e   ; c ≤ e + a   ; e ≤ a + c

As the solving triangle can always be embedded in a two-dimensional subspace of the whole space, our general problem can be reduced to a planar problem consisting of solving (10) by investigating this triangle. Thus, by some manipulations, we get

$$(13) \quad \delta(AB,CD) = \int_0^1 \sqrt{(e^2 - t.(e^2 - c^2))}\,dt \quad \text{for } a = 0 \quad \text{and}$$

$$(14) \quad \delta(AB,CD) = a.\int_0^1 \sqrt{[(t - t0)^2 + (2P/a^2)^2]}\,dt \quad \text{for } a > 0 \text{ , where}$$

$$(15) \quad t0 = (a^2 - c^2 + e^2)/2a^2 \text{ and } P = \sqrt{[s.(s-a).(s-c).(s-e)]}$$

is the famous Heron's formula for the area of triangle with s = (a + c + e)/2 . One can demonstrate, that P = 0 iff in at least one of three inequalities (12) the equality sign holds, that means, that points A, C, E are collinear and form an improper triangle. If these three points are not collinear, then in all inequalities (12) there occur only strong inequalities, i.e. P>0 and then the corresponding triangle is proper. In such a triangle we can also introduce angles α, τ, ε in usual way (FIGURE 1). This consideration enables us to discuss systematically various possibilities how to solve (13) or (14).

An empirical approach to the problem of distance of linear segments AB,CD is illustrated in FIGURE 2 by the idea of dividing both segments AB,CD in n intervals of equal length, connecting the corresponding n+1 division points with segments and evaluating the arithmetic mean of their lengths. This is obviously a finite approximation of (13) and (14); these integrals are limits of such values, if n tends to infinity.

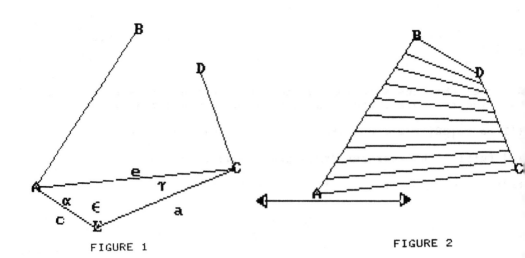

FIGURE 1   FIGURE 2

4. Discussion of Distance Formulas

CASE 0 : If a = 0, then from (11) we get C = E and e = c.
Applying (9) we can infer, that AC = BD and AB = CD, i.e. ACDB
is a parallelogram. By substituting these values in formula (13) we
get

(16) $\delta(AB,CD) = e = c$

CASE 1: If not a = 0 and c = e + a, then P = 0 and t0 = -e/a.
By substituting in (14) we get

(17) $\delta(AB,CD) = e + a/2 = c - a/2$

As AC is parallel to BD, we get a trapezoid ACDB. This case can be
also characterized by the condition, that there exists a real
number β, such that EA = β.EC with $\beta \geq 1$. In the special case β
= 1 we get A = C and e = 0 and the trapezoid degenerates to a
triangle ADB. Then formula (17) returns the value a/2.

CASE 2: If not a = 0 and e = a + c, then P = 0 and t0 = e/a $\geq$
1. By substituting in (14) we get

(18) $\delta(AB,CD) = c + a/2 = e - a/2$

Similarly, as in CASE 1, we get a trapezoid ACDB and this case may
be characterized by $\beta \leq 0$. For $\beta = 0$ (t0=1,a=e) is A = E, i.e.
c=0, B=D and we get a triangle ACB with $\delta(AB,CD) = a/2 = e/2$. From
(17) and (18) we see, that the condition not a=0 was substantial
only for derivation of the formulas, but the formulas themselves
can be used also for a=0. Thus the trapezoidal cases 1 and 2
degenerate not only to triangles, but also to parallelograms of t
CASE 0. To illustrate e.g. the CASE 2, we choose two segments AB,CD
(FIGURE 3), construct the point E (FIGURE 4) and estimate the
distance $\delta(AB,CD)$ by evaluating the mean value of lengths of 31
connecting segments (FIGURE 5). The table (FIGURE 6) gives us a
chance to compare estimated and exact values by (18).

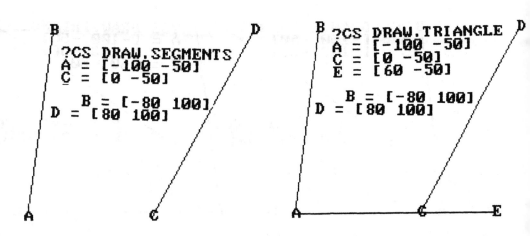

FIGURE 3   FIGURE 4

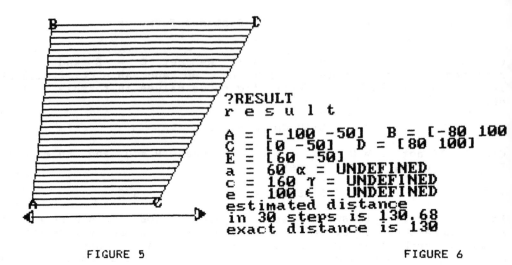

```
?RESULT
r e s u l t

A = [-100 -50]   B = [-80 100]
C = [0 -50]    D = [80 100]
E = [60 -50]
a = 60  α = UNDEFINED
c = 160  γ = UNDEFINED
e = 100  ε = UNDEFINED
estimated distance
in 30 steps is 130.68
exact distance is 130
```

FIGURE 5   FIGURE 6

After these "normal" trapezoidal cases we shall study an "exotic" case of "crossed trapezoid":

CASE 3: If not $a = 0$ and $a = c + e$, then $P = 0$ and $t0 = e/a \leq 1$. By substituting in (14) we get

$$(19) \qquad \delta(AB, CD) = (c^2 + e^2)/2a$$

This "crossed trapezoid" CABD is characterized by $0 \leq \beta \leq 1$. The transient cases of $\beta = 0$ or $\beta = 1$ were already treated under CASE 1 and CASE 2; they represent, as we already know, the limit triangles and are decribed also by formula (19). For illustration we observe the corresponding segments (FIGURE 7), the position of the point E (FIGURE 8), estimate the distance by means of connecting segments (FIGURE 9) and compare with the exact distance (FIGURE 10).

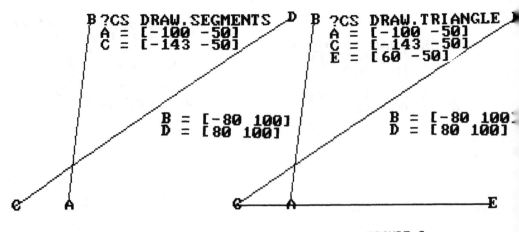

FIGURE 7   FIGURE 8

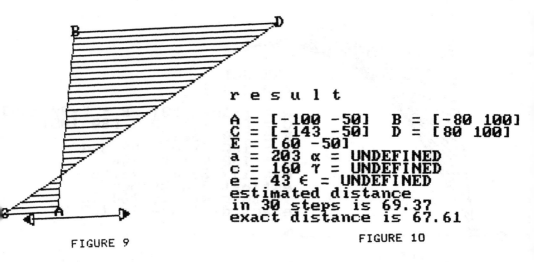

result

A = [-100 -50]   B = [-80 100]
C = [-143 -50]   D = [80 100]
E = [60 -50]
a = 203 α = UNDEFINED
c = 160 γ = UNDEFINED
e = 43   ε = UNDEFINED
estimated distance
in 30 steps is 69.37
exact distance is 67.61

FIGURE 9   FIGURE 10

CASE 4: If not a = 0 and P > 0, the points A, C, E are not collinear and form a proper triangle with area P. After substituting in (14), we get -after relatively tedious manipulations- a general formula

(20)
$$S(AB,CD)=\{c^2.\cos\varepsilon+e^2.\cos\tau-c.e.\sin\tau.\sin\varepsilon.\ln[\tan(\tan(\tau/2).\tan(\varepsilon/2)]\}/2$$

This formula may be illustrated by FIGURES 11-14 representing the general quadrangle ADCB.

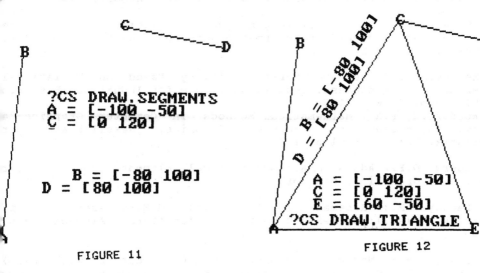

?CS DRAW.SEGMENTS
A = [-100 -50]
C = [0 120]

B = [-80 100]
D = [80 100]

?CS DRAW.TRIANGLE
A = [-100 -50]
C = [0 120]
E = [60 -50]

B = [-80 100]
D = [80 100]

FIGURE 11   FIGURE 12

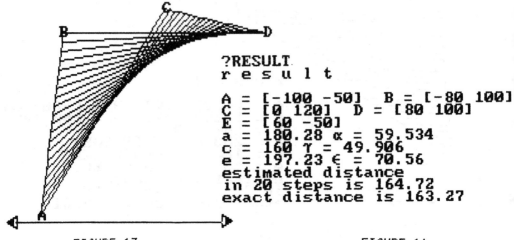

FIGURE 13   FIGURE 14

    Detailed mathematical manipulations leading to formulas (16)-(20) as well as LOGO programs, which execute their applications and have drawn the FIGURES 1-14, are omitted for lack of space, but can be easily worked out by any interested reader. A thorough inspection of general formula (20), which is the chief result of our investigation, gives us, besides of aesthetic satisfaction, some feeling for this most important element of polygonal approximation of curves.

5. Bibliography

[1] Cesàro, E.: Lezioni di geometria intrinseca, Napoli, 1900

[2] Kowalewski, G.: Vorlesungen über Allgemeine natürliche Geometrie und Liesche Transformationsgruppen, Walter de Gruyter, Berlin/Leipzig, 1931

[3] Mehlum, E.: Curve and Surface Fitting Based on Variational Criteriae for Smoothness, Central Institute for Industrial Research (CIIR), Oslo, Norway, 1969

[4] Woodsford, P.A.: Mathematical Methods in Computer Graphics- a Survey, Symposium on Computer Graphics, Gesellschaft für Informatik, Vol. 5, Berlin, 1971

[5] Rogers, D.F./ Adams, J.A.: Mathematical Elements for Computer Graphics, McGraw-Hill, New York, 1976

[6] Lansky, M.: Kinematik in LOGO- Trial and Error Approach. In: Melezinek, A.(ed.): Medien und Technik, Leuchtturm, Alsbach, 1986, p.423-426

[7] Lansky, M.: Natürliche Geometrie mit LOGO/ Natural (Intrinsic) Geometry with LOGO. In: Melezinek, M./ Kornhauser, A./ Sturm L.(ed.): Technik und Informationsgesellschaft, Leuchtturm, Alsbach, 1987

[8] Rogers, D.F.: Computer Graphics in Engineering Education, Pergamon Press, Oxford, GB, 1982

[9] Lansky, M.: On Parameter Invariance of Plane Curves in Computer Geometry, Proceedings of the IV th International Conference TAKIS (Int.Ass. for Cybernetics, Informatics and Theory of Systems), San Marino, 1988

List of Contributors

Ackermann, David, Swiss Federal Institute of Technology, ETHZ,
Lehrstuhl für Arbeits- und Organisationspsychologie,
CH-8092 Zürich, Switzerland   137

Anghern, Albert, Swiss Federal Institute of Technology, ETHZ,
Institut für Operations Research, CH-8092 Zürich, Switzerland   137

Arnoldi, Massimo, Swiss Federal Institute of Technology, ETHZ,
Institut für Operations Research, CH-8092 Zürich, Switzerland   137

Böcker, Heinz-Dieter, Projekt INFORM, Institut für Informatik,
Universität Stuttgart, Herdweg 51, D-7000 Stuttgart, FR Germany   16

Brandenburg, Franz J., Lehrstuhl für Informatik,
Universität Passau, Innstr. 33, D-8390 Passau, FR Germany   1

Dix, Alan J., Human-Computer Interaction Group,
Department of Computer Science, University of York,
York YO1 5DD, United Kingdom   241

Fehrle, Thomas, Institut für Informatik, Universität
Stuttgart, Azenbergstr. 12, D-7000 Stuttgart 1, FR Germany   27

Gimnich, Rainer, IBM Wissenschaftliches Zentrum Heidelberg,
Tiergartenstr.15, D-6900 Heidelberg, FR Germany   227

Goodstein, L.P., Riso National Laboratory, Department
of Information Technology, P.O. Box 49, DK-4000 Roskilde, Denmark   149

Guest, Steven P., LUTCHI Research Centre, Department of
Computer Studies, University of Technology,
Loughborough, LE11 3TU, United Kingdom   82

Harrison, Michael D., Human-Computer Interaction Group,
Department of Computer Science, University of York,
York YO1 5DD, United Kingdom   241

Herczeg, Jürgen, Projekt INFORM, Institut für Informatik,
Universität Stuttgart, Herdweg 51, D-7000 Stuttgart, FR Germany   16

Herczeg, Michael, Projekt INFORM, Institut für Informatik,
Universität Stuttgart, Herdweg 51, D-7000 Stuttgart, FR Germany   16

Kunkel, Klaus, Institut für Informatik, Universität
Stuttgart, Azenbergstr. 12, D-7000 Stuttgart 1, FR Germany   183

Lüthi, Hans-Jakob, Swiss Federal Institute of Technology, ETHZ,
Institut für Operations Research, CH-8092 Zürich, Switzerland   137

Vol. 408: M. Leeser, G. Brown (Eds.),Hardware Specification, Verification and Synthesis: Mathematical Aspects. Proceedings, 1989. VI, 402 pages. 1990.

Vol. 409: A. Buchmann, O. Günther, T. R. Smith, Y.-F. Wang (Eds.), Design and Implementation of Large Spatial Databases. Proceedings, 1989. IX, 364 pages. 1990.

Vol. 410: F. Pichler, R. Moreno-Diaz (Eds.), Computer Aided Systems Theory – EUROCAST '89. Proceedings, 1989. VII, 427 pages. 1990.

Vol. 411: M. Nagl (Ed.), Graph-Theoretic Concepts in Computer Science. Proceedings, 1989. VII, 374 pages. 1990.

Vol. 412: L. B. Almeida, C. J. Wellekens (Eds.), Neural Networks. Proceedings, 1990. IX, 276 pages. 1990,

Vol. 413: R. Lenz, Group Theoretical Methods in Image Processing. VIII, 139 pages. 1990.

Vol. 414: A.Kreczmar, A. Salwicki, M. Warpechowski, LOGLAN '88 – Report on the Programming Language. X, 133 pages. 1990.

Vol. 415: C. Choffrut, T. Lengauer (Eds.), STACS 90. Proceedings, 1990. VI, 312 pages. 1990.

Vol. 416: F. Bancilhon, C. Thanos, D. Tsichritzis (Eds.), Advances in Database Technology – EDBT '90. Proceedings, 1990. IX, 452 pages. 1990.

Vol. 417: P. Martin-Löf, G. Mints (Eds.), COLOG-88. International Conference on Computer Logic. Proceedings, 1988. VI, 338 pages. 1990.

Vol. 418: K. H. Bläsius, U. Hedtstück, C.-R. Rollinger (Eds.), Sorts and Types in Artificial Intelligence. Proceedings, 1989. VIII, 307 pages. 1990. (Subseries LNAI).

Vol. 419: K. Weichselberger, S. Pöhlmann, A Methodology for Uncertainty in Knowledge-Based Systems. VIII, 136 pages. 1990 (Subseries LNAI).

Vol. 420: Z. Michalewicz (Ed.), Statistical and Scientific Database Management, V SSDBM. Proceedings, 1990. V, 256 pages. 1990.

Vol. 421: T. Onodera, S. Kawai, A Formal Model of Visualization in Computer Graphics Systems. X, 100 pages. 1990.

Vol. 422: B. Nebel, Reasoning and Revision in Hybrid Representation Systems. XII, 270 pages. 1990 (Subseries LNAI).

Vol. 423: L. E. Deimel (Ed.), Software Engineering Education. Proceedings, 1990. VI, 164 pages. 1990.

Vol. 424: G. Rozenberg (Ed.), Advances in Petri Nets 1989. VI, 524 pages. 1990.

Vol. 425: C. H. Bergman, R. D. Maddux, D. L. Pigozzi (Eds.), Algebraic Logic and Universal Algebra in Computer Science. Proceedings, 1988. XI, 292 pages. 1990.

Vol. 426: N. Houbak, SIL – a Simulation Language. VII, 192 pages. 1990.

Vol. 427: O. Faugeras (Ed.), Computer Vision – ECCV 90. Proceedings, 1990. XII, 619 pages. 1990.

Vol. 428: D. Bjørner, C. A. R. Hoare, H. Langmaack (Eds.), VDM '90. VDM and Z – Formal Methods in Software Development. Proceedings, 1990. XVII, 580 pages. 1990.

Vol. 429: A. Miola (Ed.), Design and Implementation of Symbolic Computation Systems. Proceedings, 1990. XII, 284 pages. 1990.

Vol. 430: J. W. de Bakker, W.-P. de Roever, G. Rozenberg (Eds.), Stepwise Refinement of Distributed Systems. Models, Formalisms, Correctness. Proceedings, 1989. X, 808 pages. 1990.

Vol. 431: A. Arnold (Ed.), CAAP '90. Proceedings, 1990. VI, 285 pages. 1990.

Vol. 432: N. Jones (Ed.), ESOP '90. Proceedings, 1990. IX, 436 pages. 1990.

Vol. 433: W. Schröder-Preikschat, W. Zimmer (Eds.), Progress in Distributed Operating Systems and Distributed Systems Management. Proceedings, 1989. V, 206 pages. 1990.

Vol. 435: G. Brassard (Ed.), Advances in Cryptology – CRYPTO '89. Proceedings, 1990. XIII, 634 pages. 1990.

Vol. 436: B. Steinholtz, A. Sølvberg, L. Bergman (Eds.), Advanced Information Systems Engineering. Proceedings, 1990. X, 392 pages. 1990.

Vol. 437: D. Kumar (Ed.), Current Trends in SNePS – Semantic Network Processing System. Proceedings, 1989. VII, 162 pages. 1990. (Subseries LNAI).

Vol. 438: D. H. Norrie, H.-W. Six (Eds.), Computer Assisted Learning – ICCAL '90. Proceedings, 1990. VII, 467 pages. 1990.

Vol. 439: P. Gorny, M. Tauber (Eds.), Visualization in Human-Computer Interaction. Proceedings, 1988. VI, 274 pages. 1990.